Learning SQL:
A Step by Step
Guide Using Oracle®

RICHARD EARP AND SIKHA BAGUI

Learning SQL: A Step by Step Guide Using Oracle®

RICHARD EARP AND SIKHA BAGUI

Addison
Wesley

Boston San Francisco New York
London Toronto Sydney Tokyo Singapore Madrid
Mexico City Munich Paris Cape Town Hong Kong Montreal

Senior Acquisitions Editor	Maite Suarez-Rivas
Executive Editor	Susan Hartman Sullivan
Project Editor	Katherine Harutunian
Executive Marketing Manager	Michael Hirsch
Production Supervisor	Marilyn Lloyd
Project Management	Argosy Publishing
Copyeditor	Shannon Leuma
Proofreader	Kim Cofer
Composition and Art	Argosy Publishing
Text Design	Sandra Rigney
Cover Design	Gina Hagen Kolenda
Design Manager	Gina Hagen Kolenda
Prepress and Manufacturing	Caroline Fell

Access the latest information about Addison-Wesley titles from our World Wide Web site: *http://www.aw.com/cs*.

Many of the designations used by manufacturers and sellers to distinguish their products are claimed as trademarks. Where those designations appear in this book, and Addison-Wesley was aware of a trademark claim, the designations have been printed in initial caps or all caps.

The programs and applications presented in this book have been included for their instructional value. They have been tested with care, but are not guaranteed for any particular purpose. The publisher does not offer any warranties or representations, nor does it accept any liabilities with respect to the programs or applications.

Library of Congress Cataloging-in-Publication Data

Earp, Richard W.,
  Learning SQL : A Step by Step Guide Using Oracle / by Richard W. Earp
and Sikha S. Bagui.
       p. cm.
Includes index.
  ISBN 0-201-77363-5 (pbk. : alk. paper)
  1. SQL (Computer program language) 2. Oracle (Computer file) I.
Bagui, Sikha S., II. Title.
  QA76.73.S67 E27 2002
  005.75'65--dc21

                          2002021516

Contents

Preface

In recent years, we have seen a dramatic increase in the popularity of Oracle—in fact, it is now the most widely used database on the market. Due to this dramatic increase in popularity, more and more schools and training organizations are using Oracle in their database courses to teach database principles and concepts. And given the current technological climate, the computer industry needs application developers who can write Oracle SQL code efficiently. However, despite this need, there are still no Oracle books that employ a step-by-step systematic approach to learning Oracle SQL. Most books on the market today discuss several SQL concepts, but they are scattered throughout the book, making it very difficult for a beginner to grasp them. In addition, they are written for people who already know SQL.

This situation has generated a need for a concise book on Oracle/SQL programming, tied in with database principles and concepts. This book hopes to meet this need. It starts by presenting the simplest Oracle SQL concepts, and slowly moves into more complex query development and PL/SQL. Each chapter includes numerous examples, and, if readers wish, they can run these examples themselves using Oracle. Each chapter ends with a series of exercises that reinforce and build on chapter material. (We recommend that the exercises be performed at a pace of one chapter per week.) In presenting these exercises, it is our hope that readers will improve their proficiency with SQL. In writing this book, we have kept database principles and concepts and the novice reader in mind.

ORACLE and SQL

SQL is an abbreviation for SEQUEL (Structured English Query Language), and was originally an IBM product. Since the 1970s, when SEQUEL was introduced, it has become the de facto standard "language" for accessing relational databases. SQL is not really a language as much as it is a database query tool used to access relational databases. In this book, we will concentrate on using the Oracle database engine interactively.

SQL allows you to define a relational database and to create tables (in this sense, SQL is a Data Definition Language [DDL]). SQL also allows you to tell Oracle which information you want to select, insert, update, or delete. Oracle also provides a utility to load the database, the SQL*Loader. After creation, SQL provides a way to modify the database definition (using DDL); it also allows you to query the relational database in a most flexible way as well as change the data (that is, perform data manipulation and therefore, in this sense, SQL is a Data Manipulation Language [DML]).

This book covers SQL as it is invoked via SQL*Plus, a command-line system to launch interactive queries. SQL*Plus is a powerful Oracle product that takes your instructions for Oracle, checks them for correctness, submits them to Oracle, and then modifies or reformats the response Oracle gives. In short, SQL*Plus aids in interacting with Oracle smoothly and easily.

> The book was originally written for a class in which students are Personal Oracle users on the Windows operating system. However, if you are a UNIX user, Appendix 1 will get you started on Oracle.

Audience and Coverage

We use this book in our introduction to databases course along with the textbook by Elmasri/Navathe, *Fundamentals of Database Systems*, (3rd Edition, Addison-Wesley, 2000). In our course, students learn database theory and apply it as they learn SQL. The book can be used in a course such as this. It can also be used in a course just on SQL as a "stand-alone" text to learn SQL and Oracle. For this latter scenario, we included Chapter 0. This chapter provides the basic database background needed to begin using SQL.

> This book will work with Oracle versions 7 and higher.

This book can be divided into two parts. Part I (Chapters 0–10) covers topics meant for introductory-level database classes or a beginning SQL/Oracle class. Part II (Chapters 11–13) is a *preview* of advanced topics, usually covered in advanced database classes, and is really meant for more advanced students. Part II assumes that students have some programming background, or have had at least one programming course.

Chapter 0 introduces some of the database terms that will be used throughout the book and shows how and why the relational database model fits into the database world of today. Chapter 1 begins in a step-by-step manner, signing the user into Oracle, and then covers basic Oracle/SQL topics such as SELECT, INSERT, DELETE, and so on. Simple editing concepts are also introduced in this chapter. Chapter 2 covers more beginning SQL commands, while Chapter 3 introduces joins. Chapters 4 and 5 get into basic Oracle functions and query development, the use of views, and other derived structures. Chapter 6 covers simple set operations, while Chapters 7, 8, and 9 cover subqueries, aggregate functions, and correlated subqueries. Chapters 10 through 13 introduce more advanced SQL concepts, such as the load utility, start files, reports, some introductory PL/SQL, and triggers. As we mentioned earlier, we have included exercises at the end of every chapter, which test the material in the respective chapters and incorporate a review of previous chapters.

As noted above, we have included Appendix 1 for users in the UNIX environment. Appendix 2 covers data dictionary concepts, while Appendix 3 lays out the Student-course tables and other tables that have been used throughout the book. Appendix 4 lists and briefly describes some important improvements in Oracle 8*i* and 9*i*. In addition, we have provided a Glossary of Terms and a Glossary of Important Commands and Functions for your reference. Finally, an Index of Important Commands and Functions and an Index of Terms have been provided for easy reference.

Overall, although this book does not discuss advanced features such as performance tuning issues or advanced PL/SQL, it is ideal for a beginning Oracle user to get an overview of what SQL and Oracle entails. The book gives a very good "feel" for what Oracle is and the many ways Oracle can be used. It certainly can be considered a starting point for what Oracle has to offer.

Supplements

The exercises at the end of each chapter are drawn from databases that we created and that can be downloaded from the Addison-Wesley site for this book (www.aw.com/cssupport) and from www.cs.uwf.edu/~rearp or www.cs.uwf.edu/~sbagui. The download instructions are also available at these Web sites.

In addition, solutions are available exclusively to qualified instructors only. Please contact your local sales representative or send email to aw.cse@awl.com for access information.

Acknowledgements

Our special thanks are due to our editors, Katherine Harutunian and Maite Suarez-Rivas for their invaluable guidance and assistance during this project. We would also like to thank Susan Hartman Sullivan, Executive Editor; Michael Hirsch, Executive Marketing Manager; Marilyn Lloyd, Production Supervisor; Sally Boylan, Project Manager; Laura Hemrika, Associate Project Manager; Shannon Leuma, Copyeditor; Kim Cofer, Proofreader; Sandra Rigney, for Text Design; Gina Hagen Kolenda, Design Manager; and Caroline Fell in Prepress and Manufacturing, for all their expertise and care during the final production of this book.

We are also indebted to the following reviewers Rocky Conrad, San Antonio College; Rose Endres, City College of San Francisco; Le Gruenwald, The University of Oklahoma; Arijit Sengupta, Indiana University; Munindar P. Singh, North Carolina State University; Junping Sun, Nova Southeastern University; and Salih Yurttas, Texas A&M University who have taken their time and effort to meticulously review this work and make helpful comments and suggestions.

Finally we would like to thank all our colleagues in the Department of Computer Science at The University of West Florida; special thanks goes to the Chair of the Department, Dr. Mohsen Guizani, Dr. Ed Rodgers, and Dr. Norman Wilde, for their encouragement and support.

The Software Engineering Process and Relational Databases

This chapter is provided for those students who wish to study SQL and database topics but feel that they lack sufficient computer experience. This chapter is not intended to replace a course about databases; a theoretical database course is often taught concurrently with a study of this material.

The chapter begins with some preliminary definitions and a short history of databases, followed by a description of how and why the relational database model fits into the database world of today. We then delve into a more detailed description of relational databases and normal forms. Finally, we provide a brief explanation of software engineering. Some knowledge of how software (SQL "programs," if you will) might be developed is useful in understanding why we suggest using some formats and conventions in this book.

What Is a Database?

Data—facts about something—must be stored in some fashion in order for it to be useful (that is, in order for it to be found). A **database** is a collection of associated or related data. For example, the collection of all the information in a doctor's office could be referred to as a "medical office database"; all data in this database would refer to information that is pertinent to the operation of a medical office. Before the age of computers, databases were kept on paper (medical databases were kept in doctor's offices, personnel databases were kept in employment offices, and so on). However, databases have migrated from paper to magnetic media over the past 40 years or so, and current databases are usually stored on magnetic disks.

Regardless of the format (paper or electronic), information stored in databases is organized into files. *Files* are a collection of data about one subject. A medical office database might well have files other than patient data. One might imagine that in a doctor's office there would be a pharmaceutical file, employee files, and so on.

Individual data is stored in ***records*** within files. For example, Mr. Smith's medical *records* would be located in his doctor's patient *files*. Individual items in Mr. Smith's records would include his name, his address, and so on. Information such as name and address is referred to as a ***field*** or ***attribute***. Thus, databases contain files, files contain records, and records contain fields (attributes).

Database Models

A conceptual way of thinking about data in a database is called a ***logical model***. With a logical model, we *conceptualize* how data might be organized. The way that data is actually laid out on the disk—that is, where each bit is located—is called a ***physical model***.

Over the past 20 years or so, three basic camps of logical database models have been presented:

• the hierarchical model

• the network model

• the relational model

All three of these models represent ways of logically perceiving the arrangement of data in databases. As you will see, the hierarchical and network models can infer some knowledge of how the physical model operates, whereas the relational model virtually ignores the physical model. We will now give a little insight into each of these three main models to see how the relational model has evolved into the dominant logical model.

The Hierarchical Model

The idea in a ***hierarchical model*** is that all data is logically arranged in a hierarchical fashion (also known as a *parent-child* relationship). Suppose that your company had an employee database. Further, suppose that this database contained files about employees and files about the dependents of employees. Some employees have dependents; some do not. For those employees who do have dependents, there must be a reference in those employees' records to the location of corresponding dependent records in the dependent file.

If an employee has dependents, you can think of that employee as being the "parent" of the dependent. Thus, every dependent *would have* one employee-parent and every employee *could have* one or more dependent-children. (Please note that the "parent" and "child" inference is not necessarily meant to be a personal relationship; "child" and "parent" are not meant to be taken literally.) The connection of the employee to a dependent and vice versa is called a ***relationship***. Figure 0.1 illustrates the hierarchical model.

In logical models, all relationships between records have what is called ***structural constraints***. Structural constraints indicate how many of one type of record is related to another (also called *cardinality*) and whether one type of record must have such a relationship (also called *participation* or *optionality*).

For example, suppose that an employee *may* have *one or more* dependents, and all dependents in a database *must* be related to *one and only one* employee. We would term the cardinality of this relationship of employee to dependent as *one to many*, or 1:M. Further, since we say that an

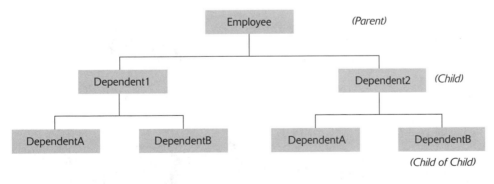

FIGURE 0.1 Hierarchical Model

employee may (or may not) have dependents, the participation constraint of the relationship from the employee side is *partial* or *optional*. Because a dependent must be associated with one employee, the participation from the dependent side is *full* or *mandatory*. Note that the words "one or more" and "one and only one" indicate cardinality. The words "may" and "must" indicate optionality or participation.

In a hierarchical model, there are either one-to-one (1:1) or one-to-many (1:M) relationships (as shown in Figures 0.2 and 0.3, respectively), but never many-to-one (M:1) relationships. The most common relationship in a hierarchical model is 1:M. In our example, a 1:M relationship means that one employee may have many dependents ("many" meaning one or more). Further, the 1:M employee-to-dependent relationship implies that each dependent has one and only one employee-parent.

Less common, but allowable in hierarchical models, is the 1:1 relationship shown in Figure 0.2. In our employee example, a 1:1 relationship would imply that one employee might have one designated dependent and a dependent would be related to only one employee. This relationship might infer a "next-of-kin" designation, for example.

Other Cardinalities

> While M usually stands for "many," M:N is used more often than M:M to stand for many-to-many because it's important not to infer that the values for M and N need be equal; in fact, they usually are not.

A *many-to-one* (M:1) relationship between employee and dependent would imply that a dependent might have multiple parents (multiple employees who "claimed" a particular dependent). However, because the relationship is M:1, it would infer that an employee could have at most one dependent. Again, the M:1 relationship is not allowed in hierarchical logical models.

FIGURE 0.2 One-to-One (1:1) Relationship

FIGURE 0.3 One-to-Many (1:M) Relationship

The very common *many-to-many* (M:N) relationship, shown in Figure 0.4, is not allowed in hierarchical database models either.

We'll discuss examples of these hierarchically unallowable relationships (M:1 and M:N) when we look at the network model.

Connecting Records

Before the advent of computers, hierarchical databases were implemented by choosing some way of *physically* connecting the parent and child records. Suppose that an employee, Mr. Smith, had three children, Sally, Ann, and Tom. If we think back to paper records, we might visualize that in the dependent file, there could be a Sally Smith record, an Ann Smith record, and a Tom Smith record. Where would these independent records be in the dependent file? Suppose we put the dependent records in a filing cabinet and put the notation in Mr. Smith's record that his dependents were Sally (file drawer 1, record 2), Ann (file drawer 3, record 12), and Tom (file drawer 2, record 13). Here, we are using a system to "point to" the dependent records from Mr. Smith's employee record. This scheme is called a *multiple-child pointer scheme.*

On a disk, one has little choice but to "point to" physical locations for the dependent records. Yet there are multiple ways to implement this hierarchical model. In addition to using a disk address instead of "file drawer x, record y," a *different* way to implement the employee-dependent relationship would be to have an employee record point to a disk location for a dependent record. That dependent record would in turn point to the disk location of the next dependent, and so on. In this example, Mr. Smith would point to Sally, Sally would point to Ann, and Ann would point to Tom. This is called a *linked list of child-records,* or, in older database books, a *chain* of records because they can be thought of as record-links that are chained together.

The hierarchical model has two major drawbacks:

• The choice of the way in which the files are physically linked impacts the way underlying database software is developed and hence impacts database performance both positively and negatively.

FIGURE 0.4 Many-to-Many (M:N) Relationship

• Not all situations fall into parent-child (hierarchical) formats. What if you wanted to have a dependent (a child record) point to multiple employees (multiple parent records) and vice versa (that is, an M:N relationship)? This would not fit the hierarchical database model well.

To see a way around these drawbacks, let's take a look at the network model.

The Network Model

The *network model* alleviates the multiple parent concern of the hierarchical model. In the network model, you are not restricted to having one parent per child—a many-to-one (M:1) and a many-to-many (M:N) relationship is acceptable. As an example, if your network-modeled database consisted of your employee-dependent situation as in the hierarchical model but it was necessary to allow multiple parents for each dependent person, then a dependent could have two or more "parents." Therefore, a dependent could relate to one or more employees. In this case, we would say that the relationship was many-to-many (M:N). An employee *may* have many dependents (*zero or more*) and a dependent *must* have a relationship to many (*one or more*) employees.

Implementing the employee-dependent M:N database in hierarchical databases involves creating redundant files. However, in network databases, you can simply have two or more connections or links from the dependent-child to however many parents there are. If you considered the multiple-child pointer scheme or the chaining system we described earlier in a network setting, you might imagine that the pointing schemes in networked databases are very complex. Indeed they are.

To illustrate the network model, suppose we consider a database of employees and projects to which they are assigned. Figure 0.5 is an example of a network model in which employees may be working on

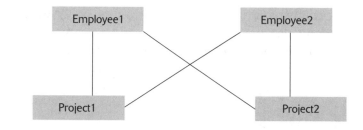

FIGURE 0.5 Network Model

many projects, and the projects may have many employees working on them. This is a *many-to-many* (M:N) relationship between employee and project.

Connecting Records

As in the hierarchical model, the database software in the network model must be designed using some pointing scheme; one would have to choose some method of connecting or linking records. This choice of record connection then presents a hardware-implemented connection, which impacts performance both positively and negatively. Further, as the database becomes more complicated, the paths of connections and the maintenance problems with all the links become exponentially more difficult for the software to manage. As you can imagine, networked linking is more complicated than hierarchical linking. As records are updated, inserted, or deleted, all links must be maintained. The more complicated the system, the more danger there is for dead links (that is, corrupted links or lost addresses).

Contemporary Databases: The Relational Model

Dr. Edgar F. Codd introduced the ***relational model*** around 1970 (Codd, 1970b). The relational model is based on the idea that if you ignore the way data files are connected and arrange your data into simple two-dimensional, unordered tables, then you can develop an algebra for queries and focus on the data as data, not as a physical realization of a logical model.

Before we delve into the details of the relational model, however, it's important that you understand some changes in terminology as databases evolved from file systems to relational databases. As you may know, current terminology refers to an *entity* as something we record information about. For example, we record information (data, facts) about employees; hence, an employee is an entity. Whereas we used to refer to the *employee file*, we now refer to the set of employee entities, or an *employee entity set*. Likewise, employee records (now called *entities*) contain employee information fields (now called *attributes*) of the employee entity. The reason for using the terms *entity set*, *entity*, and *attribute* instead of *file*, *record*, and *field*, respectively, is to disconnect the idea of a physical file, record, and field from the logical notion of these things.

The relational model is truly logical in that one is no longer concerned with how data is physically stored. Rather, files (called *entity sets* in the relational model) are simply unordered, two-dimensional tables of simple data values (or sets of rows). Necessarily, there are rules that govern the way these tables "store" data. The first rule is that the data itself must be atomic—that is, not broken down into component parts. The tables of data are called *relations,* and because the data is stored in tables, each table has columns (which represent the attributes) and rows (which represent the instances of each entity). A collection of tables is referred to as a ***relational database.*** Table 0.1 shows an example of an Employee relation (a table with data in it).

Table 0.1: Example of an Employee Table

Employee		
name	address	project#
Smith	123 4th St.	101
Smith	123 4th St.	102
Jones	5 Oak Dr.	101

Employee is a table (that is, a relation), and name, address, and project# are attributes (that is, column names). The rows, such as <Smith, 123 4th St, 102>, represent an employee entity occurrence (data about a person named Smith, Smith's address, and the project# that Smith is working on). In relational databases, the ordering of the rows in the table is not defined. The rows are considered a set of rows and sets do not have to have an order. Rows are either *in* the set or they or not, but *where* they are in the set is irrelevant. Thus, Table 0.2 is equivalent to Table 0.1.

Table 0.2: A Re-ordered Employee Table

Employee		
name	address	project#
Smith	123 4th St.	102
Jones	5 Oak Dr.	101
Smith	123 4th St.	101

Obviously, databases contain more data than is illustrated in this Employee table. To arrive at a workable way of deciding which pieces of data go into which tables and to arrange the tables so that Codd's relational algebra would work, Codd proposed something he referred to as *normal forms* (Codd, 1970a, Codd, 1970c, Codd, 1971). He originally defined three normal forms: the first, second, and third normal forms. We'll look at each of these next.

The First Normal Form

The *first normal form (1NF)* requires that data in tables be atomic and be arranged in a two-dimensional layout. Atomicity implies that there be no column containing repeating groups. A *repeating group* refers to columns that may contain multiple occurrences of data. A repeating group is an example of non-atomic data and violates the definition of a relational table. A problem with putting data in tables with repeating groups is that the table cannot be easily indexed or arranged in such a way that data in the repeating group can easily be found. Put another way, data in repeating groups cannot be found without searching each row individually.

An example of a table *not* in 1NF is where there is an employee entity with attributes (fields) name, address, and dependent name, as shown below:

```
Employee (name, address, {dependent name}),
```

Here, {dependent name} implies that the attribute is repeated, with rows containing data as illustrated below:

```
Smith, 123 4th St., {John, Mary, Paul, Sally}
Jones, 5 Oak Dr., {Mary, Frank, Bob}
Adams, 33 Dog Ave., {Alice, Alicia, Mary}
```

What do you do if you want to store data about employees and their dependents? Before tackling the problem of dealing with non-1NF data, it is helpful to understand the concept of a key. A *key* in a table is an attribute or group of attributes that identifies a row—a unique handle whereby one can find information in a table. In Table 0.2, the key could be the employee's last name. For example, if you wanted information about Jones, you would access Jones's row. Clearly, if there were two Joneses, you would have to come up with a better key, such as adding an employee number to the key, for example.

To resolve the non-1NF problem (and other NF problems that you will encounter), databases must be *normalized*. The normalization process involves splitting tables into two or more tables (a process called *decomposition*). Data can be reunited from decomposed tables with a relational operation called a **join**. We will illustrate the normalization process by first solving the non-1NF problem. To eliminate the non-1NF problem, we do the following:

Non-1NF to First Normal Form (1NF): The repeating group is moved to a new table with the key of the table from which it came.

We will assume that the last name of the employee is the key in this version of Employee.

```
Non-1NF:
Smith, 123 4th St., {John, Mary, Paul, Sally}
Jones, 5 Oak Dr., {Mary, Frank, Bob}
Adams, 33 Dog Ave., {Alice, Alicia, Mary}
```

is decomposed into 1NF tables with no repeating groups, as shown in Table 0.3a and Table 0.3b.

Table 0.3a: Employee Table in 1NF

Employee1	
name	address
Smith	123 4th St
Jones	5 Oak Dr
Adams	33 Dog Ave

Table 0.3b: Dependent Table in 1NF

Dependent	
dependentName	employeeName
John	Smith
Mary	Smith
Paul	Smith
Sally	Smith
Mary	Jones
Frank	Jones

Table 0.3b: Dependent Table in 1NF

Dependent	
dependentName	employeeName
Alice	Adams
Alicia	Adams
Mary	Adams

In Table 0.3a, `name` is the key of `Employee1`—it uniquely identifies the rows. We would call `name`, as used here, a ***primary key***. A primary key is the key that we choose to uniquely identify a row or tuple. In Table 0.3b, the primary key is a combination (concatenation) of `dependentName` and `employeeName`. Neither the `dependentName` nor the `employeeName` is unique in Table 0.3b, and hence both attributes are required to uniquely identify a row in the table. The `employeeName` in Table 0.3b is called a ***foreign key*** because it references a primary key: `name` in Table 0.3a. Note that the original data

```
Non-1NF:
Smith, 123 4th St., {John, Mary, Paul, Sally}
Jones, 5 Oak Dr., {Mary, Frank, Bob}
Adams, 33 Dog Ave., {Alice, Alicia, Mary}
```

could be reconstructed by combining all the rows in Table 0.3a with the corresponding rows in Table 0.3b where the names were equal. The combination of tables based on the equality of some attribute is called an *equi-join* in a relational database.

The Second Normal Form

The ***second normal form (2NF)*** requires that data in tables depend on the whole key of the table. If a data item depends on only part of a compound key, it is said to be a *partial dependency*. Partial dependencies are not allowed in the second normal form. Consider, for example, a table called `Employee2` with attributes `name`, `job`, `salary`, and `address`, as shown below:

```
Employee2(name, job, salary, address)
```

Further suppose that it takes a combination of the `name` and `job` fields (which can also be shown as `name + job`) to identify a `salary` field, but the `address` field depends only on the `name` field. `Name + job`, a concatenated key, then, is the primary key of this table. *Dependence* here means identification; "address depends on `name`" means that if you know the `name`, this will identify the person's `address` in this data. We would say that the dependence of `address` on `name` is a partial dependency because `name` is only part of the primary key of the table. Table 0.4 shows some sample data for the `Employee2` table.

Table 0.4: A Non-2NF Table

| Employee2 | | | |
name	job	salary	address
Smith	Welder	14.75	123 4th St.
Smith	Programmer	24.50	123 4th St.
Smith	Waiter	7.50	123 4th St.
Jones	Programmer	26.50	5 Oak Dr.
Jones	Bricklayer	34.50	5 Oak Dr.
Adams	Analyst	28.50	33 Dog Ave.

Can you see the problem developing here? The `address` is repeated for each occurrence of a `name`. This repetition is called ***redundancy*** and leads to anomalies. An ***anomaly*** means that there is a restriction on doing something due to the arrangement of the data. There are insertion anomalies, deletion anomalies, and update anomalies. The key of this table is `name + job`. This is clear because neither attribute will, by itself, identify information in a particular row—it takes both the `name` and `job` fields to identify a `salary`. (Try to answer the question, "What is Smith's salary?" without saying what the `job` is). However, `address` depends only on the `name`, not the `job`. This is an example of a partial dependency. `Address` depends on only part of the key of this table.

An example of an insertion anomaly would be where you would want to insert a person into the preceding table (Table 0.4) but the person to be inserted is not, as yet, assigned a `job`. You cannot make this insertion because a value would have to be known for the `job` attribute. A further rule of a relational database is that no part of the primary key of a relation may be a null or have an unknown value (this is known as the *entity-*

integrity constraint). What's wrong with null values in keys? If a null were allowed in a key, the key would have a non-unique value and hence not be a key at all.

An example of an update anomaly would be where one of the employees changed their `address`. Suppose the person named Smith had a change of address. You would have to change three rows to accommodate this one change.

An example of a delete anomaly would be that if Adams quits, Adams' row is deleted; however, the information that the analyst pay is $28.50 is also lost. Therefore, a delete anomaly deletes more than is desired. How do we decompose a non-2NF table to fix these problems?

Non-2NF to 2NF: To make a non-2NF table a 2NF table, partial dependency has to be removed to a new table. The attributes or fields that are fully dependent of the primary key (primary key here being `name` + `job`) are put together with the primary key (as shown in Table 0.5a). The `salary` is dependent on both parts of the primary key (`name` and `job`), so the `salary` is placed with the `name` and `job` fields in Table 0.5a.

Table 0.5a: Employee Salary Table

EmployeeSalary		
name	job	salary
Smith	Welder	14.75
Smith	Programmer	24.50
Smith	Waiter	7.50
Jones	Programmer	26.50
Jones	Bricklayer	34.50
Adams	Analyst	28.50

The fields that are not fully dependent on the primary key are then placed with the part of the primary key that they are dependent on. In this case, the `address` field (which is only dependent on part of the primary key) is placed with `name` (the part of the primary key that `address` is dependent on). This is shown in Table 0.5b.

Table 0.5b: Employee Information Table

EmployeeInformation	
name	address
Smith	123 4th St.
Jones	5 Oak Dr.
Adams	33 Dog Ave.

Hence the non-2NF table, Table 0.4, is decomposed to the 2NF tables, Table 0.5a and Table 0.5b.

The key of the `EmployeeSalary` table (Table 0.5a) is as before—the `name` and the `job` taken together. The key of the `EmployeeInformation` table (Table 0.5b) is just the `name`. Note that the "other" non-key attributes in both tables now depend on the key (and only on the key). Also, note the removal of unnecessary redundancy and the ending of possible anomalies. For practice, try adding, deleting, and updating rows and note that the anomalies are gone.

The Third Normal Form

The **third normal form (3NF)** requires that data in tables depend on the primary key of the table. 2NF problems only appear when there is a concatenated key to begin with; 3NF problems do not require a concatenated key. 3NF problems occur when some non-key data item is more properly identified by something other than the key of the table. A classic example of non-3NF relation could be shown by the `Employee3` table shown below. `Employee3` has the attributes `name`, `address`, `project#`, and `project-location`.

    Employee3(name, address, project#, project-location)

In `Employee3` we will assume that the `name` field is the primary key. Suppose that `project-location` in `Employee3` means the location from which a project is controlled, and is defined by the `project#`. Some sample data will illustrate the problem with this table, as shown in Table 0.6.

Table 0.6: A Non-3NF Table

Employee3			
name	address	project#	project Location
Smith	123 4th St.	101	Memphis
Smith	123 4th St.	102	Mobile
Jones	5 Oak Dr.	101	Memphis

Note the redundancy in Table 0.6. Project 101 is controlled from Memphis, but every time a person is recorded as working on project 101, the fact that they work on a project that is controlled from Memphis is recorded again. The same anomalies—insert, update, and delete—are also present in this table. You cannot add a `project#–project location` unless you have a `name`. (Remember that `name` cannot be null.) If you deleted Smith's working on project 102 in the preceding table, the "102, Mobile" information is also deleted. Suppose project 101's control is moved to Tuscaloosa? How many changes would this require?

The `name`, `project#`, `project-location` situation is called a ***transitive dependency***. This transitive dependency is relieved by decomposing into 3NF as follows.

Non-3NF to 3NF: To make a non-3NF table into a 3NF table, transitive dependency has to be removed to a new table. Thus, Table 0.6 is decomposed into two tables, Table 0.7a and Table 0.7b.

Table 0.7a: Employee Table in 3NF

Employee3a		
name	address	project#
Smith	123 4th St.	101
Smith	123 4th St.	102
Jones	5 Oak Dr.	101

Table 0.7b: Project Table in 3NF

Project	
project#	project Location
101	Memphis
102	Mobile
101	Memphis

Again, observe the removal of the transitive dependency and the anomaly problem.

Before leaving the topic of normal forms, note that there are other cases of non-normality that are beyond the scope of this brief overview. These other cases are not common, and a "good" relational database may be thought of as one that is in the 3NF.

In summary, there are rules that define a relational database. All data is laid out in two-dimensional tables. The tables have no sense of ordering of rows. In fact, the tables are often called "sets of rows." All data is atomic. A primary key is a chosen unique row-identifier; if you want information from a row in a table, you get it by the primary key value. The 3NF means that the data in a relation depends only on the primary key of the relation. Data in 3NF is assumed to be in the 1NF and 2NF. Data that is decomposed into the 3NF will avoid most redundancy and anomaly problems.

What Is the Software Engineering Process?

As a further bit of orientation to the material contained in this book, we wish to present some insight into how software is developed. The term *software engineering* refers to a process of specifying, designing, writing, delivering, maintaining, and, finally, retiring software. Many excellent references on the topic of software engineering (including Norman, 1996, and Schach, 1999) are available to the interested reader.

A basic idea in software engineering is that to build software correctly, a series of standardized steps or phases are required. The steps ensure that a process of thinking precedes action. That is, thinking through "what is needed" precedes "what is written." One common version of presenting the thinking-before-acting scenario is referred to as a *waterfall model*, as described in Schach, (1999), as the phases are supposed to flow from one another in a directional way without retracing.

Software production is like a life-cycle process—it is created, used, and eventually retired. The "players" in the software development life cycle may be placed into two camps, often referred to as the *user* and the *analyst*. Software is designed by the *analyst* for the *user*.

There is no general agreement among software engineers as to the exact number of phases in the waterfall-type software development model. Models vary depending on the interest of the author in one part or another in the process. A very brief description of the software process goes like this:

Step 1 (or Phase 1). *Requirements*: find out what the user wants/needs.

Step 2. *Specification*: write out the user wants/needs as precisely as possible.

Step 3. *Software is designed* to meet the specification from Step 2.

Step 4. *Software is written (developed).*

Step 5. *Software is turned over to user (implementation).*

Step 6. *Maintenance* is performed on software until it is retired.

In most software engineering models, some feedback loops are allowed. For example, when completing Step 2, it is possible to go back to Step 1 if the analyst does not understand the user's requirements.

For SQL users, the software process is involved in accessing data from a database. As mentioned earlier, a database is a collection of facts stored on some medium—normally a magnetic disk. Often the question in SQL is "What does some user want to know"? This question is called a *query* in a database because it is a question directed at the information contained in the database.

What does software engineering have to do with writing queries? We can draw a number of implications from the software engineering process. In the normal business world, the person who writes SQL queries is often not the person who wants to know something. Imagine a supervisor telling a SQL programmer to find the names of all the customers who spent over $1,000 this month. The SQL programmer must design a query for this request. Does the SQL programmer understand the nature of the question? (requirements) Did the SQL-programmer provide feedback to the supervisor and verify what he or she thinks the question is? (specification) What kind of query will the SQL programmer decide upon? (design) Once the query is written, is it efficient? Does it answer the original question? Is the execution of the query ready for turning over the result to the supervisor? (development/implementation) What if the supervisor now wants to change the amount in the query or the month or the format of the names? (maintenance)

Thus, queries should be written so that other people can immediately understand what the writer intended. Most of the money spent on software is on maintenance. Maintenance is a very time-consuming and expensive part of the software process—particularly if the software engineering process has not been done well. Maintenance involves correcting hidden software faults as well as enhancing the functionality of the software.

One of the goals of this text is to teach you not only how to write queries, but how to write them so that other SQL programmers will know that you understood the requirements and so that your queries are open to maintenance. We also have tried to suggest ways to audit your query results. As with other programming, computers only do what you tell them to do. If you ask for garbage, you will get garbage. If your query is not correctly formed, SQL may give you an answer, but the answer may not be correct or make sense. You must ask yourself, does the query really answer the question that was originally asked? Will other SQL programmers understand my query?

REFERENCES

Codd, E.F., (1970a). "Notes on a Data Sublanguage," IBM internal memo (January 19, 1970).

Codd, E.F., (1970b). "A Relational Model of Data for Large Shared Data Banks," *CACM 13*, No. 6 (June, 1970).

Codd, E.F., (1970c). "The Second and Third Normal Forms for the Relational Model," IBM technical memo (October 6, 1970).

Codd, E.F. (1971). "A Data Base Sublanguage Founded on the Relational Calculus," IBM Research Report RJ893 (July 26, 1971).

Norman, R.J., (1996). *Object-Oriented Systems Analysis and Design.* Upper Saddle River, NJ: Prentice Hall.

Schach, S.R., (1999). *Classical and Object Oriented Software Engineering,* WCG McGraw-Hill, New York.

Getting Started with Oracle 8 in the Windows Environment

In this chapter, we'll cover some elementary commands, statements, and procedures that will allow us to use Structured Query Language, or SQL. We'll look at generic operations that we can do with SQL and specific statements that pertain to the principal delivery system, Oracle. We'll be concentrating on SQL*PLUS (often called SQLPLUS and henceforth referred to as such), which is used to generate, store, and edit SQL queries and to control the database environment.

The database model that we will use throughout this workbook is the Student-Course database example (shown in Appendix 3). We'll call this our "standard" database to distinguish it from tables you will have to create "on the fly." You can download this database from www.cs.uwf.edu/~rearp or www.cs.uwf.edu/~sbagui. (The download instructions are available at these Web sites.)

> In this book, we'll concentrate on the Windows version of Oracle. For information on using Oracle in the UNIX operating system, see Appendix 1.

Getting Started on Oracle

Once you have installed Oracle on your personal computer system, you are ready to start. In this first section, you'll learn how to sign onto Oracle.

Signing onto Oracle

To start Oracle in the Windows environment, go to the START menu, select PROGRAM, ORACLE-ORAHOME81, APPLICATION DEVELOPMENT, and then SQL PLUS, as shown in Figure 1.1. You will then see the screen shown in Figure 1.2.

To log in as the system administrator, type in `System` for the userid, and `Manager` for the password. To log in as a user, the default userid (that comes with Oracle) is `scott` and the password is `tiger`.

At this point, you should download the script ("load_all2.sql") from the Web site into Oracle's bin directory, and run it before proceeding. (Follow the instructions on the Web site.) After you have run the "load_all2.sql" script, you'll have created a unique Oracle userid and password. From this point on, you should use this userid and password to sign on to Oracle. Normally, you would use only your own userid and password in a real-world database (that is, not the defaults).

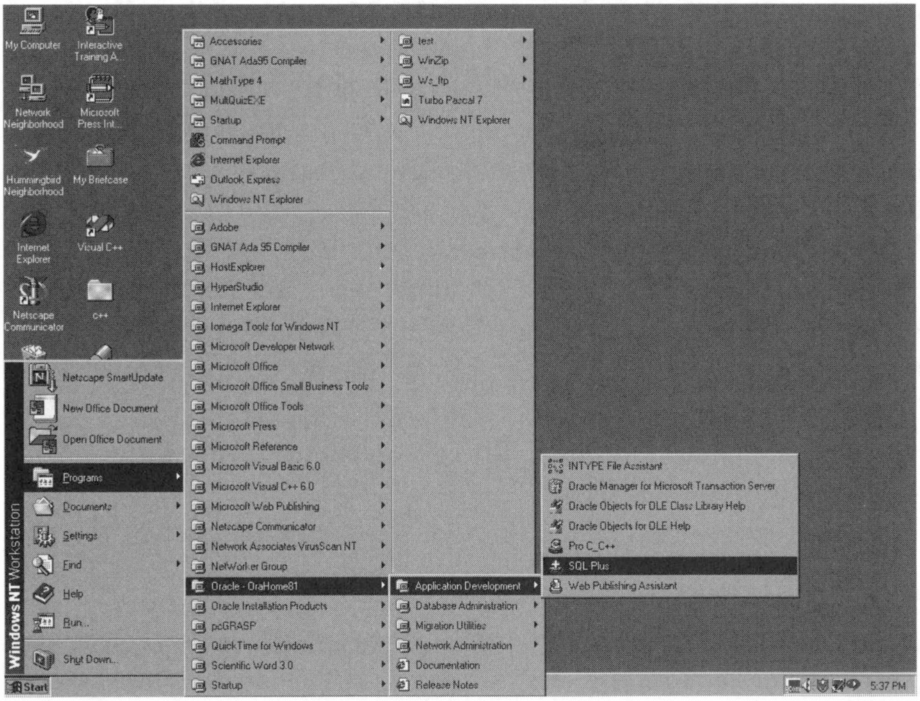

FIGURE 1.1 Signing on to Oracle

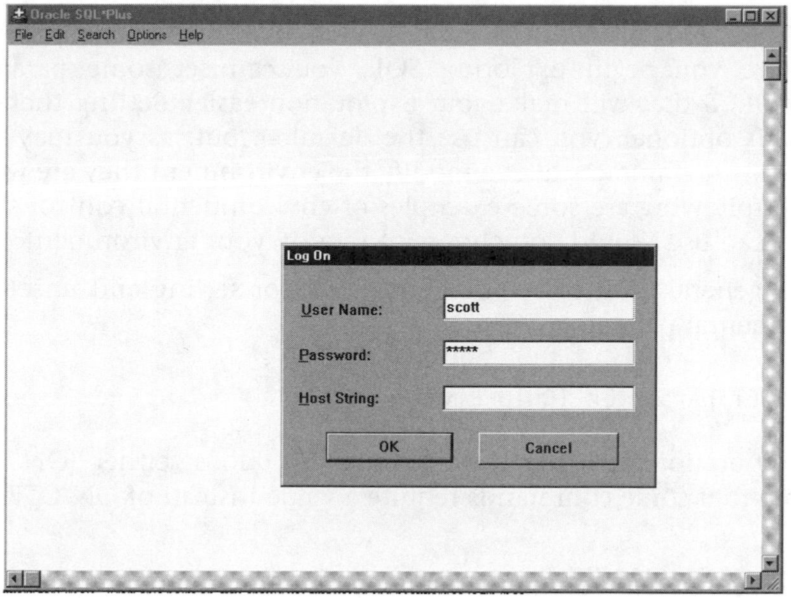

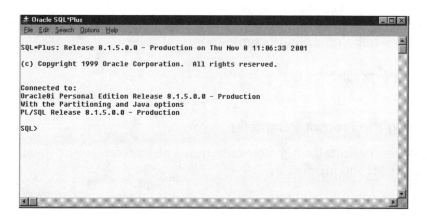

FIGURE 1.2 The Oracle Sign on Screen

Once you have correctly signed on, SQLPLUS will announce that you are connected to ORACLE and will display the SQL prompt. The default SQL prompt is

```
SQL>
```

This is shown in the screen in Figure 1.3.

You are now in SQLPLUS, and it awaits your instructions.

FIGURE 1.3 The Default SQL Prompt

Setting Your System Parameters

Before you begin exploring SQL, you can set some parameters in SQLPLUS that will make your exploration easier. Setting these parameters is optional (you can use the defaults), but, as you may be aware, many programmers like to modify the environment they are working in. The following are some examples of environmental control statements you can use should you choose to modify your environment.

The general form of the SET command for setting and unsetting environmental parameters is:

```
SET parameter [ON|OFF|value]
```

The notation [ON|OFF] means you are to choose either "ON" or "OFF." Note that some commands require a value instead of ON/OFF.

Setting the PAUSE Parameter

The first useful parameter we will illustrate is PAUSE. When you execute a command that has a long output, the screen view of the result will scroll by very quickly. To keep your screen from scrolling, you can pause the screen and view results by the "screenfull" by pressing the <Enter> key to move to the next screen. The command is

```
SQL> SET PAUSE ON
```

> Oracle is case *insensitive* to *commands*, so "SET PAUSE ON" is the same as "Set pause on" or "set pause on." However, Oracle is case *sensitive* to *data*, as we will illustrate later.

This is shown in the screen in Figure 1.4.

If you have a long result and you wish to terminate the command and you have "pause on," you can use <Ctrl>C and <Enter>. If you wish to reset "SET PAUSE ON" to where the screen will keep scrolling (that is, not pause) when you execute commands, you type:

```
SQL> SET PAUSE OFF
```

Setting the Prompt Parameter

Another personalized parameter that can be set is the prompt. The default for the prompt is:

```
SQL>
```

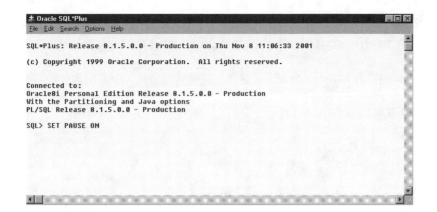

FIGURE 1.4 Oracle SQLPLUS Screen—Setting the PAUSE Parameter

To change the default SQL prompt, you can type something like the following:

```
SQL> SET SQLPROMPT "Enter command ->"
```

This SET command will set the prompt so that it will look like the screen shown in Figure 1.5.

To get back to the "regular" prompt, you can type:

```
SQL> SET SQLP SQL>
```

Note that here, SETPROMPT may be abbreviated as SETP.

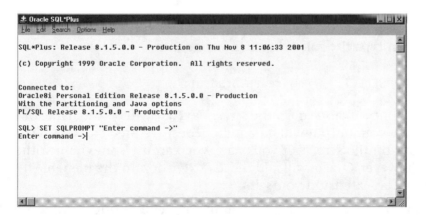

FIGURE 1.5 Setting the Prompt Parameter

Showing Timing Statistics

To show timing statistics for each SQL command that is executed, type:

```
SQL> SET TIMING ON
```

To reset the preceding, type:

```
SQL> SET TIMING OFF
```

Viewing a List of System Parameters

To view a list of all your system parameters, type:

```
SQL> SHOW ALL
```

Obviously, there are plenty of other SET commands. We'll look at additional commands later in the chapter.

Printing and Using HOST

To print the result of a query or a command, you can use the SPOOL command to create a file of your output, and then print the spooled file.

The SPOOLed file will be available through the operating system you are using (for example, Windows). To activate SPOOL, you enter the following:

```
SQL>SPOOL ex1
```

You then type the following SQL statement:

```
SQL> SELECT * from rearp.Student;
```

> You can also use the Windows cut and paste method with NOTEPAD or Word, but cutting and pasting is a poor substitute for the SPOOLing method described here.

The output will appear on the screen. *ex1.lst* will be the name of the file to which your output will be simultaneously redirected as it executes and displays on the screen. If you want, you can use some name other than *ex1*; however, Oracle will add the *.lst* extension to the filename if you do not add an extension yourself.

When you execute a series of commands, such as one or more SELECTs, you can examine the result from *ex1.lst*, as well as modify it or print it from the host operating system.

The command to turn off the spooler is

```
SQL>SPOOL OFF
```

You can use HOST from SQLPLUS to temporarily exit to your host operating system, use the operating system commands to do whatever you need to do, and then from the host operating system prompt type EXIT, which will put you back into SQLPLUS.

The following is a sequence of commands that shows how you would get to the host, use it, and get back to SQLPLUS.

At the SQL prompt, type:

```
SQL> HOST
```

Oracle under Windows uses DOS, so this will take you to the Oracle\BIN directory:

```
F:\Oracle\Ora81\BIN>
```

This is shown in the screen in Figure 1.6.

To see a directory listing of the files that you had spooled from within SQLPLUS, type:

```
F:\Oracle\Ora81\BIN> DIR *.lst
```

This is shown in the screen in Figure 1.7.

> There is a SPOOL OUT command as well, which will automatically route the output of the SPOOLer to a printer and turn off the SPOOLing at the same time. However, *most* of the time it is easier to control the spooled output via SPOOL OFF rather than SPOOL OUT.

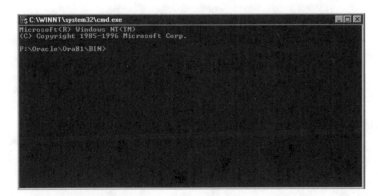

FIGURE 1.6 The Host Screen

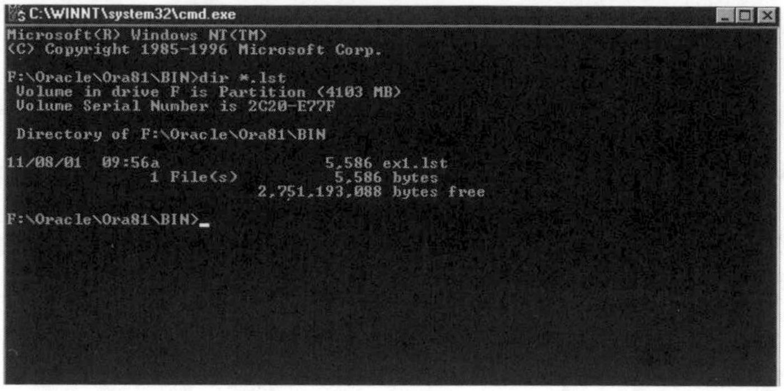

FIGURE 1.7 Viewing Spooled Files from Host

To view the *ex1.lst* file that you had spooled from SQLPLUS, type:

    F:\Oracle\Ora81\BIN> TYPE ex1.lst

To make a copy of your spooled file (for example, if you wanted to copy *ex1.lst* to a backup file called *ex1.bak*), type:

    F:\Oracle\Ora81\BIN> COPY ex1.lst ex1.bak

To get back to SQLPLUS from the host prompt, type:

    F:\Oracle\Ora81\BIN> EXIT

This should take you back to the SQL prompt:

    SQL>

You must turn off the SPOOLer before you can open the spooled file to read or copy it in the operating system.

Signing Off from Oracle

To exit SQLPLUS, type:

    SQL>EXIT

or

    SQL>QUIT

> If you turn off the SPOOLer and then later turn it back on in the sequence SPOOL ex1 then SPOOL OFF, and then you SPOOL ex1 again, you will write over the first version of *ex1.lst* with *no* warning, so be careful! Remember to use a new filename with the SPOOL command the next time you use it.

Using Oracle Commands

We will now begin looking into the syntax and semantics of the SQL language.

Understanding SQL and its Sub-Language

What we call "SQL" has several "sub languages," and as you grow more familiar with SQL programming, you will want to distinguish between them:

• *SQLPLUS (SQL*PLUS)* (typified by SPOOL, HELP, LIST, HOST, SET, and so on) is an Oracle application language from which Oracle commands are launched.

• *PL/SQL (as in BEGIN..END, EXIT, LOOP, IF, and so on)* is a procedural language we will explore later in this text. Note that SQL is a set language as opposed to a procedural language.

In addition, SQL itself is further subdivided into the following classes:

• *SQL—data definition language (DDL)* (for example, ALTER, CREATE, DROP)

• *SQL—data manipulation language (DML)* (for example, SELECT, INSERT)

• *SQL—security control* (for example, GRANT, REVOKE)

• *SQL—session control* (for example, ALTER SESSION, SET ROLE)

• *SQL—system control* (for example, ALTER SYSTEM, COMMENT)

• *SQL—transaction control* (for example, COMMIT, ROLLBACK)

SQL allows us to tell Oracle which pieces of information we want to:

• SELECT (retrieve) from a table

• INSERT (add data) to a table

• UPDATE (modify data) in a table

• DELETE (remove data) from a table

In fact, these four verbs are the primary SQL commands that we will use to deliver Oracle instructions. SELECT is the main query verb.

Using SELECT Statement Syntax

The syntax of the SELECT statement is:

```
SELECT result set FROM table
```

The "result set" is what we want to see. The result set is drawn from the list of columns that are available in a table. The "table" is the name of the table from which the data will be taken. The keywords SELECT and FROM are *always* present in a SELECT statement. Statements in Oracle are terminated by a semicolon, so to display a table called Student from our database you would enter:

```
SQL>SELECT * FROM rearp.Student;
```

Here, the "*" means "all columns" of the table Student.

If the Student table had a column called "sname" and you wanted to see only the names of the students, you could type:

```
SQL>SELECT sname FROM rearp.Student;
```

> If your screen appears frozen, press the <Enter> key. The freezing screen is probably due to the "SET PAUSE ON" command if you are using "pause on."

Re-Executing a Command

It is common to want to re-execute a command. Each command you issue from the SQL prompt is stored in a buffer. To re-execute a command from the buffer (that is, without typing it back in), you can use a "/". At the SQL prompt, if you type the following you will re-execute the last command you ran:

```
SQL> /
```

> As mentioned earlier, Oracle commands are case insensitive, so SELECT Sname or SELECT SNAME will also work.

Accessing Tables

As will often be the case, the table in the example mentioned earlier was created by another user—here, Richard Earp, who is identified under Oracle as rearp. Oracle allows you to control access to tables. In this case, you have been given the privilege to view a table called Student, which was created by rearp. To view the table, you need the name of the creator and the actual name of the table. You "qualify" the table name with the creator name, hence "rearp.Student" is used.

Suppose your name is S. Brown. If you had created a similar table under your own account, sbrown, and called it Student1, my statement (as executed from my account) would be SELECT * FROM sbrown.Student1; (assuming you gave me permission to view your table). You do not need to qualify your own tables; if you are sbrown and are logged in as sbrown, you would use SELECT * FROM Student1; from your own account to access your own table.

In Oracle, you can use as many lines as you wish to enter a statement. Oracle SQL acts like a "free-form" language. The system will not process an SQL statement until you enter a semicolon in a statement or a "/" on a line by itself in the first position. Actually, it is advantageous to use several lines to enter statements in Oracle because it makes the statements easier to change and re-execute. So, you could enter the previous statement as:

```
SQL> SELECT *
    2 FROM rearp.Student;
```

This format, in which we capitalize keywords such as SELECT and FROM and use lowercase letters for user-supplied words, is preferred by many SQL programmers and is an excellent convention to follow.

Adding Comments in Statements

Software engineering suggests that we write statements in a standard and understandable way. To aid in statement elucidation, comments are often used. Comments are ignored by SQLPLUS but are very useful to programmers in determining what a statement does, when it was written, who wrote it, and so on. Comments can be put into multi-line statements like this:

```
SQL>SELECT *              -- this statement shows only "seniors"
   2 FROM rearp.Student        -- due to use of WHERE clause
   3 WHERE class = 4;
```

The WHERE clause in this example is a *row filter*. The result set in this query consists of all the columns in the table Student, but only the columns WHERE the value of the Class attribute is equal to 4 (that is, seniors) are selected for the result set.

> The "-- comment" cannot be on the same line with the semicolon.

Another way to comment SQL is to use /* ... */. The following is an example of a commented statement that uses this format:

```
SQL>SELECT sname, class         /* get the sname and class */
FROM rearp.Student              /* from the Student table */
;
```

In some versions of Oracle, you cannot start a command with a comment as your first word because you need a keyword such as SELECT for correct syntax.

A Few More Examples and Further Comments about Case

As mentioned earlier, although SQL is **not** case sensitive for commands, SQL **is** case sensitive for data. The following statements, which basically ask to show all information about people whose name is "Smith," are equivalent as far as SQL is concerned:

```
SELECT * FROM rearp.Student WHERE sname = 'Smith';
Select * from rearp.Student where sname = 'Smith';
Select * FROM rearp.Student Where Sname = 'Smith';
```

However, the following examples would **not** retrieve any data:

```
SELECT * FROM rearp.Student WHERE sname = 'smith';
Select * from rearp.Student where sname = 'SMITH';
```

The reason for the non-return of data is that you need to match data in the database exactly. If the sname is stored as "Smith," then "SMITH" or "smith" won't match.

Editing SQL Statements

You will often need to edit SQL statements, and several methods of editing statements are available. The most common method is to use an editor (such as NOTEPAD). However, you can also edit a statement using SQLPLUS commands (for example, CHANGE, HOST, EDIT APPEND, INPUT, and DELETE [or some combination of these]). Although you should use whichever method you are most comfortable with, you should become familiar with both basic methods.

Option 1: Editing SQL Statements Using an Editor

If a statement is entered at the SQL prompt and if a change is desired, most programmers use an editor. For Windows, the default is NOTEPAD. However, if your default editor is not already defined, you can define an editor for your system. You can do this in Oracle 8 in the Windows environment by selecting EDIT, EDITOR, DEFINE EDITOR from the top menu. Then, in the screen that appears, type in whatever you would like to use as your default editor (if you don't want to use NOTEPAD).

Suppose you typed the following statement at the SQL prompt:

```
SQL> SELECT *
   2 FROM rearp.Student;
```

Now suppose you wanted to change the statement to look at the Course table instead of the Student table. There are actually two ways to edit using an editor: you can edit the buffer or you can edit a named file. Editing the buffer implies that you execute the preceding statement and then type:

```
SQL>EDIT
```

Or, more simply:

```
SQL>ED
```

You will then see the screen shown in Figure 1.8.

Typing ED calls up the default editor, NOTEPAD, from which you would EDIT the command. You would then choose FILE and SAVE from the top menu, EXIT the editor, and execute the changed buffer with a /. When

FIGURE 1.8 Edit Screen

you SAVE and EDIT and run the command in the command buffer, the file will have the default name "afiedt.buf."

Saving a Query

Editing the buffer is fine for "quick and dirty" work, but it is risky because you will inevitably write over your buffer command as you develop queries. This is because the buffer holds only one query when working with SQL in this way; thus, when you execute a second query, the first one is overwritten. So how do you save a query?

Again, operating from the SQL prompt, to save a query to a file, you can either:

• name the query from NOTEPAD using FILE and SAVE AS from the FILE pull-down menu, or

• use the SAVE command from the SQL prompt.

From NOTEPAD, if you have a file you want to name "something" and you do not add an extension, the file will be saved as "something.txt." *It is best when naming files in this way to choose "all files" from the combo box within NOTEPAD and name the file with the extension ".sql."* Oracle works best when commands have the ".sql" extension.

An alternative way to create a file for a query in the buffer is to use the SAVE command from the SQL prompt. For example, before invoking the editor, you can type:

```
SQL> SAVE ex23
```

This will create a file named *ex23.sql*. Then, you can edit the file from SQL using the command:

```
SQL> ED ex23
```

Because you now have a named file, you may also have occasion to enter the operating system using HOST and edit the *ex23.sql* file using whatever editor you choose (most likely NOTEPAD if you are using Windows).

Running a Stored Query

To run a query you have stored as a named file, type:

```
SQL> START ex23
```

or

```
SQL> @ex23
```

Naming Statements

When using SQL, it is a good practice to name every statement before it is written. For example, rather than write statements from the SQL prompt, write each statement in the editor in the first place. Rather than writing a statement at the prompt, type:

```
SQL> ed ex25.sql
```

NOTEPAD will respond that *ex25.sql* does not exist and then it will ask you if you want to create the file. Answer *yes* and then type your statement into NOTEPAD. When you exit NOTEPAD, the file *ex25.sql* is created and ready to be executed or edited. When proceeding in this way, you will not "/" (or execute) statements, but rather execute them using the START (@) command as follows:

```
SQL> @ex25
```

Using the GET Command

Finally, if you have stored a statement, you can edit it directly or bring it into the command buffer with the GET command. For example, you can type:

```
SQL> GET trial1.sql;
```

> The ";" after the GET statement is not required.

When would you use GET? If you have a statement (particularly an extensive one) and you want to create a new statement from within SQL and model it after the old one, you can either copy the old query file to a new file or you can bring the old statement into the buffer to "play with" using GET.

Option 2: Editing SQL Statements Using SQLPLUS

SQLPLUS supplies several commands to make minor changes to statements.

Using the CHANGE Command

If your change is simple (such as a misspelled word), you can use the CHANGE command. The format for CHANGE is:

```
CHANGE /old string/new string/
```

> The last "/" after "new string" is not required.

The CHANGE command works on one line at a time. For example, if you type:

```
SQL> SELECT * FROM rearp.Studens;
```

You get an error message that you determine means that you misspelled "Student" as "Studens." You change the query by typing:

```
SQL> CHANGE /ens/ent/
```

This will repair the current last line of the statement in the buffer. You should then display the buffer from which you "/" the statement to re-execute it.

Using the LIST Command

If the statement is multi-line, you should use LIST first to see the whole statement. Then, put in the line number you want to CHANGE, CHANGE the line, type LIST again, and then "/" to re-execute the statement. For example, if you type:

```
SQL> SELECT cou      [you press <Enter>]
FROM rearp.Prereq;   [you press <Enter>]
```

you get an error on "SELECT cou" because "cou" is not a valid attribute name. To correct the error with the line editor, complete the following steps:

1. To see the whole buffer, type:

```
SQL> LIST
```

This will give you:

```
1 SELECT cou
2* FROM rearp.Prereq
SQL>
```

2. To correct line 1 of the buffer, type:

```
SQL> 1 <Enter>
```

This will give you:

```
1* SELECT cou
```

3. To change cou to course_number, type:

```
SQL> CHANGE /cou/course_number/
```

This will give you:

```
1* SELECT course_number
```

4. To see the whole buffer, use LIST. In this case, you will see lines 1 and 2:

```
SQL> LIST
```

This will give you:

```
1 SELECT course_number
2* FROM rearp.Prereq
SQL>
```

This is shown in the screen in Figure 1.9.

5. Finally, to re-execute the corrected statement, type:

```
SQL> /
```

You will see the output shown in Figure 1.10.

Using Other Commands

As stated earlier, most SQL programmers use an editor only to make changes other than simple modifications. In addition to the CHANGE [c] and LIST [l] commands, you can use other line editor commands (although their use is rare nowadays). For example, if you want to add one line to the last line of a SQL statement, you can use APPEND. In addition, you can use the INPUT command to add a line to a statement

> SQLPLUS commands like CHANGE, LIST, APPEND, INPUT, and DELETE can be abbreviated. You need only type the single letter c for CHANGE, l for LIST, a for APPEND, i for input, and del for DELETE. Also, the command CHANGE will accept non-letter separators other than /. For example, the command CHANGE /ens/ent can be entered as c.ens.ent.

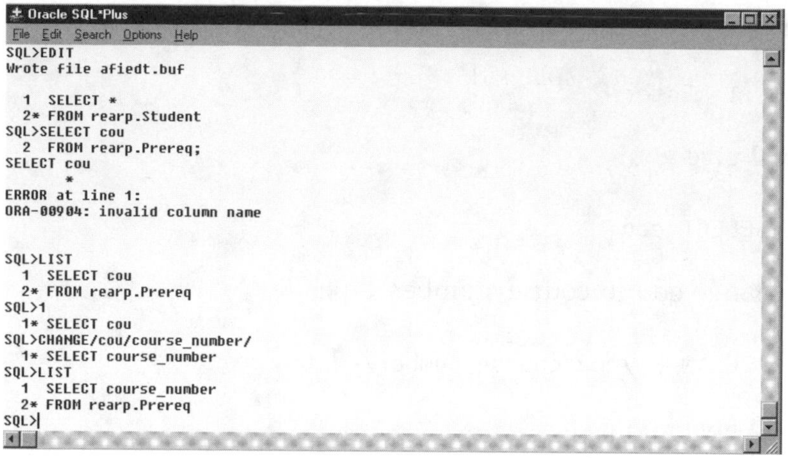

FIGURE 1.9 Editing Using SQLPLUS

anywhere, and the DELETE command will allow you to use the line editor to delete a line from a SQL statement.

Displaying the "Student-Course" Database

It is now time to explore the actual database you will be using to do the exercises in this book. We begin our exploration with simple, sample queries. The exercises will ask you to modify these sample queries to produce other results.

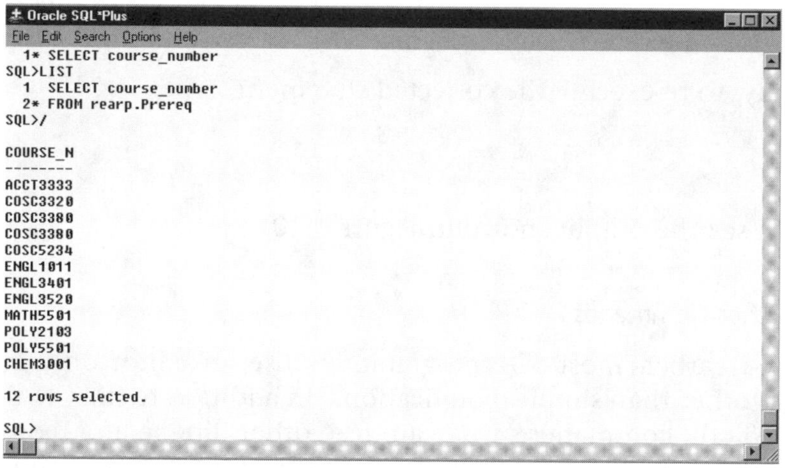

FIGURE 1.10 Output of Query

Displaying the Course Table (the Course Relation)

The statement that displays the `Course` table is:

```
SELECT *
FROM rearp.Course;
```

You will then see the screen shown in Figure 1.11.

Note that:

- The word SELECT is necessary for all queries.
- The * means all columns (attributes) will be in the result set.
- The word FROM is necessary for all SELECT commands as it defines the table from which you are SELECTing.
- `Course` is the name of the table you want to see. The "rearp." part of the table name is a necessary qualifier for our table.

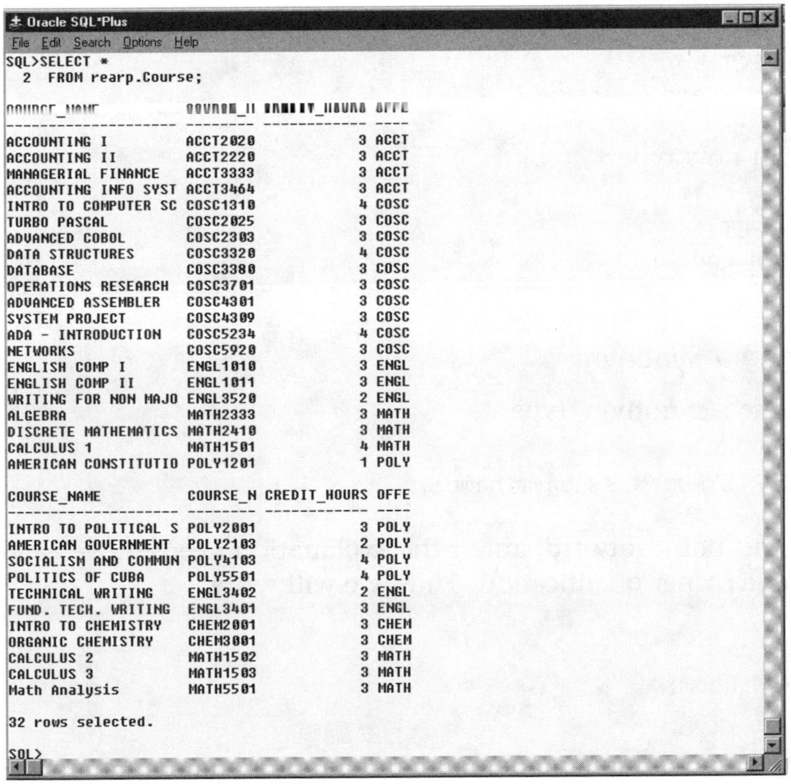


```
SQL>SELECT *
  2  FROM rearp.Course;

[illegible]
-------------------- -------- ------------ ----
ACCOUNTING I         ACCT2020            3 ACCT
ACCOUNTING II        ACCT2220            3 ACCT
MANAGERIAL FINANCE   ACCT3333            3 ACCT
ACCOUNTING INFO SYST ACCT3464            3 ACCT
INTRO TO COMPUTER SC COSC1310            4 COSC
TURBO PASCAL         COSC2025            3 COSC
ADVANCED COBOL       COSC2303            3 COSC
DATA STRUCTURES      COSC3320            4 COSC
DATABASE             COSC3380            3 COSC
OPERATIONS RESEARCH  COSC3701            3 COSC
ADVANCED ASSEMBLER   COSC4301            3 COSC
SYSTEM PROJECT       COSC4309            3 COSC
ADA - INTRODUCTION   COSC5234            4 COSC
NETWORKS             COSC5920            3 COSC
ENGLISH COMP I       ENGL1010            3 ENGL
ENGLISH COMP II      ENGL1011            3 ENGL
WRITING FOR NON MAJO ENGL3520            2 ENGL
ALGEBRA              MATH2333            3 MATH
DISCRETE MATHEMATICS MATH2410            3 MATH
CALCULUS 1           MATH1501            4 MATH
AMERICAN CONSTITUTIO POLY1201            1 POLY

COURSE_NAME          COURSE_N CREDIT_HOURS OFFE
-------------------- -------- ------------ ----
INTRO TO POLITICAL S POLY2001            3 POLY
AMERICAN GOVERNMENT  POLY2103            2 POLY
SOCIALISM AND COMMUN POLY4103            4 POLY
POLITICS OF CUBA     POLY5501            4 POLY
TECHNICAL WRITING    ENGL3402            2 ENGL
FUND. TECH. WRITING  ENGL3401            3 ENGL
INTRO TO CHEMISTRY   CHEM2001            3 CHEM
ORGANIC CHEMISTRY    CHEM3001            3 CHEM
CALCULUS 2           MATH1502            3 MATH
CALCULUS 3           MATH1503            3 MATH
Math Analysis        MATH5501            3 MATH

32 rows selected.

SQL>
```

FIGURE 1.11 SQL Query and Output

Creating a Synonym for the Course Table

As mentioned earlier, because the tables you will use were created by someone else, you must qualify the table name by indicating the table creator (owner) (for example, rearp.Course). Here, "rearp" is the owner (the creator) of the table Course. Qualifying the name of the tables you use frequently becomes tiresome. Therefore, most programmers find it useful to create a synonym for the qualified table names. The command for creating a synonym is:

```
CREATE SYNONYM x FOR y;
```

where x is the name you want to use, and y is the table you want to reference. For example, to create a synonym called cou for the Course table you would type:

```
CREATE SYNONYM cou FOR rearp.Course;
```

So, instead of typing:

```
SELECT *
FROM rearp.Course;
```

You can now type:

```
SELECT *
FROM cou;
```

> It is a good idea to use meaningful synonym names, but simple names such as "test1" or even "x" are syntactically acceptable.

Deleting a Synonym

To delete a synonym, type:

```
DROP SYNONYM synonym_name;
```

From this point forward, unless the explanation needs it, we will not use the table owner qualification. Thus, we will write:

```
SELECT *
FROM Room;
```

instead of:

```
SELECT *
FROM rearp.Room;
```

Introducing the Oracle Data Dictionary

The Oracle Data Dictionary is a vast set of tables and views that we will explore in measured steps. At this point we want to introduce you to the dictionary. As you learn more SQL "tricks," we will look at the dictionary in more detail.

The dictionary holds descriptions of tables and objects that have been created by individual users, the system, and the Database Administrator (DBA). The tables in the dictionary are prefixed so that you can find:

- objects that are created by you, prefixed by *user_*, like user_tables,

- objects that are created by others but where you have permission to query, prefixed by *all_*, like all_objects

- objects that are created by the system or the dba, prefixed by *dba_*

- some dynamic tables, which have names like V$parameter (which are not prefixed), and

- a few other tables, which have "odd" names like role_role_privs.

To see the synonyms you have created, you can type:

```
SELECT *
FROM user_synonyms;
```

This is shown in the screen in Figure 1.12.

You can also type:

```
SELECT *
FROM all_synonyms
WHERE table_owner = 'sql-id';
```

where 'sql-id' stands for your userid.

> You may still need the table owner qualification to access the tables in the Student_course database because you are not the owner of these tables.

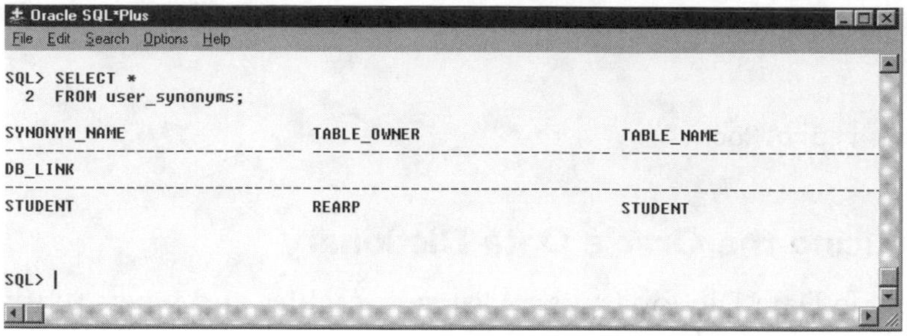

```
± Oracle SQL*Plus                                                      _□×
File  Edit  Search  Options  Help

SQL> SELECT *
  2   FROM user_synonyms;

SYNONYM_NAME                     TABLE_OWNER              TABLE_NAME
------------------------------   ----------------------   ----------------
DB_LINK
------------------------------   ----------------------   ----------------
STUDENT                          REARP                    STUDENT


SQL> |
```

FIGURE 1.12 A Data Dictionary Screen

> Your 'sql-id' is case sensitive because you must exactly match the stored value for 'your sql-id.' The stored value in system (dictionary) tables is in all-caps, such as SBAGUI (if the table's owner is SBAGUI).

Assuming that your userid is SBAGUI, you can type:

```
SELECT *
FROM all_synonyms
WHERE table_owner = 'SBAGUI';
```

Another command you will find useful is:

```
SELECT *
FROM user_tab_columns;
```

This will give you all the information about the columns you have created in tables. This table is very long, so a much more useful command in Oracle is:

```
SELECT *
FROM tab;
```

This gives you the tables and synonyms you have created. "tab" is a public synonym for a view of the dictionary.

If you wanted to use "obj," you could also type:

```
SELECT *
FROM obj;
```

However, as with "tabs," you would be overwhelmed with information. To find out what "obj" stands for, look up "obj" in the dictionary table all_synonyms.

> Actually the use of "tab" is now considered old-fashioned. "tab" is a synonym that has been grand-fathered into Oracle 7 and beyond. The latest version of "tab" could be considered "tabs" (a synonym for a Data Dictionary table called `user_tables`) or "obj" (a synonym for `user_objects`). "tabs" contains a lot more information than "tab," but this presents a display problem. "tabs" contains 18 columns, which you are invited to study, but for a simple version of "What tables do I have?" you can still use the SELECT * FROM tab.

For a display that looks like "tab," you could type:

```
SELECT SUBSTR(object_name,1,15) Name, object_type Type
FROM obj;
```

You could alternatively use SELECT * FROM tab; if it is supported.

Using DESC

To see the attribute names in a table, use DESCRIBE *table name*. DESC is a synonym for DESCRIBE. To use this very common command, type:

```
DESC Student
```

You will then see a screen like that shown in Figure 1.13.

There is also a synonym, DICT, for a table called `Dictionary`, owned by user SYS. To look over all the tables you can "see," type:

```
SELECT *
FROM dict;
```

> A semicolon after the DESC Student command is not necessary, but it is allowed.

> The result set is long, so you might consider setting the "pause on."

```
± Oracle SQL*Plus                                              _ □ X
File  Edit  Search  Options  Help
SQL>DESC Student;
Name                                    Null?     Type
-------                                 --------  -----------
STNO                                    NOT NULL  NUMBER(3)
SNAME                                             VARCHAR2(20)
MAJOR                                             CHAR(4)
CLASS                                             NUMBER(1)
BDATE                                             DATE

SQL>
```

FIGURE 1.13 Description of a Table

Employing a Convention for Writing SQL Statements

Although there is no fixed rule for writing SQL statements, we suggest you follow a convention that will help you as your statements become more involved. The convention is this:

1. Use uppercase for the keywords like SELECT, FROM, and WHERE. Use lowercase for user-supplied words.

2. Align the keywords SELECT, FROM, and WHERE on separate lines like this:

```
SELECT *
FROM Student
WHERE class = 1;
```

CHAPTER 1 EXERCISES

To save your work to "hand in," you may want to create a file using SPOOL. It is a good idea to spool each exercise as SPOOL ex11, SPOOL off, SPOOL ex12, SPOOL off, and so on.

1. Print a "display" of the Course table. By "display" we mean to use DESC Course to show meta-data and SELECT statements to display the actual data.

2. Create a synonym for the Student and "display" the table using the synonym (DESC and SELECT). (A reminder: You must use "rearp." in front of all tables because you aren't the owner of these tables. Thus, you must type rearp.Student instead of Student in your query.)

3. We have supplied a Student-Course database with the following tables (these tables are shown in Appendix 3 of this text):

   ```
   Student
   Course
   Section
   Prereq (for prerequisite)
   Grade_report
   Department_to_major
   Room
   ```

   (There are other tables that will be used later in other exercises [such as Cap, Plants, Worker and AA] but they are not tables connected with the Student-Course database.) Create synonyms for the Student-Course tables because we will use them extensively. You can shorten the name of the table in your synonym, if you like, for example:

```
CREATE SYNONYM d2m FOR Department_to_major;
```

Using the synonym and DESC, show the first few lines of all the Student-Course tables. To show the column variables and types (meta-data), use DESC. To display the first few lines of the table, use a WHERE on the table name like this:

```
SELECT *
FROM Student
WHERE rownum < 5;
```

Assume you created a synonym, Stu, for the Student table. Rownum is a *built-in* row counter (also called a *pseudo variable*). You can also use rownum in the result set of the query like this:

```
SELECT rownum, sname, major
FROM Stu
WHERE major = 'ACCT';
```

4.   Using line editing

   a.   Type in and run the statement, SELECT * FROM Prereq;

   b.   Use c (the CHANGE command) to edit the statement and display the Course table instead of the Prereq table.

   c.   Edit and then run the previous statement by appending a new line that says:

```
WHERE offering_dept = 'COSC'
```

   Your query should now read:

```
SELECT *
FROM Course
WHERE offering_dept = 'COSC';
```

   d.   Edit the above query (use a line number and c) to select only course_name in the result set. (Hint: Change from * to course_name.)

   e.   Delete the last line (WHERE offering_dept = 'COSC') of your query and re-run the query.

5. You can access system parameters using a dummy table called "dual." Run the following statement:

   ```
   SELECT sysdate, user FROM dual;
   ```

   Oracle provides Dual as a convenient table guaranteed to return at least one row and one column.

   The system also keeps the time. You can show it like this:

   ```
   SELECT TO_CHAR (sysdate,'dd-Mon-yyyy hh24:mm:ss') FROM dual;
   ```

   Other date formats are also available and will be discussed later in this text.

More "Beginning" SQL Commands

In this chapter, we expand the power of the SELECT command and illustrate how to create a table, insert values into a table, update tables, and delete from tables. We also discuss the ROLL-BACK, COMMIT, and SAVEPOINT, which can be used if you make a mistake and want to undo whatever work you have done in your database. The chapter closes with a discussion of data types available in Oracle, and an extended discussion of the DATE data type.

An Extended SELECT Statement

The SELECT is *usually* the first word in an SQL statement. The SELECT statement instructs the database engine to return information from the database as a set of records, or a *result set*. The SELECT displays the result on the computer screen, but does not save the results. The simplest form of the SELECT syntax is as follows:

```
SELECT attributes FROM Table;
```

This gives us a result set that is drawn from the list of columns (or attributes or fields) that are available in a table. Note that in this syntax, "Table" is the name of the table from which the data will be taken and "attributes" shows only the selected columns (attributes) from the table.

Note also that the keywords SELECT and FROM are *always* present in a SELECT statement.

If we were to use an asterisk (*) in place of the "attributes," we would indicate that we want to list all the attributes (or columns) of the table. Consider the following example in which "*" means "all columns" of the table, Student:

```
SELECT *
FROM Student;
```

SELECTing Attributes (Columns)

You do not have to show all the attributes (columns) or all of the tuples (rows) with a SELECT statement. What *is* shown is called the result set. You can SELECT attribute names from a table, provided you know the name of the attribute. To find out the name of the attributes, use "DESC *tablename,"* as we discussed in Chapter 1. For example, to show a listing of only the customer balances, we use the following syntax:

```
SELECT "attribute name" FROM "Table"
```

An example of this is as follows:

```
SELECT balance
FROM Customer;
```

The output of this query will be all the customer balances of the Customer table.

> Note that the Customer table has not been created for you. In order to run the examples in this section, you'll first have to create the Customer table (as shown in the section that discusses creating tables later in this chapter).

Using ORDER BY

As noted above, the output of the preceding query will be all the customer balances of the Customer table. However, the customer balances will not be ordered since a relational table does not keep its rows in any particular order. To show the contents of a table in any particular order, you can order the display with the ORDER BY clause. For example, the following query will show the customer numbers and balances of the Customer table, ordered by customer number (cno). Here the output will be ordered in ascending order of customer number (ascending order is the default of the ORDER BY clause):

```
SELECT cno, balance
FROM Customer
ORDER BY cno;
```

To order in descending order, you can append the keyword DESC as follows:

```
SELECT balance, cno
FROM Customer
ORDER BY cno DESC;
```

This will give you the same output as above, but the output will now be ordered in descending order by customer number.

In addition, you can order within an order. For example, in the following example, you would order principally by customer_type in descending order and then by balance within customer_type:

```
SELECT customer_type, balance
FROM Customer
ORDER BY customer_type DESC, balance;
```

SELECTing Tuples (Rows)

You can restrict the output of tuples (rows) in the result set by adding a WHERE clause. When the WHERE clause is used, the database engine selects the rows from the table that meet the conditions listed in the WHERE clause. If no WHERE clause is used, the query will return all rows from the table. In other words, the WHERE clause acts as a *row filter*.

The simplest form of the WHERE clause would be:

```
SELECT fields or attributes or columns
FROM Table
WHERE criteria;
```

For example, to list the balances of only those customers with a balance less than 100, we would type:

```
SELECT balance
FROM Customer
WHERE balance < 100;
```

> All SQL statements require semicolons. SQLPLUS commands do not require semicolons or a terminating character, but if you use one, SQLPLUS is usually forgiving and will execute the command correctly anyway. In addition, DESC does not require a semicolon, while SELECT does.

> As noted earlier, the ascending order is the default order of the ORDER BY clause; that is, if no direction (ASC for ascending or DESC for descending) is specified, the ORDER BY clause will produce the output in ascending order.

All of the following comparison operators are available:

> (greater than),

<> not equal,

= equal,

> = greater than or equal to, and so on

Other common operators include IN, EXISTS, and BETWEEN (which we'll discuss later in the text).

A Simple CREATE TABLE Command

The CREATE TABLE command allows you to create a table in which you can store data. A simplified syntax of the command is as follows (we will expand the syntax with more options in a later chapter):

```
CREATE TABLE "tablename"
("attribute name," "type," "attribute name," "type," and so
on);
```

In Example 1 below, we are creating a table called Customer. The table has two attributes: cno and balance. As you can see, the type of cno is a fixed-length character with a length of 3. The type of balance is numeric with five digits and no decimals. The appendage "DEFAULT 0" means that if no value is specified for balance when rows are put in the table, balance will be equal to zero:

```
CREATE TABLE Customer
  (cno CHAR(3), balance NUMBER(5) DEFAULT 0);
```

Of course, we can use other data types as well, the most common of which is VARCHAR2(n), which is a variable-length character string of length *n* and DATE. (We'll discuss these and other date types in more detail later in the chapter.) In Example 2 below, we are creating a table of names:

```
CREATE TABLE Names
  (name VARCHAR2(20));
```

This table, Names, has one field called name. name is of data type VARCHAR2 (which means varying length character), and can have a maximum size of 20 characters.

> In this example, if "DEFAULT 0" were not used, bal-ance would default to null. Null means "empty" and is Oracle's way of signifying that no value is present.

> Older versions of SQL used a type called VARCHAR (without the 2), but Oracle now uses and recommends the use of VAR-CHAR2. Although it currently allows you to use the older name VAR-CHAR, it may not do so in the future, so it's wise to use VARCHAR2 instead.

Inserting Values into a Created Table

You can insert values into a created table using several methods, including:

- INSERT INTO .. VALUES

- INSERT INTO .. SELECT

- SQLLOADER

In this section, we'll look at INSERT INTO .. VALUES and INSERT INTO .. SELECT. We'll discuss SQLLOADER later in this text.

INSERT INTO .. VALUES

One method of inserting values into *one* row of a table is by using the INSERT command with the VALUES option. An example using the table of names we created in Example 2 is as follows:

```
INSERT INTO Names
VALUES ('Joe Smith');   [semicolon required]
```

where

- "INSERT" is the name of the command.

- "INTO" is a necessary keyword.

- "Names" is the name of an existing table.

- "VALUES" is another necessary keyword.

- 'Joe Smith' is a string of letters corresponding to the type (see Example 2 above).

If you created a table with *n* attributes, you usually would have *n* values in the INSERT .. VALUES in the order of the definition. For example, if you have created a table called Employee, as follows:

```
CREATE TABLE Employee (name            VARCHAR2 (20),
                       address         VARCHAR2 (20),
                       employee_number NUMBER (3),
                       salary          NUMBER (6,2));
```

The INSERT INTO .. VALUES to insert a row would match column for column and would look like this:

```
INSERT INTO Employee
VALUES ('Joe Smith', '123 4th St.', 101, 2500);
```

This is shown in the screen in Figure 2.1.

An INSERT that looks like the following is incorrect because it doesn't include all four attributes of Employee:

```
INSERT INTO Employee
VALUES ('Joe Smith', '123 4th St.');
```

However, you can write an INSERT like the following to insert a row with less than all the attributes:

```
INSERT INTO Employee (name, address)
VALUES ('Joe Smith', '123 4th St.');
```

In this case, the row will contain nulls or default values for the values you left out.

An INSERT that looks like the following is incorrect because it doesn't have the values in the same order as the definition of the table:

```
INSERT INTO Employee
VALUES (2500, 'Joe Smith', 101, '123 4th St.');
```

If the data had to be specified in this order, the statement could be corrected by specifying the column names like this:

```
INSERT INTO Employee (salary, name, employee_number, address)
VALUES (2500, 'Joe Smith', 101, '123 4th St.');
```

FIGURE 2.1 Creating a Table and Inserting into a Table

The following INSERT would also be legal if the `address` and the `salary` were unknown when the row (tuple) was created, provided that the `address` and `salary` attributes allowed nulls:

```
INSERT INTO Employee
VALUES ('Joe Smith', null, 101, null);
```

INSERT INTO .. SELECT

With INSERT INTO .. VALUES, you insert only one row at a time into a table. With this INSERT INTO .. SELECT option, you may (and usually do) insert *many* rows into a table at one time. The syntax of the INSERT INTO .. SELECT is:

```
INSERT INTO Newcustomer
  "SELECT clause"
```

For example, the following statement will insert all the values from the Customer table into another table called `Newcustomer`:

```
INSERT INTO Newcustomer
  SELECT *
  FROM Customer;
```

But note that before doing this INSERT INTO .. SELECT statement, you'll have to first create the table `Newcustomer`; and, though the attributes of `Newcustomer` do not have to be named exactly what they are named in `Customer`, the data types and sizes must match. The size of the attributes that you are inserting into—that is, the size of the attributes of `Newcustomer`—must be at *least* as big as the size of the attributes of `Customer`.

You may embellish the SELECT and load less than the whole table—fewer rows or columns, as necessary. Some examples of restricted SELECTs for the INSERT command follow.

Suppose you have a table with only one attribute, which was created as follows:

```
CREATE TABLE Namelist
  (customer_name VARCHAR2(20));
```

> If you use non-numeric types like CHAR (fixed character size) or VARCHAR2 (variable character size), you must use single quotes in the INSERT command. If you use numbers, you should not use quotes. Oracle will convert these character strings to numbers, but it is never good to let a system do something that you should do yourself.

Assume that a second table exists that has the following structure:

```
Customer (cname, cnumber, amount) where cname is VARCHAR2 (20)
```

You can populate the Namelist table with the name from the Customer table as follows:

```
INSERT INTO Namelist
 SELECT cname
 FROM Customer;
```

This copies all the names from Customer to Namelist. However, you don't have to copy all the names from Customer because you can restrict the SELECT as follows:

```
INSERT INTO Namelist
 SELECT cname
 FROM Customer
 WHERE amount > 100
```

As with the INSERT .. VALUES, if you create a table with n attributes, you usually would have n values in the INSERT .. SELECT in the order of definition. Suppose that you had a table like the following:

```
Employee (name, address, emp_num, salary)
```

Further suppose that you wanted to load a table called Emp1 from Employee with the following attributes, where the attributes stand for address, salary, and employee number, respectively:

```
Emp1 (addr, sal, empno),
```

As with INSERT .. VALUES, the INSERT .. SELECT must match column for column and would look like the following:

```
INSERT INTO Emp1
 SELECT address, salary, emp_num
 FROM Employee;
```

An INSERT that looked like the following would fail because Employee has four attributes and Emp1 has only three:

```
INSERT INTO Emp1
  SELECT * FROM Employee;
```

An INSERT that looked like the following would be wrong because the order of the SELECT must match the order of definition in Emp1:

```
INSERT INTO Emp1
  SELECT address, emp_num, salary
  FROM Employee;
```

As you might guess from the last INSERT .. VALUES example, you can load fewer attributes than the whole row of Emp1 with a statement like the following:

```
INSERT INTO Emp1 (address, salary)
  SELECT address, salary
  FROM Employee;
```

However, this would leave the other attribute, emp_num, with a value of null or with a default value. Therefore, although loading less than a "full row" is syntactically correct, you must be aware of the result.

One final caution: INSERT .. SELECT could succeed if the types of the SELECT matched the types of the attributes in the table to which you're INSERTing. For example, if name and address were both VARCHAR2 types and if Emp2 were defined as name, address, and if you executed the following, the command *could* succeed, but you would have an address in a name attribute and vice versa:

```
INSERT INTO Emp2
  SELECT address, name
  FROM Employee;
```

> We say the command *could* succeed here because there are ways to prevent integrity violations of this type, but we have not introduced them yet.

Be careful with this INSERT .. SELECT command: unlike INSERT .. VALUES (which inserts one row), you almost always insert multiple rows. If types match, the insert will take place regardless of whether it makes sense.

The UPDATE Command

Another common command in setting/changing data values is the UPDATE command. As with INSERT .. SELECT, you often UPDATE more than one row. The table must exist, so following a CREATE TABLE command and the insertion of some data, you might want to set or reset a value in some column. This can be done with UPDATE as follows.

We have created a table called Customer, like this:

```
CREATE TABLE Customer
  (cno CHAR(3), balance NUMBER(5), date_opened DATE);
```

Suppose that you have added some values to the table. Suppose further that you would like to set *all* balances in the table to zero. You can do this with one UPDATE command, as follows:

```
UPDATE Customer
SET balance = 0;
```

> Beware—this can be a dangerous command. Later in the chapter we will discuss a method in which to safeguard against its misuse using the ROLLBACK command.

This command sets all balances in all rows of the table to zero, regardless of their previous value.

It is often useful to include a WHERE clause on the UPDATE command so that you set values selectively. For example, the updating of a particular customer might be done with the following statement:

```
UPDATE Customer
SET balance = 0
WHERE cno = 101;
```

This would update only customer number 101's row(s). You could also set particular balances to zero with a statement like the following:

```
UPDATE Customer
SET balance = 0
WHERE date > '01-JAN-96';
```

The DELETE Command

In addition to inserting and updating rows in tables, it is also common to delete rows. An example of the DELETE command is this:

```
DELETE FROM Customer
WHERE (condition)
```

The (condition) determines which rows to delete.

An example from our sample Customer table might be:

> Again, because multiple rows can be affected by this command, it can be a dangerous command. Be careful when using it.

```
DELETE FROM Customer
WHERE balance < 0;
```

or

```
DELETE FROM Customer
WHERE date_opened < '01-JAN-83';
```

ROLLBACK, COMMIT, and SAVEPOINT

When we make modifications to our database—typically when we use some insert, delete, or update commands—we perform what is called a *transaction*. A transaction ends with a COMMIT command. Under certain conditions, if you make a mistake, you can undo whatever modification you have done to your database with a ROLLBACK command. In this section, we'll discuss how to perform a commit and a rollback, as well as discuss the conditions for un-doing a transaction.

All transactions have a beginning and an end. To set a "begin point," you either have to just have logged on or you have to issue a ROLLBACK or COMMIT command in the middle of a session. To set a point from which you want to be sure that you cannot ROLLBACK, you issue the COMMIT command.

If you start with a COMMIT, a transaction in a database is what you do between COMMITs. When you log off of your SQL session, you implicitly COMMIT your work. When you log onto your account, you begin a *session*. If you log on and do numerous commands and then log off, your transaction may span the time from when you logged on until when you logged off, provided you do only data manipulation commands (SELECT, INSERT, and so on). If you issue a COMMIT during a session, your transaction ends at that point and a new one begins. Data definition commands are implicit COMMITs and end and restart a new transaction. Therefore, several transactions may take place within a single session.

Sometimes, you need to divide your work into separate transactions. COMMIT and ROLLBACK are explicit transaction-handling commands. Suppose you had a table of values and you deleted some of the tuples. You can undo (by using ROLLBACK) the delete action (assuming you have not otherwise terminated the transaction explicitly or implicitly). For example, suppose you have a table called `Customer`, which has 100 tuples in it. Suppose that you issued the following DELETE command:

```
DELETE FROM Customer
WHERE balance < 500;
```

This deletes all tuples in the `Customer` table where balances are less than 500. Then you note that your boss actually said to delete customers where the `balance` was less than 50, not 500. You can ROLLBACK the previous command with:

```
ROLLBACK;
```

If you did not want to ROLLBACK, you could type COMMIT and the table would not be "ROLLBACK-able."

We mentioned that ROLLBACK would work under certain conditions. You can use ROLLBACK except

• when you use Data Definition Language (DDL) commands (DDL commands define [or create] or delete [or drop] database objects. Examples of such commands include CREATE VIEW, CREATE TABLE, CREATE INDEX, DROP TABLE, RENAME TABLE, ALTER TABLE.)

• in situations where you explicitly or implicitly issue a COMMIT.

• when you log off of SQL, implicitly COMMITting your work.

Of course, for valuable tables, an explicit backup (or two) would be made and permissions for update and delete would be judiciously managed by the table owner.

As an intermediate COMMIT/ROLLBACK action, you can also name a transaction milestone called a SAVEPOINT. For example, you can use the following command to mark a point in a transaction with a name, *point1*:

```
SAVEPOINT point1
```

You can then ROLLBACK to *point1* with the following command:

```
ROLLBACK TO SAVEPOINT point1
```

The naming of the COMMIT point allows you to have several points in a series of transactions—"milestones" if you will. These milestones allow partial ROLLBACKs. COMMIT is much stronger than a SAVEPOINT because it commits all actions and basically wipes out the SAVEPOINTs.

The following is an example of a transaction that includes a SAVEPOINT, ROLLBACK, and COMMIT.

Suppose we had a table, CustA, with fields name and balance, defined as VARCHAR2(20) and NUMBER(5,2), respectively. Further suppose that we type:

```
SELECT *
FROM CustA;
```

We will the get the following output:

NAME	BALANCE
Mary Jo	25.53
Sikha	44.44
Richard	33.33

If we insert another record into CustA, as follows:

```
INSERT INTO CustA
VALUES ('Brenda',40.02);
```

We will get the following message:

```
1 row created.
```

We can now use this as a milestone, creating a SAVEPOINT by typing:

```
SAVEPOINT pointA;
```

We will then get the following message:

```
Savepoint created.
```

Now if we type:

```
SELECT *
FROM CustA;
```

We will get the following output:

NAME	BALANCE
Mary Jo	25.53
Sikha	44.44
Richard	33.33
Brenda	40.02

If we type:

```
DELETE FROM CustA
WHERE balance < 35;
```

We will get the following message:

```
2 rows deleted.
```

If we type:

```
SELECT *
FROM CustA;
```

We will get the following output:

```
NAME        BALANCE
_____       _____
Sikha       44.44
Brenda      40.02
```

We could make this our next milestone, calling it *pointB*, by typing:

```
SAVEPOINT pointB;
```

Again, we will get the following message:

```
Savepoint created.
```

If we then type:

```
DELETE FROM CustA;
```

We will get the following message:

```
2 rows deleted.
```

If we then type:

```
SELECT *
FROM CustA;
```

We will get the following message:

```
no rows selected
```

If we feel that we have made a mistake, we can, at this point, ROLLBACK the transaction as follows:

```
ROLLBACK TO SAVEPOINT pointB;
```

We will get the following message:

```
Rollback complete.
```

If we then type:

```
SELECT *
FROM CustA;
```

We will get the following output:

NAME	BALANCE
Sikha	44.44
Brenda	40.02

We can update CustA by typing:

```
UPDATE CustA
SET BALANCE = 55.55
WHERE name like 'Si%';
```

This will give us the following message:

```
1 row updated.
```

If we then type:

```
SELECT *
FROM CustA;
```

We will get the following output:

```
NAME        BALANCE
------      -------
Sikha       55.55
Brenda      40.02
```

If we want to rollback to *pointA*, we type:

```
ROLLBACK TO pointA;
```

We will then get the following message:

```
Rollback complete.
```

If we then type:

```
SELECT *
FROM CustA;
```

We will get the following output:

```
NAME        BALANCE
------      -------
Mary Jo     25.52
Sikha       44.44
Richard     33.33
Brenda      40.02
```

At this point, if we COMMIT, we will basically wipe out the SAVEPOINTs and we won't be able to rollback.

We now issue a COMMIT as follows:

```
COMMIT;
```

We get the following message:

```
Commit complete.
```

This completes the transaction in terms of making it impossible to rollback.

The ALTER TABLE Command

In addition to adding, changing, and deleting rows with INSERT, UPDATE, and DELETE, you can also add and change (modify) *columns* in a table. The appropriate command to do so is ALTER TABLE, which has the following syntax:

For adding a column:	Example:
ALTER TABLE tablename	ALTER TABLE Customer
ADD column-name type	ADD address VARCHAR2 (20);

For changing a column's type:	Example:
ALTER TABLE tablename	ALTER TABLE Customer
MODIFY column-name new_type	MODIFY balance NUMBER (8,2);

We'll discuss several other uses of the ALTER TABLE command later in the text. For example, using the ALTER TABLE command, you can define or change a default column value, enable or disable an integrity constraint, manage internal space, and so on. You can also add columns with little difficulty.

Data Types

A *data type* defines the kind of data attributes we will have for values as well as the operations we can perform on attributes with those values. We commonly use the NUMBER data type for numbers and the CHAR and VARCHAR2 data types for character strings. In this section, we will explore these and other commonly used data types.

Number Data Types

In Oracle, the data type of NUMBER, by itself with no parentheses, defaults to a number that is up to 38 digits long with 8 decimal places. Other available numeric data types include INTEGER and SMALLINT. INTEGER holds whole numbers of various sizes. SMALLINT is basically the same as NUMBER, with less precision (that is, with 38 digits and no decimals). Usually, you enter a maximum length or a format for your numbers with entries such as NUMBER(3) or NUMBER(6,2). The NUMBER(3) implies you will have three digits and no decimal places. NUMBER(6,2) means that the numbers you store will be similar to 1234.56 or

> If you modify a column, you can only make it bigger, not smaller, unless there is no data; all the data in the database must conform to your modified type.
>
> If you add a column, it will contain null values until you put data into it with an UPDATE command to change the values in the new column.

> There is also a FLOAT data type, which allows large exponential numbers to be stored, but it is rarely used.

12.34, with a decimal before the last two digits in a field that has a maximum of six numbers.

CHAR Data Type

CHAR (pronounced "care") is a fixed-length data type. You can use this data type when you will always have the requisite number of characters or digits in the value. For example, major codes that will always be four characters long should be encoded as CHAR(4). Social security numbers are also good candidates for this type because they should always contain nine digits and therefore use CHAR(9). If you do not have the requisite number of characters or digits, the field will be padded on the right with blanks. For example, if you define the social security number as CHAR(10) instead of CHAR(9), there will be one blank space on the right of every social security number. The default (that is, the minimum size) for CHAR is 1 byte; its maximum size is 2000 bytes.

VARCHAR2 Data Type

> As we mentioned earlier in the chapter, older versions of Oracle and other SQLs used VARCHAR (without the "2") as the type for varying strings. VARCHAR is considered old-fashioned and may not be supported in future versions of the query language, so we advise you to use VARCHAR2 instead.

As we mentioned earlier in the chapter, VARCHAR2 (pronounced "varcare") is Oracle's variable-length string. Maximum string lengths should be specified, as in VARCHAR2(20), for a string of zero to twenty characters. When varying sizes of data are stored in an Oracle VARCHAR2, only the necessary amount of storage is allocated. This practice makes the internal storage of Oracle data more efficient. In fact, some Oracle gurus suggest using only VARCHAR2(n) instead of CHAR(n). The minimum size for VARCHAR2 is 1 byte; the maximum size is 4000 bytes. Since there is no default size for VARCHAR2, you must specify a size.

LONG, RAW, LONG RAW, and BOOLEAN Data Types

The LONG data type is similar to VARCHAR2 and has a variable length of up to 2Gb. However, there are some restrictions in the access and handling of LONG data types:

• Only one LONG column can be defined per table.

• LONG columns may not be used in subqueries, functions, expressions, WHERE clauses, or indexes.

A RAW or LONG RAW data type is used to store binary data, such as graphics characters or digitized pictures. The maximum size for RAW is 2000 bytes and the maximum size for LONG RAW is 2 gigabytes. Thus, LONG RAW allows for larger sets of binary data.

Large Object (LOB) Data Types

As of Oracle 8, four new large object (LOB) data types are supported: BFILE and three LOB data types—BLOB, CLOB, and NCLOB. BFILE is an external LOB data type that only stores a locator value that points to the external binary file. BLOB is used for binary large objects, CLOB is used for character large objects, and NCLOB is a CLOB data type for multi-byte character sets.

Data in the BLOB, CLOB, or NCLOB data types is stored in the database, although LOB data does not have to be stored with the rest of the table. Single LOB columns can hold up to 4Gb in length, and multiple LOB columns are allowed per table. In addition, Oracle allows you to specify a separate storage area for LOB data, greatly simplifying table sizing and data administration activities for tables that contain LOB data. Note that LOB data types consume large quantities of space.

Abstract Data Types

In Oracle 8 you can define and use abstract data types. A data type defines a *range* of values and *operations* that can be performed on data declared to be of that type. An ***abstract data type*** (ADT) defines the operations explicitly (in methods) and should allow you to only access data of that type via the defined method. ADTs are created with the CREATE TYPE statement.

The CREATE TYPE command allows you to create more complicated data types that are somewhat abstract. For example, Oracle *collection types* allow you to put a table within a table or allow a varying array in a table. Both of these concepts are non-third normal form (non-3NF) constructions and should be used only with a strong need to violate the 3NF assumption for relational database—perhaps because of a performance problem, for example.

> In Oracle, there is also a BOOLEAN data type with values TRUE, FALSE, and NULL. However, it is only available when running the procedural language PL/SQL. We'll discuss PL/SQL in Chapter 11.

More "Beginning" SQL Commands

> A complete treatment of CREATE TYPE and abstract data types is a more advanced topic we will discuss later in this text. We mention CREATE TYPE here only so that you are aware of its existence as an Oracle data type.

The DATE Data Type and Type Conversion Functions

A DATE data type allows you not only to store dates but also to manipulate them (add, take differences between dates, convert to a four-digit year, and so on) by using a date function such as TO_DATE. Suppose you define a date type in a table like the following:

```
CREATE TABLE xx       (today          DATE,
                       amount         NUMBER (6,2),
                       name           VARCHAR2 (20));
```

> The format of the DATE data type can be changed by the DBA, but dd-Mon-yy is common.

Data is entered into the today date field, in the character format 'dd-Mon-yy,' which automatically converts the character string to a date format.

If your CREATE TABLE were just as above, then some examples of INSERTs would be:

```
INSERT INTO xx (today)
    VALUES ('10-oct-02')   -- valid;
INSERT INTO xx (today)
    VALUES ('10-OCT-02')   -- valid (month not case sensitive);
INSERT INTO xx (today)
    VALUES (10-oct-02)     -- invalid (needs quotes);
INSERT INTO xx (today)
    VALUES (sysdate)       -- valid (system date);
INSERT INTO xx (today)
    VALUES ('10-RWE-02')   -- invalid (bad month);
INSERT INTO xx (today)
    VALUES ('32-OCT-02')   -- invalid bad day);
INSERT INTO xx (today)
    VALUES ('31-OCT-02')   -- valid;
INSERT INTO xx (today)
    VALUES ('31-SEP-02')   -- invalid (bad day);
```

> Oracle keeps up with the correct days per month.

For other than "standard" dates in the form dd-Mon-yy, you can use the TO_DATE function to insert values in other ways. The TO_DATE function has two arguments: TO_DATE (a,b), where "a" is the string you are using to enter the date and "b" is a recognizable Oracle character format. For example, to insert the date '2-1-02' in the format 'mm-dd-yy,' you would type:

```
INSERT INTO xx (today) VALUES
        (TO_DATE ('2-1-02', 'mm-dd-yy'))
```

Likewise, to enter the date '2/1/2002' in the format 'mm/dd/yyyy,' you would type:

```
INSERT INTO xx (today) VALUES
        (TO_DATE ('2/1/2002', 'mm/dd/yyyy'));
```

To convert a DATE data type to a character data type, you need another function, TO_CHAR. Here, if we are dealing with a date type and if we store the months as 1, 2, and so on in 12 rows as follows:

```
INSERT INTO xx (today) VALUES
        (TO_DATE(1,'mm'));
INSERT INTO xx (today) VALUES
        (TO_DATE(2,'mm'));
INSERT INTO xx (today) VALUES
        (TO_DATE(3,'mm'));
.
.
.
```

and so on

Then, if we use the following SELECT:

```
SELECT TO_CHAR(today, 'dd-MON-yy')  FROM xx;
```

We would get the following output:

```
To_Char(today,'dd-mon-yy')
01-JAN-02
01-FEB-02
01-MAR-02
01-APR-02
01-MAY-02
01-JUN-02
01-JUL-02
01-AUG-02
01-SEP-02
01-OCT-02
01-NOV-02
01-DEC-02
```

The month and date can be reversed with TO_CHAR. If we type:

```
INSERT INTO xx (today)
VALUES (TO_DATE('2-1-02', 'dd-mm-yy'));
```

We will get:

```
02-JAN-02
...
```

Actually, the DATE data type stores quite a bit more information than just the month, day, and year. Consider an example in which we have expanded the date to include the hour (using a 24-hour clock) and minute. Suppose we create a table like this:

```
CREATE TABLE zz (d DATE);
```

We then INSERT some data as follows:

```
INSERT INTO zz
VALUES (TO_DATE('2-11-2002 16:05','mm-dd-yyyy hh24:mi'));
```

A simple SELECT will show only the day, month, and year, as follows:

```
SELECT d FROM zz;
```

We then get:

```
d
-----
11-FEB-02
```

However, note that the information that was stored can be fully displayed by using the TO_CHAR as follows:

```
SELECT (TO_CHAR(d,'dd-Mon-yyyy hh:mi:ss')) FROM zz;
```

We then get:

```
(TO_CHAR(D,'DD-MON-Y
-----------
11-Feb-2002 04:05:00
```

We can specify other data like this:

```
SELECT (TO_CHAR(d,'dd-Mon-yyyy hh:mi:ss j q w PM cc')) FROM
zz;
```

We then get:

```
(TO_CHAR(D, 'DD-MON-YYYYHH:MI:SSJQWPMCC
_____
11-Feb-2002 04:05:00 2452317 1 2 PM 21
```

where

- The *j* is the "Julian" days since Dec. 31, 4713 BC (here, 2452317).
- The *q* is the quarter of the year (1st quarter).
- The *w* is the week of the month (2nd week of February).
- The *PM* signifies PM if PM and AM if AM.
- The *cc* specifies the century (21st).

Entering Four-Digit Years

There will often be times when we want to enter and display four-digit years. If we type in the following, it is valid and gives the same result as mm-dd-yy in converting 02 to 2002:

```
INSERT INTO xx (today) VALUES
(TO_DATE('2-1-02', 'mm-dd-yyyy'));
```

If we insert a four-digit year as 2002, we still get a two-digit result on directly displaying the date (provided the default date format is dd-mon-yy). For example, if we type:

```
SELECT today
FROM XX;
```

We will get:

```
TODAY
01-FEB-02
```

You might wonder how to enter a date like 2097 if the date entry mode is 'dd-MON-yy'. An answer is that you can enter four-digit dates, but you must use the TO_DATE function to do it.

Here is an example:

```
... VALUES (TO_DATE ('2-1-2097', 'mm-dd-yyyy'))
```

If we display our table with:

```
SELECT * FROM xx;
```

We would still get the following:

```
01-FEB-97
```

This is because date fields would be displayed directly in the two-digit year format.

If we wanted to see the four digits we stored as 2097, we would have to convert the date value into a character format with a TO_CHAR function, which in this case might be considered the "inverse" of the TO_DATE:

```
SELECT TO_CHAR (today, 'dd-mm-yyyy')
FROM xx;
```

For values INSERTED with:

```
INSERT INTO xx (today) VALUES (TO_DATE ('2-1-1997',
'mm-dd-yyyy'));
INSERT INTO xx (today) VALUES (TO_DATE ('2-1-2097',
'mm-dd-yyyy'));
```

this would display as:

```
TO_CHAR(TODAY, 'DD-MM-YYYY')
---------------------------
01-02-1997
01-02-2097
```

You can also use functions to compute MONTHS_BETWEEN and a month in the future or past with ADD_MONTHS.

Today's date can be found with a statement like this:

```
SELECT sysdate FROM dual;
```

"Dual" is a dummy table that always returns one row. It is used for testing functions such as "sysdate" or variations on sysdate such as TO_CHAR (sysdate, 'mm-day-yyyy'), as in:

```
SELECT TO_CHAR (sysdate, 'mm-Day-yyyy') FROM dual;
```

Finally, to change the default format, you can alter the way dates are formatted with a statement such as the following:

```
ALTER SESSION SET nls_date_format = 'dd-mon-yyyy';
```

CHAPTER 2 EXERCISES

1. **a.** Create a table called Cust with a customer number as a fixed-length character string of 3, an address with a variable character string of up to 20, and a numeric balance of five digits.

   b. Put values in the table with INSERT .. VALUES. Use the form of INSERT .. VALUES that requires you to have a value for each attribute; therefore, if you have a customer number, address, and balance, you must insert three values with INSERT .. VALUES.

   c. Create at least five tuples (rows in the table) with customer numbers 101 .. 105 and balances of 200 to 2000.

   d. Display the table with a simple SELECT.

2. Show a listing of the customers from Exercise 1 in balance order (high to low) and use ORDER BY in your SELECT. (Result: Five tuples or however many you created in 1.)

3. From the "standard" Student table, display the student names, classes, and majors for freshmen or sophomores (class <= 2) in descending order.

4. From your Cust table, show a listing of only the customer balances in ascending order where balance > 400. (You can choose some other constant or relation if you want, for example, balance <= 600, and so on. The results will depend on your data.)

5. **a.** Create another table with the same types as Cust but without the customer address. Call this table Cust1. Use attribute names cnum for customer number and bal for balance. Load the table with the data you have in the Cust table with one less tuple. Use an INSERT .. SELECT with appropriate attributes and an appropriate WHERE clause.

   b. Display the resulting table. If it appears okay, COMMIT your work.

   c. Assuming that you have COMMITted in step b, delete about half of your tuples from Cust1 ("DELETE FROM Cust1 WHERE bal < some value" [or bal > some value, etc.]).

   d. Show the table after you have deleted the tuples.

e.   Undelete the tuples with ROLLBACK.

f.   Display the table with the reinstated tuples.

g.   Delete one tuple from the `Cust1` table and SAVEPOINT *point1*. Display the table.

h.   Delete another tuple from the table and SAVEPOINT *point2*. Display the table.

i.   ROLLBACK to SAVEPOINT *point1*, display the table, and explain what is happening.

j.   Try to ROLLBACK to SAVEPOINT *point2* and see what happens and explain it.

6.   a.   Using the `Cust1` table from the Exercise 5, COMMIT the table as it exists.

b.   Alter the table by adding a `date_opened` column of type date.

     After each of the following, display the table.

c.   Set the `date_opened` value in all rows to '01-JAN-91' and COMMIT.

d.   Set all balances to zero, display the table, then ROLLBACK the action and display again.

e.   Set the `date_opened` value of one of your rows to '21-OCT-60' and display.

f.   Change the type of the balance attribute in `Cust1` to number (8,2). Display the table. Set the balance for one row to 888.88 and display the table again.

g.   Try changing the type of balance to NUMBER (3,2). What happens? Why does this happen?

h.   Change the values of all dates in the table to the system date using SYSDATE.

i.   When you are finished with the exercise (but be sure you are finished), DROP TABLE `Cust1` to delete the table. Use SELECT * FROM tab to be sure that you dropped `Cust1`.

The Cartesian Product, the Join, and Aliases

The purpose of this chapter is to demonstrate a very common problem with SQL queries: You get what you ask for! If you ask for nonsense, you will get nonsense. In this chapter, we'll look at the Cartesian product and joins. We'll then turn our attention to using column aliases and scripting. We'll close the chapter with a brief discussion of COUNT and Rownum.

The Cartesian Product

The **Cartesian product** is mathematically a binary operation in which two objects are combined in an "everything in combination with everything" fashion. The Cartesian product in SQL *per se* is usually not wanted. If it is requested by accident, results are spurious.

Suppose we created a table called Emps, with an employee number and a job code as follows:

Emps

empno	jobCode
101	cp
102	ac
103	de
104	cp
105	cp

> These two tables, Emps and Jobs, have not been created for you in the database. If you wish to try out this section, you will have to create the tables as shown.

Then, suppose we created a second table called Jobs, which contained a job code and a job title as follows:

Jobs

jobC	jobTitle
de	dentist
cp	computer programmer
ac	accountant

We can display the tables with SELECT * FROM Jobs or SELECT * FROM Emps. With SQL, we can retrieve the combination of both tables; however, we must be careful how we do it. If we connect the tables like this:

```
SELECT *
FROM Emps, Jobs;
```

We will get the Cartesian product—basically, all rows in Emps in combination with all rows in Jobs. The result of the above query would be:

```
EMP     JO     JO     JOBTITLE
---     -      -      --------------
101     cp     de     dentist
102     ac     de     dentist
103     de     de     dentist
104     cp     de     dentist
105     cp     de     dentist
101     cp     cp     computer programmer
102     ac     cp     computer programmer
103     de     cp     computer programmer
104     cp     cp     computer programmer
105     cp     cp     computer programmer
101     cp     ac     accountant
102     ac     ac     accountant
103     de     ac     accountant
104     cp     ac     accountant
105     cp     ac     accountant

15 rows selected.
```

There would be 15 tuples (5 times 3) in the result set with all combinations from Emps and Jobs.

The Join

To join tables, we use a SELECT command that includes both tables in the FROM clause and also a WHERE clause that ties the "connecting" fields together. Such a command could look like this:

```
SELECT *
FROM  Emps, Jobs
WHERE Emps.jobcode = Jobs.jobc;
```

This SELECT requests a result set that will contain only those resultant tuples (rows) that have `jobcode` in `Emps` equal to `jobc` in `Jobs`. This is an *equi-join* operation because the WHERE clause asks for rows in the Cartesian product where the two common columns have equal values. The result set of this join query looks like the screen shown in Figure 3.1.

> In relational algebra, a *join* is defined as a Cartesian product followed by a *relational select*. Technically, a relational select is not the same as an "SQL SELECT" (which is broader), and the behind-the-scenes workings of the SQL SELECT may or may not actually follow the "Cartesian product, followed by the 'relational select' scenario" internally for performance reasons. The *result* of the SQL-join in SQL SELECT statements (when done correctly) is the same as the sense of the relational join in relational algebra.

Compare this result to the Cartesian product on the preceding page and you will observe that the tables have the same structure but the latter one has been row-filtered by the WHERE clause to include only those rows where there is equality between `Emps.jobcode` and `Jobs.jobc`. Put another way, the latter table makes sense because it only presents those rows that correspond to one another; the former, Cartesian product result has extra, meaningless rows.

```
± Oracle SQL*Plus                                          _ □ ×
File  Edit  Search  Options  Help
SQL> SELECT *
  2   FROM Emps, Jobs
  3   WHERE Emps.jobcode=Jobs.jobc;

    EMPNO JO JO JOBTITLE
--------- -- -- --------------------
      102 ac ac accountant
      101 cp cp computer programmer
      104 cp cp computer programmer
      105 cp cp computer programmer
      103 de de dentist

SQL> |
```

FIGURE 3.1 A Join

Theta Joins

Joins with a sign other then an equal sign operator are called theta joins. Tables in **theta joins** are joined using other relational operators such as >, >=, <, <=, and <>. However, theta joins with operations other than equality are rare, and 99.9 percent of the time equi-joins are used.

Qualifiers

The phrase "Jobs.jobc" uses a qualifier of "Jobs" for "jobc"—it says take jobc from the Jobs table. In this case, the qualifiers are not needed because the column name jobc is unique to the Jobs table. The same is true for jobcode and Emps. The command will work without the qualifier, as follows:

```
SELECT *
FROM   Emps, Jobs
WHERE jobcode = jobc;
```

This gives the same result as in the preceding section:

EMP	JO	JO	JOBTITLE
102	ac	ac	accountant
101	cp	cp	computer programmer
104	cp	cp	computer programmer
105	cp	cp	computer programmer
103	de	de	dentist

Never write a multi-table SELECT without qualifiers. There are two reasons for this:

1. If the names of the attributes were the same in the two tables, you would have to use the qualifier. You never know when a table might be modified in the future; someone could add a `jobc` column to the Emps table someday.

2. When someone else looks at your statement, they should never have to figure out which attribute came from which table.

Queries Involving Multiple Tables: Using Table Aliases

A **table alias** is a temporary variable name for a table that allows us to short-hand the notation as we qualify attributes. Here is an example of a one-letter table alias:

```
SELECT  *
FROM    Emps e, Jobs j
WHERE   e.jobcode = j.jobc;
```

The table alias is defined by a letter *after* the table name, so the table alias for Jobs here is j and the table alias for Emps in this example is e. Some people prefer a short, meaningful word or expression rather than a one-letter table alias, but the one-letter alias is very common among SQL users. We will use many table aliases in future statements and in all multi-table queries. The following is an example showing statements with and without table aliases.

Without table aliases:

```
SELECT    Student.stno, Section.course_num, Grade_report.grade
FROM      Student, Grade_report, Section
WHERE     Student.stno = Grade_report.student_number
AND       Grade_report.section_id = Section.section_id;
```

With table aliases:

```
SELECT    stu.stno, sec.course_num, gr.grade
FROM      Student stu, Grade_report gr, Section sec
WHERE     stu.stno = gr.student_number
AND       gr.section_id = sec.section_id;
```

As with the one-letter example, the table aliases stu, gr, and sec are declared just after the table name in the FROM part of the SELECT.

In multi-table queries, it is not advisable to leave off qualifiers for attributes even if the database is well known. Most commonly, qualifiers are handled with table aliases. You never know when the database will be expanded or when a query will need to be analyzed by another person. Aliases are not persistent; they are only for the statement that you are doing at any time. As with many Oracle users, we will use single-letter table aliases in our examples.

More on Comments

As we mentioned in Chapter 1, and wish to repeat here, comments are often added to SQL statements to enhance their readability. As in programming languages, comments are ignored by the SQL engine but are invaluable for understanding and debugging. As you'll recall from Chapter 1, there are two ways of adding comments to SQL statements.

With the first method, you can add comments in the C style with /* and */, where everything between the two markers is ignored by the SQL parser. The /* comment */ is valid anywhere in a SELECT statement. Comments may cover several lines of code and are ignored when the statement is parsed prior to execution. An example of a commented SQL statement would be:

```
SELECT *                    /* the result set contains all
                               columns */
FROM Emps e, jobs j         /* using the Emps and the Jobs
                               tables */
WHERE e.jobcode = j.Jobc    /* this is the join condition for an
                               equi-join */
;
```

Another method of inserting comments is the dash-dash, or --. The -- may be included on any line, but it does not span lines like the /* .... */. The same example from above with -- would look like this:

```
SELECT *                    -- result set contains all columns
FROM Emps e, Jobs j         -- using the Jobs and the Emps tables
WHERE e.jobcode = j.jobc    -- join condition for an equi join
;
```

Either of these commenting tools is good programming practice as long as they do not obscure the code. In our example, the first and second comments are really superfluous because they are obvious to any SQL user. Obvious comments are annoying, whereas the comment on the join condition could be quite helpful.

Join Conditions and Comments

While Cartesian products are rarely appropriate, there are times when they may be used—in some table loads, for example. However, in creating joins, it is imperative to avoid Cartesian products. There is no warning that you have joined incorrectly except that you get an incorrect answer. In creating a join, there will always be (*n-1*) join conditions for joining *n* tables. Joins are done pair-wise.

If we join Student and Grade_report, there are two tables and one join condition as follows:

```
SELECT *
FROM   Student s, Grade_report g
WHERE  s.stno = g.student_number       /* the join condition */
;
```

If we join Student, Grade_report, and Section, there are three tables and two join conditions as follows:

```
SELECT *
FROM   Student s, Grade_report g, Section t
WHERE  s.stno = g.student_number       /* Student-Grade_report
                                          join condition */
AND    g.section_id = t.section_id     /* Grade_report-Section
                                          join condition */
;
```

Of course, it is valid and usual to include other conditions in the WHERE clause as necessary, as shown in the following example:

```
SELECT sname, grade, class
FROM   Student s, Grade_report g, Section t
WHERE  s.stno = g.student_number  /* Student-Grade_report
                                     join */
AND    g.section_id = t.section_id /* Grade_report-Section
                                     join */
AND    g.grade = 'B'
AND    s.class < 3;
```

This would be a three-table join of Student, Grade_report, and Section where the result would be students who have a B in the Grade_report table and who are sophomores or freshmen. The output of this is as follows:

SNAME	G	CLASS
Lineas	B	1
Lineas	B	1
Lineas	B	1
Brenda	B	2
Brenda	B	2
Lujack	B	1
Lujack	B	1
Lujack	B	1
Reva	B	2
Reva	B	2
Reva	B	2

```
SNAME          G    CLASS
-----------    -    -----
Harley         B    2
Lynette        B    1
Hillary        B    1
Hillary        B    1
Hillary        B    1
Sadie          B    2
Jessica        B    2
Steve          B    1
Cedric         B    2
George         B    1
Fraiser        B    1

SNAME          G    CLASS
-----------    -    -----
Fraiser        B    1
Smithly        B    2
Sebastian      B    2
Lindsay        B    1

26 rows selected.
```

We highly recommended that you:

• include a comment for each join condition in multiple table joins, and

• put each join condition on a separate line.

Outer Joins

An equi-join that was illustrated earlier is extremely common in SQL and relational database. An equi-join results from a query like the following:

```
SELECT *
FROM  Emps e, Jobs j
WHERE j.jobc = e.jobcode      -- join condition for equi-join
;
```

At times, it is desirable to include not only the rows that have matching values in another table, but all the rows in one table, matching or not. When you want all rows from one table regardless of whether they match values in the other table, the query is called an ***outer join***. In Oracle, outer joins are generated using a construction like the following:

```
SELECT *
FROM   Emps e, Jobs j
WHERE  j.jobc = e.jobcode(+)    /* outer join (Jobs is the
                                   driving table) (a.k.a., left
                                   outer join) */
;
```

This basically says to include all rows of Jobs, and if matching rows in Emps do not exist, then manufacture them (hence, the (+) on the Emps join attribute). Suppose the following jobs were added to the Jobs table from above <'tr','tree surgeon'>. The result of the outer join would then be:

```
EMP   JO   JO   JOBTITLE
--    --   --   ---------------
102   ac   ac   accountant
101   cp   cp   computer programmer
104   cp   cp   computer programmer
105   cp   cp   computer programmer
103   de   de   dentist
           tr   tree surgeon
```

This query asks for all rows of Jobs, regardless of whether there is a match in Emps. Hence the unmatched, new job—where there is no employee yet who does this work—is still reported with nulls for the Emps information. Oracle uses the idea of a "driving table." A ***driving table*** is the table that is accessed first (in our example above, the Jobs table). It "drives" the join and all of its rows *will* be included in the result set (regardless of whether they match with the other table). Syntactically, the driving table in Oracle is the one *without* the plus sign. The SQL standard and other database systems use the phrase *left outer join* to represent the same idea as illustrated here. Other systems have *right outer joins* as well as *full outer joins*, which would show all unmatched rows. As just mentioned, in Oracle, the left or right notation is dropped in favor of the idea of the driving table (which the authors laud). Oracle does not allow a full outer join directly (but there are always work-arounds).

> The use of the term "driving table" has performance implications that are beyond the scope of this material.

Column Aliases

When writing a query, it is often useful to enhance its output and readability by using a ***column alias***. A column alias is declared following the column designation in the SELECT statement. For example, for a query *without* a column alias, we would type:

```
SELECT s.sname, g.grade
FROM   Student s, Grade_report g
WHERE  s.stno = g.student_number        -- join condition
;
```

This produces the following result set:

```
SNAME          G
_____    _
BURNS          D
BURNS          F
BURNS          C
BURNS          C
```

A query *with* a simple column alias would be:

```
SELECT s.sname Name, g.grade Grade
FROM   Student s, Grade_report g
WHERE  s.stno = g.student_number        -- join condition
;
```

This produces the following result set (note the change in the column heading):

```
NAME           G
_____    _
BURNS          D
BURNS          F
BURNS          C
BURNS          C
```

You can also use more complex column aliases. For example, if there is an embedded blank, the column alias is put in double quotes as follows:

```
SELECT s.sname "Student Name", g.grade "Grade Assigned"
FROM   Student s, Grade_report g
WHERE  s.stno = g.student_number        -- join condition
;
```

This produces the following result set:

```
Student Name  G
_____   _
BURNS         D
BURNS         F
BURNS         C
BURNS         C
```

You have probably noticed a result-set presentation problem. No matter what the column alias, if the length of the output field is smaller than the alias or the name of the field, the result set display uses the field length. To make the output conform to the column alias you used, you need to execute a SQLPLUS command to format the column. The command looks like this:

```
COLUMN "Grade Assigned" FORMAT a15
```

This would set the size of the "Grade Assigned" field to 15 alphanumeric characters and make our result set look like this:

```
Student Name  Grade Assigned
_____   _____
BURNS         D
BURNS         F
BURNS         C
BURNS         C
```

> The COLUMN command should be executed just before the SELECT.

Scripting

In using column aliases, we are beginning to see output enhancements that make result sets of queries easier to read. Other formatting features can also enhance outputs (for example, in reports). At present, the use of column formats and column aliases suggests that there ought to be a way to put these two features together. The way the two are combined is to use a script. A *script* is an executable set of commands that can combine multiple SQL and SQLPLUS commands.

To put together and run a script, follow these steps:

1. At the SQL prompt, type:

```
SQL> EDIT run1;
```

This will open up an editor for a new file called run1.sql.

2. Type the following statements in the editor, as shown in the screen in Figure 3.2.

```
COLUMN "Student Name" FORMAT a20
COLUMN "Your Grade" FORMAT a20
SELECT s.sname "Student Name",
       g.grade "Your Grade"
FROM   Student s, Grade_report g
WHERE  s.stno = g.student_number      /* join condition */;
CLEAR COLUMNS
```

> You should issue a CLEAR COLUMNS after formatting columns. The purpose of the CLEAR COLUMNS is to remove the formatting from the heading "Student Name." If you do not issue a CLEAR command, then any other time you use "Student Name" as a column alias, it would be formatted as FORMAT a20. If that is what you want, then the CLEAR could be left off; however, it is good practice to leave the environment as you found it, so we recommend that whatever you format, you un-format it at the end of the script.

3. To save the file in Windows, go to the top menu and select FILE, SAVE. To quit the text editor and get back to the SQL prompt, select FILE, EXIT from the top menu.

4. To run the script you just created, type:

```
SQL>@run1
```

COUNT and Rownum

When dealing with multiple tables, it is often desirable to explore the result set without actually displaying all of it. For example, you may want to know how many rows are in a result set without actually seeing

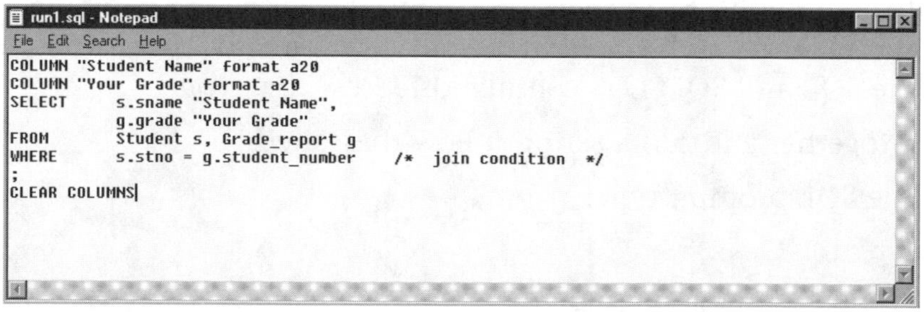

FIGURE 3.2 Typing a Script File in an Editor

the result set itself. The "row-counter" in SQL is a function called COUNT. COUNT is one of many functions Oracle provides, and although we will explore other functions later in the text, COUNT is used so commonly that we want to introduce it to you here. For example, if you execute the following statement:

```
SELECT *  -- all columns, all rows
FROM    Student;
```

You will see all the rows of the Student table plus the values for all columns in those rows. If all you want to see is the number of rows in the result set, the statement is:

```
SELECT COUNT(*)  -- count of number of rows in result set
FROM    Student;
```

This results in the screen shown in Figure 3.3.

You can also count the occurrence of attributes. For example, if you type:

```
SELECT COUNT(class)
FROM    Student;
```

It would give you:

```
COUNT(CLASS)
--------
      38
```

COUNT(class) will count the rows where class is not null.

Rownum is another handy Oracle device for exploring result sets. Rownum is called a pseudo-variable because it looks like a variable

```
± Oracle SQL*Plus                                    _ □ ×
File  Edit  Search  Options  Help

SQL> SELECT COUNT(*)
  2  FROM Student;

 COUNT(*)
---------
       48

SQL>
```

FIGURE 3.3 Using COUNT

attribute. Rownum may also be referred to as a *pseudocolumn*. The following is an example of how Rownum can be used. If you type:

```
SELECT rownum, sname
FROM  Student
WHERE rownum < 5;
```

This results in the screen shown in Figure 3.4.

There are two caveats to observe with using Rownum. First, the WHERE clause must contain an inequality—an equality will not work. More specifically, if you use Rownum in the WHERE clause, you must use either < or <=. It will not work with >, >=, =, or <>. Rownum appends a COUNT as the row is retrieved. In order for the pseudo-variable to work, it has to COUNT during retrieval, so a statement that includes WHERE rownum = 5 will not work correctly.

Second, the following query is not allowed by SQL syntax:

```
SELECT rownum, *…
```

If you wanted to see all columns plus a row number, you would have to use the Rownum pseudo-variable and then list each of the columns.

FIGURE 3.4 Using Rownum

CHAPTER 3 EXERCISES

1. Create two tables, Stu(name, majorcode) and Major(majorcode, majordesc) with the data indicated below. Use CHAR(2) for codes and appropriate data types for the other attributes.

Stu

name	majorCode
Jones	CS
Smith	AC
Evans	MA
Adams	CS

Major

majorCode	majorDesc
AC	Accounting
CS	Computer Science
MA	Math

   a. Display the Cartesian product (no WHERE clause). Use SELECT *.... How many tuples did you get? How many tuples will you always get when combining two tables with *n* and *m* tuples in them (Cartesian product)?

   b. Display an equi-join of Stu and Major on majorCode (include an appropriate WHERE clause). Use table aliases. How many tuples did you get?

   c. Display whatever you get if you leave off the column qualifiers (the aliases) on the equi-join in step b. (Note: This will give an error because of ambiguous column names.)

   d. Use the COUNT(*) function instead of SELECT * in the query. Use COUNT to show the number of rows in the result set of the equi-join and the Cartesian product. Do the equi-join first with COUNT, then comment out the WHERE clause for the second answer. (Put -- in front of the word WHERE, to include a comment.)

2. Create two tables, T1(name, jobno) and T2(jobno, jobdesc). Let jobno be data type, NUMBER(1), and use appropriate data types for the other attributes. Put three tuples in T1 and two tuples in T2. Give T1.jobno values 1, 2, 3 for the three tuples: <..., 1>,<..., 2,>,<..., 3>, where ... represents any value you choose. Give T2.jobno the values 1, 2: <1,...>,<2,...>.

   a. How many tuples are there in the equi-join (on jobno) of T1 and T2?

   b. If the values of T2.jobno were <2,...>, <2,...> (with different jobdesc values), how many tuples would you expect to get and why? Why would the tuples have to have different descriptions?

c. If the values of T2.jobno were 4, 5 as in <4,...>,<5,...>, how many tuples would you expect to get?

d. If the values of T1.jobno were <..., 1>,<..., 1>,<..., 1> (with different names) and the values of T2.jobno were <1,...>,<1...> (with different descriptions), how many tuples would you expect to get?

So, if you have two tables, what is the number of tuples you may expect from a equi-join operation (and with what conditions)? A Cartesian product? *Edit the following statement into your homework with blanks filled in:*

The answer to the equi-join question in this problem is: The number of tuples in an equi-join of two tables, whose sizes are M and N rows, is from ____ to ____ depending on these conditions:

_____.

3. Use tables T1 and T2 in this exercise. Create another table called T3(jobdesc, minpay). Let minpay be type NUMBER(6,2). Populate the table with at least one occurrence of each jobdesc from table T2 plus one more jobdesc that is not in T2. Write and display the result of a triple equi-join of T1, T2, and T3. Use an appropriate comment on each of the lines of the WHERE clause where there are equi-join conditions. Note that you will need two equi-join conditions.

a. How many tuples did you get in the equi-join?

b. Use the COUNT(*) function and display the number of tuples (rows) in the equi-join.

c. How many tuples would you get in this meaningless, triple Cartesian product? (use COUNT(*)).

Edit the following statement into your homework with blanks filled in:

In an equi-join of N tables, you always have _____ equi-join conditions in the WHERE clause.

4. The Oracle Data Dictionary contains views of dictionary tables. Recall from previous exercises that you can display the dictionary and its entries just like any other query. To look at the dictionary itself, the command is:

```
SELECT * FROM dict;
```

a. Display the number of rows in the dictionary (just the number of rows, not the content of the rows).

b. Display Data Dictionary entries for the tables you have created. To look at a table in the dictionary, use a statement like:

```
SELECT *      /* you could also choose specific columns
                  rather than all of them */
FROM X
WHERE Y
```

where X is the name of a dictionary table like USER_TABLES, ALL_SYNONYMS, and so on, and Y is whatever condition (row filter) you care to place on the query. Because USER_TABLES are *your* tables, you do not need a "Y-condition" on this query to answer this question.

c. Look at which views are available to you. Use SELECT * FROM all_synonyms. You should also try SELECT * FROM xxx, where xxx is a synonym like Tab, tabs, or syn. Tab, tabs, and syn are public synonyms for dictionary tables (note that there are others).

d. Look at the description (DESC) for user_tables, user_objects, user_views, and user_synonyms. Compare the DESC user_tables to all_tables. What data is available in all_tables that is not in user_tables? Are there any columns (attributes) that are in all_tables that are not in user_tables? What is the synonym for user_tables?

e. Display the first five rows in the following tables: dict, user_tables, and all_synonyms.

5. Write a script to generate a result set that looks like the following:

```
Student Name      Grade Assigned
_____        _____
Lineas            D
Lineas            B
Lineas            B
Lineas            A
Etc.
```

You need show only the first 10 lines of the output. (Use WHERE .. rownum < 11 .. in the WHERE clause and do not put rownum in the result set, just after the SELECT.)

You created tables T1, T2, T3, Stu, and Major. These are temporary tables you used for testing. When you have completed this exercise, delete these tables. Check the dictionary to ensure that you have deleted your tables.

REFERENCE

Earp, R., and Bagui, S. (2000). Oracle's Joins. *Oracle Internals*, Vol. 2(3), 6–14.

Functions and Matching (LIKE)

This chapter is designed to introduce more utilitarian features into the SELECT statement and to show the application of these enhancements. You can use some of the information introduced in this chapter for checking the feasibility of outputs. As we have seen, SQL does not prevent programmers from asking questions that have very long or even meaningless answers (see for example, our discussion of Cartesian products in Chapter 3).

The main thrust of this chapter is to introduce functions and to demonstrate how to find information when a row contains strings. Functions come in two general varieties: aggregate functions (such as COUNT or SUM) and row functions (such as SQRT). We will place special emphasis on string functions (row functions). We will also demonstrate how functions and other constructions allow us to retrieve information (LIKE and matching patterns).

The COUNT Function

As we have mentioned, COUNT is a function that will generate a value of *how many* of something there are. A function that returns a result based on multiple rows is called an **aggregate function** or a **group-function**. We prefer the term *aggregate* because it avoids confusion. Later, we will study a GROUP BY option in the SELECT statement that uses aggregates, but aggregates can be used without using GROUP BY. The aggregate function combines or distills an answer into a smaller set. In this case, the COUNT with an asterisk as the argument returns a COUNT of the number of rows in the result set. The following is the syntax for the COUNT function.

```
SELECT  COUNT(*)
FROM    table-name(s)    -- counts all tuples (rows) in a table
```

Consider the following example:

```
SELECT  COUNT(*)
FROM    Grade_report;
```

As we mentioned in Chapter 3, the COUNT feature can be quite useful because it can save you from unexpectedly long results. In addition, it can often be used to answer "how many" queries without looking at the data itself. Recall that in Chapter 3 we generated a Cartesian product and a join. When dealing with larger tables, it is very good form to first ask the question, "How many rows can I expect in my answer?" This question may be vital if a printout is involved. How many tuples are there in the Cartesian product of Student, Section, and Grade_report in our database? This can be answered by the following query:

```
SELECT  COUNT(*)
FROM    Student, Section, Grade_report;
```

The following output shows what the Cartesian product of the previous query would give:

COUNT(*)
321024

The COUNT from the last statement should equal the product of the table sizes of the three tables. Contrast the COUNTing-query and Cartesian product result from the previous query to this query:

```
SELECT  COUNT(*)
FROM    Student, Grade_report , Section
WHERE   Student.stno = Grade_report.student_number      /* join
                            condition of Student to Grade_report */
AND     Grade_report.section_id = Section.section_id    /* join
                            condition of Grade_report to Section */
;
```

The result of this query is:

```
COUNT(*)
-----
   209
```

What is requested here is a COUNT of a three-way equi-join rather than a three-way Cartesian product. Remember that we strongly advocate the idea of commenting the join conditions, hence the comment:

```
-- join condition of...
```

is appropriately appended to the join WHERE conditions.

SELECTing and COUNTing with DISTINCT

To SELECT all grades from the Grade_report table, type:

```
SELECT grade
FROM    Grade_report;
```

This results in 209 rows of all the grades in Grade_report.

To SELECT all *distinct* grades, type:

```
SELECT DISTINCT grade
FROM    Grade_report;
```

This results in:

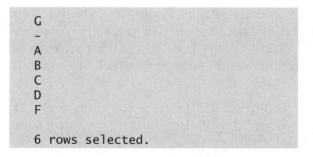

```
G
-
A
B
C
D
F

6 rows selected.
```

Observe that the syntax requires you to put the word DISTINCT first in the string of attributes because DISTINCT implies distinct rows in the result set. The previous statement also produces a row for null grades (also regarded as a DISTINCT grade). To COUNT distinct grades, we could use:

```
SELECT COUNT(DISTINCT grade)
FROM Grade_report;
```

This results in:

```
COUNT(DISTINCTGRADE)
--------------------
        5
```

This result does *not* count null values; hence, we have five distinct grades instead of six. So, the DISTINCT produces null values in the output, but the COUNT does not count the null values.

The syntax of SQL will not allow you to COUNT two columns with this query. Thus, the following query will not work:

```
SELECT COUNT (DISTINCT grade, section_id)
FROM Grade_report;
```

Additional Basic Functions

There are many more functions in SQL besides COUNT. For example, aggregate numeric functions, which work on sets of data, find table-values such as sums (SUM), averages (AVG), minima (MIN), and maxima (MAX). In addition, row-level string functions (such as LPAD, RPAD, LTRIM, RTRIM, SUBSTR, INSTR, and so on) work on values in one given row, construct, break apart, and parse strings. Row-level date functions provide interesting ways to handle date values. There are also row-level conversion functions (such as TO_CHAR and TO_DATE) that convert among dates, characters, strings, and numbers, which we saw in Chapter 2.

In this section, we will explore several of the more common aggregate functions for numbers and strings. We will also illustrate row-level functions that handle special situations that arise in SQL—notably, the problem of null values.

More Aggregate Functions

One of the more common things to ask of a database involves finding an aggregate function on a set of numeric values. We have seen the COUNT function already. The aggregate functions SUM, AVG, MIN, MAX, and others work in a similar way. For this example, suppose you have a table called `Employee` that looks like this:

Employee

name	wage	hours
Alice Adams	10	40
Barry Baker	15	30
Darrel Davis	18	
Ed Evans		10
Genny George	20	40

> This Employee table has not been created for you. You have to create it.

To find the sum of hours worked, you would use the SUM function as follows:

```
SELECT  SUM(Hours)
FROM    Employee;
```

This produces the following output:

```
SUM(HOURS)
------
    120
```

This SUM result is particularly interesting in that fields that contain null values are ignored by the SUM function (as they are by **all** aggregate numeric functions). The point about ignoring nulls can be illustrated by the following query, which also shows that several aggregate functions can be placed in the result set:

```
SELECT AVG(hours), MAX(wage), COUNT(hours)
FROM    Employee;
```

This produces the following output:

AVG(HOURS)	MAX(WAGE)	COUNT(HOURS)
30	20	4

A most interesting result may be noted in the following example. If you type:

```
SELECT name, wage*hours
FROM Employee;
```

It produces the following output:

NAME	WAGE*HOURS
Alice Adams	400
Barry Baker	450
Darrel Davis	
Ed Evans	
Genny George	800

Here, the nulls are not only ignored, but the example illustrates that if a null is contained in a calculation on a row, the result is always null!

The NVL Function

To handle this null problem, Oracle provides a row-level function that returns a value if a table-value is null: NVL. The NVL function has the following form:

```
NVL(column-value, value-returned)
```

NVL says if the "column-value" is NOT null, return the value, but if the value IS null, return "value-returned." For example, if you wanted to multiply wage by hours and avoid the null problem, the correct statement could read:

```
SELECT name, NVL(wage,0)*NVL(hours,0)
FROM Employee;
```

This produces the following output:

NAME	NVL(WAGE,0)*NVL(HOURS,0)
Alice Adams	400
Barry Baker	450
Darrel Davis	0
Ed Evans	0
Genny George	800

> NVL is not an aggregate function—it is a row/value function. It operates on values one at a time as opposed to an aggregate like SUM, which operates on multiple rows for a result.

NVL does **not** have to have a "value-returned" equal to zero. If the number of hours were assumed to be, say, 30 if the value were null, then the expression would be: … NVL(Hours, 30) …

String Functions

Unlike the functions introduced earlier in this chapter, **string functions** are not aggregates—they are row-level functions. String functions operate on a value in a row as a row is retrieved. Let's begin by looking at an example of a string function. Using the previous `Employee` table, we can list the names of the employees with a statement like this:

```
SELECT name
FROM   Employee;
```

This produces the following output:

```
NAME
____

Alice Adams
Barry Baker
Darrel Davis
Ed Evans
Genny George
```

But suppose we would like to list the names like this:

```
Adams, A.
Baker, B.
Darrel, D.
Ed, E.
Genny, G.
```

To do this, we need string functions to break down the `name` into parts and assemble those parts. The two string functions we needed in this example are SUBSTR and INSTR, as well as a concatenation operator. SUBSTR (pronounced sub-string) returns part of a string, while INSTR (pronounced in-string) finds where a pattern is in a string. SUBSTR could therefore be called a "string extractor." To build a string, we use the concatenation operator ||. (Look just under the <Backspace> key on your PC keyboard.) *Concatenation* means "to stick together." We will start the string construction process with INSTR. Consider the following example:

```
SELECT INSTR(name,' '),name
FROM Employee;
```

> There is an Oracle function similar to NVL called NVL2. NVL2 takes three arguments and returns the second if the first is not null and returns the third if the first is null.

This produces the following output:

```
INSTR(NAME,'')   NAME
--------         ---------
      6          Alice Adams
      6          Barry Baker
      7          Darrel Davis
      3          Ed Evans
      6          Genny George
```

Again, note that INSTR (like all the string functions) is not an aggregate function. Like NVL, it is a row/value function that operates on one value, one row at a time. INSTR finds the occurrence of some search-string pattern (second argument) in the string listed in the first argument. Here, the INSTR is looking for a blank space. The search-string pattern doesn't have to be only one-character long as it is in this case. If a blank space did not occur in the subject-string name, the function would return a zero.

To illustrate concatenation, consider the following example:

```
SELECT name||', Esq.'
FROM Employee;
```

This produces the following output:

```
NAME||',ESQ.'
-----------
Alice Adams, Esq.
Barry Baker, Esq.
Darrel Davis, Esq.
Ed Evans, Esq.
Genny George, Esq.
```

As mentioned earlier, SUBSTR is a row-level string-extraction function. SUBSTR in Oracle is almost identical to the same function in other programming languages. The form of the function is:

```
SUBSTR(subject-string, start, how-far)
```

"Start" indicates where to start retrieving from the subject-string and "how-far" indicated how many characters to extract. If "how-far" is absent, the function returns the rest of the string from wherever you "start." If "start" is negative, the function works from the right end of the string. Consider the following example:

```
SELECT SUBSTR(name,2,4), SUBSTR(name, 6), SUBSTR(name, -3)
FROM Employee;
```

This produces the following output:

SUBS	SUBSTR(NAM	SUB
lice	Adams	ams
arry	Baker	ker
arre	l Davis	vis
d Ev	ans	ans
enny	George	rge

Strings in Oracle are indexed from 1, not from 0 (zero). However, if we start at position 0 (zero), we get the same result as we would if we started at position 1, as shown here. If we type:

```
SELECT SUBSTR(name,0,2)
FROM Employee;
```

We get the following output:

SU
Al
Ba
Da
Ed
Ge

Likewise, if we type:

```
SELECT SUBSTR(name,1,2)
FROM Employee;
```

We get the following output:

```
SU
-
Al
Ba
Da
Ed
Ge
```

As you can see, both of these queries produce the same result.

To combine concatenation, SUBSTR, and INSTR, to write the names in a "last name, initial" format, a query like the following is required:

```
SELECT SUBSTR(name, INSTR(name,' ')+1)||',
'||SUBSTR(name,1,1)||'.'
FROM Employee;
```

This produces the following output:

```
SUBSTR(NAME,INSTR(N
_____
Adams, A.
Baker, B.
Davis, D.
Evans, E.
George, G.
```

SUBSTR(Name, INSTR(Name,' ')+1) says to extract characters from name beginning in the position one past (+1) the blank space. Because there is no third argument given, the function returns everything after the blank. If there were no blank space in the string, then characters returned would be the entire string.

In all of these examples, column aliases would "dress up" the output and provide a handle for ORDER BY and column formatting. Aliases are encouraged, so the last query, first line could read:

```
SELECT SUBSTR(name, INSTR(name,' ')+1)||',
'||SUBSTR(name,1,1)||'.' Names
```

This would produce the following output:

```
Names
_____
Adams, A.
Baker, B.
Davis, D.
Evans, E.
George, G.
```

RPAD and LPAD could also be used to pad a string to some other string (or anything else). To add something to the right end of name RPAD could be used as shown here:

```
SELECT RPAD(name,20,'.')
FROM Employee;
```

This would produce the following output:

```
RPAD(NAME,20,'.')
_____
Alice Adams.........
Barry Baker
Darrel Davis........
Ed Evans...........
Genny George........
```

This adds ... after the name until name has 20 characters.

To add something before the name, LPAD could be used as shown here:

```
SELECT LPAD(name,20,'.')
FROM Employee;
```

This would produce the following output:

```
LPAD(NAME,20,'.')
_____
.........Alice Adams
.........Barry Baker
........Darrel Davis
............Ed Evans
........Genny George
```

This adds enough ... before the name so that name now has 20 characters.

Likewise, LTRIM and RTRIM would trim a string from the left or the right end.

There is also a function called TRIM that will edit strings even more flexibly from the left or right or both ends.

To find the length of a desired string, LENGTH could be used as shown here:

```
SELECT  LENGTH(name)
FROM    Employee;
```

This would produce the following output:

```
LENGTH(NAME)
————
     11
     11
     12
      8
     12
```

Matching Substrings: Using LIKE

We often want to use part of a character attribute as a condition in a query. For example, consider the Section table, which has the following structure:

```
section_id       course_num    sem    yr      inst
85  MATH2410     FALL   86     KING
86  MATH5501     FALL   86     EMERSON
```

We might want to know something about Math courses (courses with the prefix MATH); if so we need to have a way to find a substring in an attribute. We could use SUBSTR, but there is another, more common way to handle this type of query—using the LIKE keyword. The LIKE keyword is used in two ways:

• as an existence match, and

• as a position match.

LIKE as an Existence Match

Using LIKE as an existence match entails finding whether a character string exists in an attribute—if the string exists, the tuple is SELECTed for inclusion in the result set. This existence type of LIKE query is useful when the position of the character string sought may be in various places in the substring. Oracle uses the wildcard % at the beginning or end of a string, when looking for the existence of substrings. For example, suppose we have a name attribute with a data type of CHAR(8). Suppose further that all names are in all caps. We want to find all students whose name is SMITH. We might try:

```
SELECT *
FROM Student
WHERE sname = 'SMITH';
```

We would get "no rows selected."

To find "SMITH's," we'd have to match all the blanks we put in the table, as shown below:

```
SELECT *
FROM Student
WHERE sname = 'SMITH   '        /* 8 characters inside the
                                   quotes */
;
```

Using a percentage (%) sign on both ends will find SMITH as well as people who have names with 'SMITH' in them, such as SMITH, SMITH-FIELD, SMITHSON, LOSMITH, and so on. Consider the following examples:

```
SELECT * FROM Student
WHERE sname = 'SMITH'   /* matches only a 5-character field
                           with SMITH in it */
;


SELECT * FROM Student
WHERE sname LIKE '%SMITH%'    /* finds any SMITH pattern in
                                 sname */
;
```

```
SELECT * FROM Student
WHERE sname LIKE 'SMITH%'          /* finds any pattern starting
                                      with SMITH, ending with --
                                      anything */

;
```

> We'll discuss mixed-case problems later in the chapter.

We need to point out here that using CHAR(8) for a name would be atypical. Names are usually VARCHAR2 data types and, as such, a name stored as 'SMITH' would be found with a query that included a WHERE sname = 'SMITH'. The point is that you can never count on what people will store in a database, and what you think might be 'SMITH' could be 'Smith' or ' SMith' (with a leading blank), and so on.

To find the math courses in the original question we posed with a wildcard LIKE match, we could use:

```
SELECT * FROM Section
WHERE course_num LIKE 'MATH%' /* matches any course_num start-
                                 ing with MATH */

;
```

This would produce the following output:

SECTION_ID	COURSE_N	SEMEST	YE	INSTRUCTOR	BLDG	ROOM
85	MATH2410	FALL	98	KING	36	123
86	MATH5501	FALL	98	EMERSON	36	123
107	MATH2333	SPRING	00	CHANG	36	123
109	MATH5501	FALL	99	CHANG	36	123
112	MATH2410	FALL	99	CHANG	36	123
158	MATH2410	SPRING	98		36	123

6 rows selected.

LIKE as a Positioned Match and a Wildcard

Another way to use the keyword LIKE is to find the occurrence of a given character sequence in a particular place in a string. For example, we might want to find courses that have a numeric identifier like 2xxx in the last four positions, where xxx is any letter (presumably a sophomore course). This LIKE form includes the use of the underscore character for the positions of the attribute where we don't care what the contents are. In this case, the SELECT would be:

```
SELECT *
FROM   Section
WHERE course_num LIKE '____2___';
```

This matches any character in the first four positions, then matches a 2, and then any character in the last three positions, as shown here:

```
SECTION_ID  COURSE_N  SEMEST  YE  INSTRUCTOR  BLDG  ROOM
_____  _____  _____  __  _____  ____  ____
85          MATH2410  FALL    98  KING        36    123
95          ACCT2220  SPRING  99  RODRIQUEZ   74
96          COSC2025  FALL    98  RAFAELT     79    179
101         POLY2103  SPRING  00  SCHMIDT
107         MATH2333  SPRING  00  CHANG       36    123
112         MATH2410  FALL    99  CHANG       36    123
158         MATH2410  SPRING  98              36    123
201         CHEM2001  FALL    99              58    114

8 rows selected.
```

The UPPER and LOWER functions

If database data is in all caps, then the previous queries will behave as discussed. However, if the data in the database is in mixed case or all lowercase letters, then a query that includes the phrase LIKE '%SMITH%' will not match—the query will return "no rows." The way around this is to uppercase the result set using the UPPER function. The UPPER function converts strings to all uppercase for display and testing (the database itself is unaffected). If the data in the database is in mixed case or, more usually, if you do not know what the case is, you can add UPPER to a query like this:

```
SELECT *
FROM     Student
WHERE    UPPER(sname) LIKE '%SMITH%';
```

Alternatively, you can add LOWER to a query like this:

```
SELECT *
FROM     Student
WHERE    LOWER(sname) LIKE '%smith%';
```

Both of these queries will produce the same result, as follows:

STNO	SNAME	MAJO	CLASS	BDATE
147	Smithly	ENGL	2	13-MAY-80
151	Losmith	CHEM	3	15-JAN-81
88	Smith			15-OCT-79

The Data Dictionary Revisited

In defining what a database is, we use the term *meta-data* to define "data about data." This meta-data is kept in a series of tables and views called the Data Dictionary. We have seen glimpses of the Data Dictionary earlier in this book, but here we will use the material presented in this chapter to expand our exploration.

The Data Dictionary in Oracle is arranged into views so that users, developers, analysts, and database administrators (DBAs) can determine what objects there are, how big they are, when they were created, who they were created by, and so on.

The objects that are monitored by the dictionary include tables, tablespaces (subdivisions where tables are located), views, catalogs, synonyms, and other objects (including one category called "objects").

The dictionary has four levels of access defined in views: USER, ALL, DBA, and "other." The view names are a combination of the access/owner and the object. Some examples follow:

• USER_TABLES, which holds tables created by a USER.

• ALL_VIEWS, which shows all views accessible to a user.

• DBA_CONSTRAINTS, which shows constraint definitions on all tables.

The "other" views in the dictionary contain more general information. For example, there is a view called COLUMN_PRIVILEGES that describes the grants on columns for which the user is the grantor, grantee, owner, or an enabled role or PUBLIC is the grantee.

There is a list of table synonyms in the dictionary. For example, CAT is a synonym for the view USER_CATALOG. There are also system tables that may be viewed. These tables/views have synonyms that begin with the prefix V$. You may or may not be able to view the table/view even though you may see it in the dictionary. One you can see and view is called V$VERSION, which will tell you which version of Oracle you are using.

> People often mix the terms "view" and "table" when talking about dictionary views. The correct term is "view"; however, "dictionary table" is so common that it is an accepted colloquialism.

> Spelling is critical when accessing these views because ALL_VIEW is not known, whereas ALL_VIEWS is. To avoid spelling and case problems for matching, you should always use LIKE and UPPER or LOWER appropriately.

Finally, because the dictionary contains a lot of information, it is prudent to access the views therein cautiously. There is a suggested step-by-step approach outlined in the following exercises that involves first describing and COUNTing before accessing these tables and views. Finally, note that the owner of dictionary tables and views is SYS. It is not appropriate to try to modify the dictionary directly.

CHAPTER 4 EXERCISES

1. Display the COUNT of rows (tuples) in each of the tables Grade_report, Student, and Section. How many rows would you expect in the Cartesian product of all three tables? Display the COUNT (*not* the resulting tuples) of the Cartesian product of all three and verify your result. Use SELECT COUNT(*) ...

2. Display the COUNT of section-ids from the Section table, and then the COUNT of DISTINCT section-ids from the Grade_report table. What does this information tell you? (Hint: section-id is the primary key of the Section table.)

3. Write, execute, and print a query to list student names and grades (just two attributes) using the table alias feature. Restrict the list to students that have either A's or B's in courses with ACCT prefixes only.

   Here's how to complete this problem:

   a. Get the statement to work as a COUNT of a join of the three tables, Student, Grade_report, and Section. Use table aliases in the join condition (remember to use /* join conditions */). Note that *a join of n tables requires (n-1) join conditions,* so here you have to have two join conditions—one to join Student and Grade_report, and one to join Grade_report and Section. Note the number of tuples that you get (expect no more tuples than is in the Grade_report table). Why?

   b. Modify the query and put the accounting condition in the WHERE clause. Note the number of tuples in the result—it should be a good bit less than in step a.

   c. Again, modify the query and add the grade constraints. The number of tuples should decrease again. Note that if you have WHERE x *and* y *or* z, parentheses are optional, but then the criteria will be interpreted according to precedence rules.

      The reason that we want you to "start small" and add conditions is that it gives you a check on what you ought to get and it allows you to output less nonsense. Your minimal starting point should be a COUNT of the join with appropriate join conditions. If you are unsure of the join, use Rownum and look at the first five or 10 rows as you go along.

4. Do not assume any particular case (upper or lower) for the data for this problem (or ever, for that matter!).

   a. How many students have names like "SMITH" or "Smith"?

   b. How many students have names that contain the letter sequence "SMITH"?

   c. How many student names end in "LD"?

   d. Would "SELECT * FROM Student WHERE sname LIKE 'SMITH%'" find someone whose name was:

      (i) "LA SMITH"

      (ii) "SMITH-JONES"

      (iii) "SMITH JR."

      (iv) "SMITH, JR"

   e. Would you call UPPER or LOWER an aggregate function? Why or why not?

   f. Pad all the student names in the Student table with ... on the right.

5. List the junior level COSC courses (like COSC3xxx) and the name of the course. Use the Course table.

6. Using the COUNT feature, determine whether there are duplicate names or student numbers in the Student table.

7. Assume that all math courses start with MATH. How many math courses are there in the Section table? From the COUNT of courses, does it appear that there are any math courses in the Section table that are not in the Course table? Again, using COUNTs, are there any math courses in the Course table that are not in the Section table? Does it appear that there are any courses at all that are in Grade_report, Section, or Course that are not in the others? (We will study how to ask these questions in SQL in a later chapter.) Note that a query like the following would not work:

```
SELECT g.section_id
FROM Grade_report g, Section t
WHERE g.section_id <> t.section_id;
```

Explain why WHERE .. <> .. will not work to produce the desired output.

8. Display dictionary views for the tables we have in the Student database (refer to the diagram in Appendix 3). Use "all_tables" as the dictionary view. Do the query as follows:

a. DESCRIBE the table "DESC `all_tables`;"

b. Display the number of rows in `all_tables`. Use SELECT COUNT(*) FROM `all_tables`;

Observe that when you are exploring the dictionary, it is *not* a good idea to simply SELECT * FROM *whatever*, where *whatever* is some dictionary view. Dictionary views are often long and "wide"—"wide" in that there are often many attributes and many of those attributes are not necessarily interesting.

c. Display the `owner` and `table_name` from `all_tables` where owner = 'your userid'.

d. Are the attributes different in `all_tables` and `user_tables`? What is the difference in the two views?

e. Display the first two rows (use WHERE `rownum` < 3) of the `all_tables` table.

f. Repeat this exercise (steps a, b, and c) for `all_catalog`, `all_objects`, `all_synonyms`, and `all_tab_columns` (synonym is cols). The point of this exercise is twofold:

(i) to drive home the admonition to be very careful to look at what you will get before you actually ask for it (use DESC and COUNT(*) prudently), and

(ii) to familiarize you with the dictionary contents.

g. How many objects are in the dictionary? Use "dict" for the dictionary (dict is the synonym for dictionary). How many USER tables are there? How many ALL_ tables? How many DBA_ type tables? How many other tables? (Hint: SELECT FROM dict and use LIKE appropriately for each query.)

h. Using the table `all_users`, find out your `user_id` number and when your account was created.

i. Determine what session privileges you have available (SESSION_PRIVS).

j. Determine which version of Oracle we are using. Also determine which V$ tables you can "see" in the dictionary and which you can and cannot actually view. Hint: Look at the V$ tables in dict and try to describe each one.

9. Complete and/or update the following paper table for all tables in our Student-Course database. You should make a copy for yourself.

```
Table    Attribute  Rows  Distinct Rows  Rows without Nulls
Student  stno        48   48             48
         sname            47             48
         major             8             3
         class            etc., etc.
Section  section_id etc.
```

Produce a similar table for Grade_report, Section, Room, Course, Prereq, and Department_to_major.

Hint: you can use SELECT COUNT (*) from Student where sname is null.

10. **a.** Find the count, sum, average, minimum, and maximum capacity of rooms in the database.

   b. Where there is a null value for the capacity, assume the capacity to be 40, and find the average room size again.

11. Using the Student table, display the first 10 rows (WHERE rownum < 11) with an appended initial. For the appended initial, choose the halfway letter of the name, so that if a name is Evans, the initial is A (half of the length +1). If the name is Conway, the initial is W. You do not need to round up or down, just use (LENGTH(Name)/2)+1 as the starting place in the SUBSTR function to create the initial. Use appropriate column aliases. Your result should look like this (actual names may vary depending on the current database):

```
PERSON#  NAMES
-----    ------------
   1     Lineas, E.
   2     Mary, R.
   3     Brenda, N.
   4     Richard, H.
   5     Kelly, L.
   6     Lujack, A.
   7     Reva, V.
   8     Elainie, I.
   9     Harley, L.
  10     Donald, A.
```

In Chapter 2, we introduced some date functions, namely ADD_MONTHS and MONTHS_BETWEEN. Use the MONTHS_ BETWEEN and other appropriate functions to write *one* query that returns the number of years between the oldest and youngest student in the Student table.

Query Development, Privileges, and Derived Structures

A problem in SQL—and in all programming for that matter—is the development of long queries or statements. One way to create statements is to begin modestly and to build up to or develop the query of interest. In this process of "building up" to the query of interest, parentheses often need to be appropriately placed. We will illustrate this stepwise approach by "developing" a query or two in this chapter, and we will discuss how parentheses can aid in query development.

Another way to develop queries is to use derived structures—a pseudo-table, if you will. Derived structures include temporary tables, views (both real and inline views), and snapshots (also known as *materialized views*). Each of these derived structures allows us to easily manipulate partial displays of the database, which can then be connected to answer a complicated database query. This chapter discusses these derived structures as well as the security measures that can be enabled using them.

Whether we are deriving a long query or working to devise a derived structure, we will likely need to store and retrieve queries, so we'll start our discussion on query development with a brief review of how to use the SAVE and EDIT commands.

Query Development

As we've mentioned earlier, you can handle editing in two ways: using the statement buffer or working with a named file. You can name the query file with SAVE or you can name the file initially with EDIT (which is the process the authors recommend).

Using SAVE and EDIT

Queries are sometimes developed after some initial experimentation, while other times they are the result of modifying previously stored queries. In either case, you must get used to using the SAVE and EDIT commands, which we'll discuss in this section.

Let's look at an example and illustration of how the query-building process works. Suppose we want to find the names of all students who major in computer science (COSC) and who have earned a grade of B in some course. To do so, we follow these steps:

1. From the SQL prompt, we begin by devising a query to find students who major in computer science (COSC):

```
SELECT *
FROM Student
WHERE major = 'COSC';
```

This produces the following output:

STNO	SNAME	MAJO	CLASS	BDATE
3	Mary	COSC	4	16-JUL-78
8	Brenda	COSC	2	13-AUG-77
14	Lujack	COSC	1	12-FEB-77
17	Elainie	COSC	1	12-AUG-76
121	Hillary	COSC	1	16-JUL-77
128	Brad	COSC	1	10-SEP-77
130	Alan	COSC	2	16-JUL-77
142	Jerry	COSC	4	12-MAR-78
31	Jake	COSC	4	12-FEB-78
5	Zelda	COSC		12-FEB-78

10 rows selected.

We save this query by typing:

```
SQL> SAVE q1
```

> When saving queries, note that "CRE" is the default option. Use of CRE assumes *q1* does not exist. In this example, SAVE q1 CRE would also work. The file *q1.sql* would then be created in the directory of the host operating system. SAVE q1 REP would save the new version of *q1* over the previously saved version of *q1*.

2. Whether we started with a query in the buffer (as in step 1) or we created a named query (with EDIT q1), we now need to modify the saved query, *q1*. Suppose we wish to restrict the output to just names. We call up the file that was just created by typing:

```
SQL> EDIT q1
```

We then edit the first line to:

```
SELECT sname
```

The query should now be:

```
SELECT sname
FROM Student
WHERE major = 'COSC';
```

We then save the file and close the editor.

3. We start our query by typing:

```
SQL> @q1 <Enter>
```

This produces the following output:

```
SNAME
_____
Mary
Brenda
Lujack
Elainie
Hillary
Brad
Alan
Jerry
Jake
Zelda

10 rows selected.
```

4. Because we want to see those students who major in computer science (COSC) *and* who have earned a B in some course, we must edit the query

> If we just say:

    SQL> EDIT

The default editor will open up with the last command that was in the buffer, which is not what we want to do here.

and, as the next step, add the Grade_report table by doing a join. The query now looks like this:

```
SELECT stu.sname
FROM   Student stu, Grade_report g
WHERE  stu.major = 'COSC'
AND    stu.stno = g.student_number   /* join condition Student-
                                        Grade_report */
;
```

5. Re-save q1 and re-start query q1. This will produce the following output:

```
SNAME
_____
Mary
Mary
Mary
.

.
Elainie
Elainie
Brenda
Hillary
Brad
Alan
Jerry
Jake
Zelda
Zelda
Brenda
.

.
Jerry
Jerry

48 rows selected.
```

6. To add the condition for B's, we need to add another AND clause. EDIT *q1* again and add a fifth line so that we end up with the following query:

```
SELECT      stu.sname
FROM        Student stu, Grade_report g
WHERE       stu.major = 'COSC'
AND         stu.stno = g.student_number    /* join condition
                                              Student-
                                              Grade_report */

AND         g.grade = 'B';
```

7. Restart the query again. This will produce the following output:

```
SNAME
_____

Mary
Mary
Mary
Mary
Mary
Brenda
Lujack
Lujack
Lujack
Hillary
Zelda
Brenda
Hillary
Hillary

14 rows selected.
```

This query successfully gives us all the students who are majoring in computer science (COSC) and who earned a grade of B in some class. The point of this process is that it allows us to test as we go, verify that the query works up to that point, and ensure that we have a reasonable result before we move on to the next enhancement.

Deleting a Query

We can go to the host and delete a stored query by typing the following:

```
SQL> HOST <enter>
```

This will take us to the host:

```
F:\Oracle\BIN>
```

> It's a good idea to adopt the convention of using query names like *q1*, *q2*, and so on or *q51* (for exercise 5, query1). It's also a good idea to keep old queries. You can always delete, replace, rename, copy, move, or add to them. As mentioned earlier, the queries will be stored in the host as *q1.sql*, *q2.sql*, and so on.

To get a listing of all our queries (.sql files), we type:

```
F:\Oracle\BIN> DIR *.sql
```

If we want to DELETE the query we just created, we type:

```
F:\Oracle\BIN> DEL q1.sql
```

Parentheses in SQL Expressions

In programming languages like C, we can write a statement like this:

```
x = y + z * w
```

What does this compute? It depends on precedence rules. Usually in programming languages (and in SQL), parentheses have the highest precedence. The authors of this book advocate *fully* parenthesized expressions for two reasons:

1. It makes the expression easier to debug.

2. It tells anyone else who looks at your expression that you knew what you wanted because you explicitly and unambiguously wrote the expression in a fully parenthesized way.

In SQL, the precedence problem occurs with AND and OR. For example, what does the following query request?

```
SELECT *
FROM  Student
WHERE class = 3 OR class = 4 AND stno < 100;
```

Does AND or OR have precedence, or is the rule "left to right"? The point is that we do not have to know the rule to write an unambiguous expression. If we use parentheses appropriately, we can make the expression clear and unambiguous. Consider the following examples. If we type:

```
SELECT *
FROM  Student
WHERE class = 3 OR (class = 4 AND stno < 100);
```

This will result in the following output:

```
STNO    SNAME        MAJO   CLASS   BDATE
_____   _____   __     ___     _____
3       Mary         COSC   4       16-JUL-78
13      Kelly        MATH   4       12-AUG-80
20      Donald       ACCT   4       15-OCT-77
24      Chris        ACCT   4       12-FEB-78
49      Susan        ENGL   3       11-MAR-80
62      Monica       MATH   3       14-OCT-80
122     Phoebe       ENGL   3       15-APR-80
131     Rachel       ENGL   3       15-APR-80
143     Cramer       ENGL   3       15-APR-80
31      Jake         COSC   4       12-FEB-78
151     Losmith      CHEM   3       15-JAN-81

STNO    SNAME        MAJO   CLASS   BDATE
_____   _____   __     ___     _____
160     Gus          ART    3       15-OCT-78

12 rows selected.
```

If we type:

```
SELECT *
FROM  Student
WHERE (class = 3 OR class = 4) AND stno < 100;
```

This will result in the following output:

```
STNO    SNAME        MAJO   CLASS   BDATE
_____   _____   __     ___     _____
3       Mary         COSC   4       16-JUL-78
13      Kelly        MATH   4       12-AUG-80
20      Donald       ACCT   4       15-OCT-77
24      Chris        ACCT   4       12-FEB-78
49      Susan        ENGL   3       11-MAR-80
62      Monica       MATH   3       14-OCT-80
31      Jake         COSC   4       12-FEB-78

7 rows selected.
```

In the preceding two statements, there is no ambiguity. In the first statement, the AND is preformed first; in the second statement, the OR is performed first—all of which is made clear by appropriate parentheses. In an unparenthesized set of conditions, OR is always evaluated first, then AND, and then NOT.

Derived Structures

Derived structures become necessary as queries get larger, and as we have to build queries in a more step-by-step approach. In this section, we'll discuss the most commonly used derived structure—views. We'll discuss the other derived structures, like temporary tables, inline views, and snapshots, later in this chapter.

Views

The first and most common derived structure is a view. A *view* (also called a *virtual table*) is a mechanism that procures a restricted subset of data that is accessible in ways akin to ordinary tables. We use the word "akin" because some operations on views (such as some updates and deletes) may be restricted where they would not be if they were performed on the database itself. A view serves several purposes: it is a convenient way to develop a query by isolating parts of it, and it is used to restrict a set of users from seeing part of the database, which is a security issue.

Using the CREATE OR REPLACE VIEW Statements

The simple version of the CREATE VIEW syntax is:

```
CREATE OR REPLACE VIEW view-name AS subquery
```

It is good and ordinarily preferred Oracle syntax to use the phrase CREATE OR REPLACE for views (and for other objects, as we will see later in the chapter). We could use the phrase CREATE VIEW (if a view did not exist) and we could DROP an existing view and re-create it with another CREATE VIEW (although we cannot say "REPLACE VIEW" by itself). However, the usual development scenario is to either CREATE OR REPLACE VIEW when we write it or develop it. So, if we wanted to create a view of students called "Namemaj," which was just names and majors, we could write:

```
CREATE OR REPLACE VIEW Namemaj AS
 SELECT sname, major
 FROM   Student;
```

We could then get our list of names and majors by using the viewname in a query like this:

```
SELECT  *
FROM    Namemaj;
```

This will produce the following output:

```
SNAME       MAJO
----------  --

Lineas      ENGL
Mary        COSC
Brenda      COSC
Richard     ENGL
Kelly       MATH
Lujack      COSC
Reva        MATH
Elainie     COSC
Harley      POLY
Donald      ACCT
Chris       ACCT


SNAME       MAJO
----------  --

Lynette     POLY
Susan       ENGL
Monica      MATH

.

.

.

48 rows selected.
```

As with a table, the view can be filtered and used in a SELECT just like an ordinary table, as follows:

```
SELECT  n.major Major, n.sname "Student Name"
FROM    Namemaj n, Department_to_major d
WHERE   n.major = d.dcode
AND     UPPER(d.dname) like 'COMP%';
```

This will produce the following output:

```
MAJO    Student Name
--      ------
COSC    Mary
COSC    Brenda
COSC    Lujack
COSC    Elainie
COSC    Hillary
COSC    Brad
COSC    Alan
COSC    Jerry
COSC    Jake
COSC    Zelda


10 rows selected.
```

Adding ORDER BY to CREATE OR REPLACE VIEW Statements

If we want to order our output, we can add an ORDER BY to a CREATE OR REPLACE VIEW statement (in Oracle 8 and beyond), as shown here:

```
CREATE OR REPLACE VIEW Namemaj AS
 SELECT sname, major
 FROM   Student
 ORDER BY sname;
```

If we then type:

```
SELECT *
FROM Namemaj;
```

We will get the output ordered by name, as follows:

```
SNAME         MAJO
----------    --
Alan          COSC
Benny         CHEM
Bill          POLY
Brad          COSC
Brenda        COSC
Cedric        ENGL
Chris         ACCT
```

```
Cramer      ENGL
Donald      ACCT
Elainie     COSC
Fraiser     POLY
Francis     ACCT
Genevieve   UNKN
George      POLY
Gus         ART
Harley      POLY
Harrison    ACCT
Hillary     COSC
Holly       POLY
Jake        COSC
Jake        MATH
  .
  .
  .

SNAME       MAJO
----------  --
Smithly     ENGL
Stephanie   MATH
Steve       ENGL
Susan       ENGL
Thornton
Zelda       COSC

48 rows selected.
```

Developing a Query Using Views

One way to "develop" a query using views is to get the query working by typing the following:

```
SELECT sname, major
FROM   Student;
```

Suppose we call this query *q2*. We can then create the view by editing in a line before the SELECT in *q2* so that the query looks like this:

```
CREATE OR REPLACE VIEW Namemaj AS
 SELECT sname, major
 FROM   Student;
```

We can then start q2 (@q2) to create the view.

Creating Special View Column Names

We can create special view column names that are different from the names of the columns in the underlying table for use with the view. Column names can be placed just after the named view in the definition command as follows:

```
CREATE OR REPLACE VIEW Namemaj (name, maj) AS
 SELECT  sname, major
 FROM    Student;
```

Now if we type:

```
SELECT *
FROM Namemaj;
```

We will get the following output:

```
NAME            MAJ
----------      --
Lineas          ENGL
Mary            COSC
Brenda          COSC
Richard         ENGL
Kelly           MATH
Lujack          COSC
Reva            MATH
Elainie         COSC
Harley          POLY
Donald          ACCT
Chris           ACCT

NAME            MAJ
----------      --
Lynette         POLY
Susan           ENGL
Monica          MATH
  .
  .
  .

48 rows selected.
```

When the view definition has column names, the column names must be used to access the view. If we type the following:

```
SELECT    maj, name
FROM      Namemaj
WHERE     maj like 'CO%';
```

We will get the following output:

```
MAJ       NAME
--        ----------
COSC      Mary
COSC      Brenda
COSC      Lujack
COSC      Elainie
COSC      Hillary
COSC      Brad
COSC      Alan
COSC      Jerry
COSC      Jake
COSC      Zelda

10 rows selected.
```

> Oracle has different forms available on the CREATE VIEW command. The optional
> WITH CHECK OPTION keeps you from creating a view that you could not use because
> of other security issues. The WITH CHECK OPTION guarantees that inserts and
> updates performed through the view will result in rows that the view subquery can
> select. The FORCE option allows you to create a view if the underlying tables do not
> exist or if you do not have privileges on the underlying table. Note that you should not
> need FORCE at this time.

Views can also be created using aliases instead of column names. The same effect as listing column names would be had if the CREATE statement were this:

```
CREATE OR REPLACE VIEW Namemaj AS
 SELECT sname name, major maj
 FROM   Student;
```

GRANTing and REVOKEing Privileges on Tables and Views

Security is an issue in the access of a table from a foreign account. The creator of the account has no restrictions on access and may or may not pass along manipulation privileges to others. The SQL statements controlling security are GRANT and REVOKE. The version of the GRANT command we will use looks like this:

```
GRANT {priv|ALL}
ON object-name
TO {specific user|PUBLIC}
```

To allow another user to see the tables we created—that is, to allow any user to be able to SELECT data from the Student table—we must run a command like the following for each table:

```
GRANT SELECT
ON Student
TO PUBLIC;
```

If we want to disallow public access to a table such as Student, we would type:

```
REVOKE SELECT
ON Student
FROM PUBLIC;
```

Instead of PUBLIC, we can identify individuals in either case (GRANT or REVOKE) with statements like:

```
GRANT SELECT
ON Student
TO jsmith;
```

One of the great benefits of views involves security. A person can create a view, grant access to the view, and revoke access to the underlying table. For example, if the Student table contained some information that we did not want Joe Smith (an imaginary person) to see, we could create a view of Student containing the information that Joe was allowed to see. We could then grant Joe access to that view and then revoke all privileges on the underlying Student table from him.

Query Development and Derived Structures

In this section, we'll first look at query development and then will show how derived structures can be used in query development. We will list the names, student numbers, and department name of students who are freshmen or sophomores and computer science majors from our standard database, the `Student_Course` database. In Step 1 we will develop a query, and in Step 2 we will show how to use this query with a derived structure. (Option 1 shows how the query can be turned into a view; Option 2 shows how the query can be turned into a temporary table; Option 3 shows how the query can be turned into an inline view; and Option 4 shows how to create a snapshot.)

Step 1: Develop a Query Step by Step

1. The first step in developing a query step by step is to see which attributes we need and in which tables these attributes are found. Because we want to list the names, student numbers, and department name of students who are freshmen or sophomores and computer science majors from our standard database, the `Student_Course` database, we need student names (`sname`) and numbers (`stno`), which are found in the `Student` table. Department names (`dname`) are found in the `Department_to_major` table. In order to find the department names that correspond to the student majors, we must JOIN the `Student` table and the `Department_to_major` table. To JOIN these two tables, we must JOIN where `major` from the `Student` table JOINs with the `dcode` from the `Department_to_major` table as follows (since the statements will be eventually filtered by `class`, we will include `class` in the result set):

```
SELECT s.sname, s.stno, d.dname, s.class
FROM   Student s, Department_to_major d
WHERE  s.major = d.dcode;
```

Once we type in the above query and run it we will get:

SNAME	STNO	DNAME	CLASS
Lineas	2	English	1
Mary	3	Computer Science	4
Brenda	8	Computer Science	2
Richard	10	English	1
Kelly	13	Mathematics	4
Lujack	14	Computer Science	1
Reva	15	Mathematics	2
Elainie	17	Computer Science	1
Harley	19	Political Science	2
Donald	20	Accounting	4
Chris	24	Accounting	4
Lynette	34	Political Science	1

```
Susan        49      English            3
Monica       62      Mathematics        3
Bill         70      Political Science
Hillary      121     Computer Science   1
Phoebe       122     English            3
Holly        123     Political Science  4
Sadie        125     Mathematics        2
Jessica      126     Political Science  2
Steve        127     English            1

SNAME        STNO    DNAME              CLASS
----------   -----   -----------        -----

Brad         128     Computer Science   1
Cedric       129     English            2
Alan         130     Computer Science   2
Rachel       131     English            3
George       132     Political Science  1
Jerry        142     Computer Science   4
Cramer       143     English            3
Fraiser      144     Political Science  1
Harrison     145     Accounting         4
Francis      146     Accounting         4
Smithly      147     English            2
Sebastian    148     Accounting         2
Jake         31      Computer Science   4
Losmith      151     Chemistry          3
Genevieve    153
Lindsay      155                        1
Stephanie    157     Mathematics
Benny        161     Chemistry          4
Gus          160     Art                3
Zelda        5       Computer Science
Mario        7       Mathematics

SNAME        STNO    DNAME              CLASS
----------   -----   -----------        -----

Romona       9       English
Ken          6       Political Science
Jake         191     Mathematics        2
45 rows selected.
```

2. Save this query as stucosc.

3. The next step is to edit stucosc and find all the freshmen and sophomores (class 1 and 2) from the Student table. To do so, add "AND (s.class = 1 or s.class = 2)" to stucosc so that stucosc now reads:

```
SELECT s.sname, s.stno, d.dname, s.class
FROM    Student s, Department_to_major d
WHERE s.major = d.dcode
AND (s.class=1 or s.class=2);
```

This query will now give the following output:

SNAME	STNO	DNAME	CLASS
Lineas	2	English	1
Brenda	8	Computer Science	2
Richard	10	English	1
Lujack	14	Computer Science	1
Reva	15	Mathematics	2
Elainie	17	Computer Science	1
Harley	19	Political Science	2
Lynette	34	Political Science	1
Hillary	121	Computer Science	1
Sadie	125	Mathematics	2
Jessica	126	Political Science	2
Steve	127	English	1
Brad	128	Computer Science	1
Cedric	129	English	2
Alan	130	Computer Science	2
George	132	Political Science	1
Fraiser	144	Political Science	1
Smithly	147	English	2
Sebastian	148	Accounting	2
Lindsay	155		1
Jake	191	Mathematics	2

21 rows selected

4. Resave this query. You can use:

```
SAVE stucosc REP;
```

Now we have the department names of all the freshmen and sophomores. To find the computer science majors from this group, edit stucosc again, and add "AND s.major = 'COSC'" to the query stucosc so the query now reads:

```
SELECT s.sname, s.stno, d.dname, s.class,
FROM    Student s, Department_to_major d
WHERE   s.major = d.dcode
AND     (s.class = 1 or s.class = 2)
AND     s.major = 'COSC';
```

This finally give us the student names, student numbers, and department names of students who are (freshmen or sophomores) and computer science majors, as shown below:

```
SNAME        STNO    DNAME                CLASS
_____   _____   _____          _____
Brenda       8       Computer Science     2
Lujack       14      Computer Science     1
Elainie      17      Computer Science     1
Hillary      121     Computer Science     1
Brad         128     Computer Science     1
Alan         130     Computer Science     2

6 rows selected.
```

5. Resave this query as stucosc:

```
SAVE stucosc REP;
```

Step 2: Using a Derived Structure

For the next step, we will see how you can use the query that we developed above and turn it into a derived structure like a view, temporary table, inline view, or snapshot. Each one of these derived structures will produce the same end-results, so as you develop your own queries you may use whichever derived structure you become most comfortable with.

Option 1: Make Your Query a View

Views are quite useful when you want to simplify frequently used queries or use certain security applications. They are also useful when you need to develop complex queries. In addition, views in Oracle occupy practically no disk space, making them even more desirable. When you use a view for queries, you use it just as you would the underlying tables. Although views depend on the underlying tables, the data in views is not stored as a separate table. Therefore, a view is like a mask over an underlying table.

To create a view from the query we just developed, `stucosc`, follow these steps:

1. EDIT `stucosc` so that it reads:

```
CREATE OR REPLACE VIEW vustu as
SELECT s.sname, s.stno, d.dname
FROM  Student s, D2m d
WHERE s.major = d.dcode   -- join condition
AND   (s.class = 1 or s.class = 2)
AND   s.major = 'COSC';
```

Here we created a view called "vustu."

2. Save this query as `vustu`. You can really call this query anything at this point; it doesn't have to be called `vustu`. We just didn't call it `stucosc` to avoid writing over the original `stucosc`.

3. Start `vustu` by typing:

```
@vustu
```

This will create the view.

4. You can then just SELECT from the view:

```
SELECT *
FROM vustu
WHERE UPPER(sname) like 'SMI%';
```

Option 2: Create a Temporary Table

If you were going to use the view of names, student numbers, and department names of freshmen and sophomore computer science majors *often*, and you did not need absolutely current information, you might want to create a ***temporary table*** rather than a view. A drawback of the temporary table is that if data is changed, it will not be changed in the temporary table, whereas in a view, there is no extra table; thus, whatever "happens" in the table "happens" in the view. On the plus side, a temporary table can be indexed, queries can change the ORDER BY (or not), and/or views of the temporary table can be made—sort of a hierarchy of views.

You can create a temporary table from the query developed in Step 1 by following these steps:

1. Edit `stucosc` so that it now reads:

```
CREATE TABLE Tempstu as
SELECT s.sname, s.stno, d.dname
FROM   Student s, D2m d
WHERE  s.major = d.dcode        /* join condition Student-D2m */
AND    (s.class = 1 or s.class = 2)
AND    s.major = 'COSC'
```

2. Save this query as `Tempstu`. Once again, you can really call this query anything at this point; it doesn't have to be called `Tempstu`. We didn't call it `stucosc` to avoid writing over the original `stucosc`.

3. Start `Tempstu` by typing:

```
@Tempstu
```

This will create the temporary table. Here, `Tempstu` is the name of the temporary table you created. `Tempstu` doesn't have to be previously created (it is created right here on the fly), and it will have the attributes sname, stno, and dname.

4. You could then query:

```
SELECT *
FROM Tempstu;
```

This would produce the following output:

```
SNAME           STNO    DNAME
_____     _____   _____

Brenda          8       Computer Science
Lujack          14      Computer Science
Elainie         17      Computer Science
Hillary         121     Computer Science
Brad            128     Computer Science
Alan            130     Computer Science

6 rows selected.
```

This is the same result (output) that option 1 gave. However, we must repeat the caveat: *the data in a temporary table is only as current as the last time it was refreshed.* Maintenance of the temporary table falls to the creator, so the creator should arrange to refresh the table. When everyone is finished with the table, the creator should DROP it.

Option 3: Use an Inline View

You can also put a query in the FROM clause of a SELECT statement and hence create what is called an ***inline view***. An inline view exists only during the execution of a query. The main purpose of an inline view is to simplify the development of a query. A person would probably devise the inline view, inner select, test it, examine the result and wrap it in parentheses, and continue with the development by using the inline view.

Let's look at an example of an inline view in our sample problem. In this example, we create the view inline—that is, we create the view on the fly, give it an alias, v, and use it just as we would a stored table or view. Thus, edit `stucosc` so that it now reads:

```
SELECT v.name, v.dname
FROM
 (SELECT s.sname   name, s.stno, d.dname
 FROM    Student s, D2m d
 WHERE   s.major = d.dcode   /* join condition Student-D2m */
 AND     (s.class = 1 or s.class = 2)
 AND     s.major = 'COSC') v;
```

Again, save this query by giving this query another name like `inline1` to avoid writing over `stucosc`.

In this example, notice that a column alias is used for the student name (name), whereas the other columns in the inline view result set are not aliased. In the final result set of the outer query, the column names reference the names used or aliased in the inline view result set—v.name corresponds to the alias of s.sname, *name*, and v.dname corresponds to *d.dname*.

It is better to use column aliases throughout in the inline view to avoid confusion. Therefore, you may want to use something like the following:

```
SELECT v.iviewname, v.iviewdname
FROM
 (SELECT s.sname iviewname,
         s.stno iviewstno, d.dname iviewdname
 FROM    Student s, D2m d
 WHERE   s.major = d.dcode   /* join condition Student-D2m */
 AND     (s.class = 1 or s.class = 2)
 AND     s.major = 'COSC') v;
```

Option 4: Use a Snapshot

> To create a snapshot, the table needs to have a primary key defined.

Snapshots (also known in Oracle as *materialized views*) are a sort of middle ground between temporary tables and views. Snapshots are usually used in distributed databases, where a table is kept at some remote location and where a current version of data is not needed right away. Snapshots can also be created locally and can serve as non-current views of data. In "snapshoting," the data can be automatically updated periodically so that the entity acts like a view and somewhat like a temporary table at the same time. By using a snapshot, the user is seeing the table as it was (yesterday or an hour ago or last week, and so on), but the database doesn't have to refresh a view each time the snapshot is used. Likewise, the user doesn't have to see what is always an old "snapshot" as they would in a temporary table.

> All the tables in our Student_Course database have a primary key already defined.

To add a primary key to a table, type the following:

```
SQL> ALTER TABLE Tablename
add(constraint name_pk PRIMARY KEY (attribute_name));
```

You can then type in the statement for creating a snapshot as follows:

```
CREATE SNAPSHOT qsnap1
REFRESH COMPLETE NEXT SYSDATE + 7
AS
SELECT * FROM Student WHERE stno < 20;
```

Here, the snapshot "view" is SELECT * FROM Student WHERE stno < 20. The snapshot is named qsnap1. The difference between this "view" and other derived structures is the REFRESH clause, which says to re-do the query every seven days (SYSDATE + 7) from the time the snapshot is first created. If you wanted a refresh every day, then the NEXT clause would read "…SYSDATE + 1." If you wanted an hourly refresh, it would read "…SYSDATE + (1/24)."

Snapshots are used just like views with statements like SELECT * FROM qsnap1. Unfortunately, CREATE OR REPLACE is not allowed, so to develop a snapshot you must DROP the snapshot and re-create it. Snapshots are not widely used except in situations where a database is distributed. Creating snapshots requires privileges that may not be typically granted to users. Also, the DBA (Database Administrator) may have to execute special scripts to allow snapshots.

The details of when the snapshot was created and last updated, what the query is, and so on may be found in the dictionary view user_snapshots or all_snapshots. In later versions of Oracle, the appropriate dictionary view is x_mviews, where x could be user, all, or DBA. However, the SELECT ANY TABLE privilege is required to see all_snapshots.

CHAPTER 5 EXERCISES

1. Develop and execute a query to find the names of students who had HERMANO as an instructor and earned a grade of B or better in the class. Develop the query by first finding sections where HERMANO was the instructor. Save this query. Then, recall (EDIT) it and modify the query to join Section with Grade_report. Then add the grade constraint. Save this query (with the REPLACE option). Then, recall and go from there. Show all steps on your output.

2. Create a duplicate table (call it Stutab) in your account from the Student table that contains all tuples from Student. Hint: Use DESC Student to see "student" attributes. Create the Stutab table with a CREATE TABLE command. INSERT INTO Stutab... SELECT to populate it.

    a. List student names and majors from Stutab for students who are juniors or seniors only.

    b. List student names and computer science (COSC) majors from Stutab.

    c. Create a view (call it vstu) that contains student names and majors, but only for COSC majors. (Use CREATE OR REPLACE VIEW.)

    d. List the student names and majors from the vstu view in descending order by name.

    e. Modify a tuple in your view of your table so that a student changes his or her major.

    f. Re-execute the display of the view. Did modifying your vstu view also change the parent-table, Stutab?

    g. Try to modify the view again, but this time change the major to 'COMPSC'—an obviously invalid field in Stutab because the attribute was defined as four characters. Can you do it? What happens?

3.   **a.** Repeat the CREATE VIEW part of the exercise in 2c with a column name in the CREATE OR REPLACE VIEW statement like this:

```
CREATE OR REPLACE VIEW vx (Na, Ma) AS SELECT ...
```

using the `Stutab` table you created in Exercise 2. Display the view. What is the effect of the (Na, Ma)?

b. Repeat Exercise 3a, but this time use column aliases in the view definition. Are there any differences noted between explicitly defining the view-columns in the heading part of the statement versus using a column alias?

4.   Perform an experiment to determine the precedence in a query with three conditions linked by AND and OR. Find out whether AND, OR, or left-to-right take precedence. Use statements like this (actual attribute names may be found using "DESC Student"):

Run this query:

```
SELECT *
FROM Student
WHERE stno < 100 AND major = 'COSC' OR major = 'ACCT';
```

Then run the following two queries and answer whether the non-parenthesized statement gives you:

```
SELECT *
FROM Student
WHERE (stno < 100 AND major = 'COSC') OR major = 'ACCT';
```

or:

```
SELECT *
FROM Student
WHERE stno < 100 AND (major = 'COSC' OR major = 'ACCT');
```

What happens if you put the OR first instead of the AND and run the query without parentheses?

5.   Develop a query to find the instructor name and course name for computer science courses (use the `Section` table). Order the table by instructor name.

a. Convert your query into a view.

b. Remove the ORDER BY clause and convert the query into an inline view with column aliases and test it.

c. Put the ORDER BY clause outside of the inline view in the main query and run your query again.

6. Repeat the dictionary exercise from the previous chapter for user_views and all_views. Be careful to DESCRIBE and COUNT(*) before (and if) you run the "SELECT * ..." version. How many rows are there in the user_ version? How many rows are there in the all_ version? Are the two views (all_ and user_) the same? If not, what is different?

7. Type:

```
DESC all_snapshots;
```

Use this information to answer the following questions:

a. When was the snapshot qsnap1 last updated?

b. Query the snapshot qsnap1 (the first five rows is fine).

Who is the owner of qsnap1?

CHAPTER  6

Set Operations

In previous chapters, we looked at how data can be retrieved from multiple tables using joins. As we'll discuss in this chapter, data can also be retrieved from multiple tables using set operations. In this chapter, we'll look at the different set operations available in SQL. We'll also look at the IN and NOT..IN predicates as well as the difference operation.

Introducing Set Operations

A *set* is a collection of objects. In relational databases, a table can be regarded as a set of rows, and a row can be regarded as a set of one or more columns. Elements in a set do not have to be ordered.

There are three explicit set operations used in SQL: UNION, INTERSECT, and MINUS (set difference). A *binary union* is a set operation on two sets where the result contains all the unique elements of both sets. A *binary intersection* generates unique values in common between two sets. Finally, a *binary set difference* tells us values in one set less those contained in another.

Relations are sets of rows. The set statements allow us to combine two distinct sets of data (two relations, two result sets) provided we ensure union compatibility. The term *union compatibility* is the commonly used SQL terminology for *set compatibility* and means that when set operations are used, both sets must match in number of items and must have compatible data types.

As we will see, forcing union compatibility can happen in several ways, such as:

• unioning (or another appropriate set operation) two tables that have identical attributes (which implies the same domains)

• taking two subsets from a table and combining them

• using two views from two tables with the attributes chosen so that they are compatible

Example of a Set Operation in Use

The format of a set statement is as follows:

```
set OPERATOR set
```

where OPERATOR is UNION, MINUS, or INTERSECT and where "set" is defined by a SELECT.

Example of Using a UNION

The following is an example of the UNION set operation being used:

```
SELECT sname
FROM Student
WHERE major = 'COSC'
 UNION
SELECT sname
FROM Student
WHERE major = 'MATH';
```

The resulting display contains the names of students who are majoring in either computer science (COSC) or math (MATH):

```
SNAME
----------
Alan
Brad
Brenda
Elainie
Hillary
Jake
```

```
Jerry
Kelly
Lujack
Mario
Mary

SNAME
----------
Monica
Reva
Sadie
Stephanie
Zelda

16 rows selected.
```

If you actually do this query, you'll find that the result set is sorted and contains no duplicate values. This is because UNION resolves duplicates and in the process sorts each result set.

The IN and NOT..IN Predicates

Although Oracle has both a MINUS and an INTERSECT predicate, many implementations of SQL don't have operators for difference (minus) or intersect per se. However, most SQLs will have an IN predicate and a corresponding NOT..IN predicate. We will begin looking at the IN and NOT..IN predicates from a set point of view. Through these IN and NOT..IN predicates, we can create differences and intersections. Set differences can be defined as follows: if we find the objects from set A that are not in set B, we have found the difference of set A and set B. Set intersections can be defined as follows: if we find the objects from set A that are also in set B, we have found the intersection of set A and set B.

A simple IN predicate with constants in a SELECT statement might look like this:

```
SELECT    sname
FROM      Student
WHERE     class IN (3,4);
```

In this example, the "IN (3, 4)" is called a *subquery-set*, where the (3, 4) is the set in which we are testing membership. This query says: "Find all

> Oracle includes an additional predicate, UNION ALL, which does not resolve duplicates. If you are willing to accept an unsorted result set that contains duplicates, UNION ALL is more efficient because no sorting is required.

student names from the Student table where the class is in the set (3, 4)." This query produces the following output:

```
SNAME
----------
Mary
Kelly
Donald
Chris
Susan
Monica
Phoebe
Holly
Rachel
Jerry
Cramer

SNAME
----------
Harrison
Francis
Jake
Losmith
Benny
Gus

17 rows selected.
```

There are usually several ways to get information via SQL. The preceding query produces the same output as the following query:

```
SELECT  sname
FROM    Student
WHERE   class = 3 OR class = 4;
```

Using IN

We can expand the IN predicate's subquery-set part to be an actual query. For example, consider the following query:

```
SELECT Student.sname
FROM   Student
WHERE Student.stno IN
 (SELECT g.student_number
  FROM    Grade_report g
  WHERE   g.grade = 'A');
```

Note that:

• WHERE `Student.stno` references the name of the column (the attribute) in the `Student` table.

• `g.student_number` is the column name in the `Grade_report` table.

• `stno` in the `Student` table and `student_number` in the `Grade_report` table have the same domain.

Note also that you must have exact column headings (usually qualified column names) and retrieve the information from same domains (again, this gets at the idea of union compatibility).

The preceding query produces the following output:

```
SNAME
----------
Lineas
Mary
Brenda
Richard
Lujack
Donald
Lynette
Susan
Holly
Sadie
Jessica

SNAME
----------
Steve
Cedric
Jerry

14 rows selected.
```

Note that you could view the preceding query as a result derived from the intersection of the sets A and B, where set A is the set of student numbers in the student set (the `Student` table) and set B is the set of student numbers in the grade set (the `Grade_report` table) that have A's.

To make this command behave like a set, you can add the DISTINCT qualifier to the statements as follows:

```
SELECT DISTINCT (Student.sname)
FROM Student
WHERE Student.stno IN
 (SELECT DISTINCT (g.student_number)
 FROM Grade_report g
 WHERE g.grade = 'A');
```

This produces the following output:

```
SNAME
----------
Brenda
Cedric
Donald
Holly
Jerry
Jessica
Lineas
Lujack
Lynette
Mary
Richard
Sadie
Steve
Susan

14 rows selected.
```

Oracle does this for you and doesn't return duplicates, so DISTINCT in this case is superfluous. In this example, using IN is preferable to using Oracle's INTERSECT from a performance standpoint. To use INTERSECT, you can use the following command:

```
SELECT s.stno FROM Student s
 INTERSECT
SELECT g.student_number
FROM Grade_report g
WHERE g.grade = 'A';
```

This produces the following output:

```
        STNO
        ____
         2
         3
         8
        10
        14
        20
        34
        49
       123
       125
       126

        STNO
        ____
       127
       129
       142

    14 rows selected.
```

This output contains the same information as the previous IN, but gives student numbers instead of names.

> In some implementations of SQL, the use of IN is preferred to joins. Any situation that uses an IN can be achieved with a join, but not vice versa. In Oracle, it's usually better to use a join than a subquery from a performance standpoint. INTERSECT and MINUS are rarely used in SQL because they can be performed with IN more efficiently. UNION is sometimes used, but again, unless you cannot find another way to work a problem, IN or a join is usually preferred.

The following command will *not* work:

```
SELECT s.sname, s.stno FROM Student s
  INTERSECT
SELECT g.student_number
FROM Grade_report g
WHERE g.grade = 'A';
```

This query will not work because the set operation has been modified to intersect a name and a number from the Student table and just a number from the Grade_report table. Again, because of union compatibility, you must have like types in the same order in the result set to complete a set operation.

> Instead of using NOT..IN, it is often preferable to use NOT EXISTS or the outer join techniques we will demonstrate later.

Using NOT..IN

In this section, we will discuss how to use NOT..IN, to complete the logical negative of IN. Before looking at the NOT..IN predicate, be forewarned that Oracle processes NOT..IN poorly. In the process of running a query, Oracle uses a program called the *optimizer*. The optimizer evaluates a query and chooses the most efficient way to proceed. For example, when you use NOT..IN in a query, you prevent the Oracle optimizer from using indexes. This is because the NOT..IN part of the query must test the outer set with all values in the subquery to find out what is not in the set. For smaller tables, no difference in performance will likely be detected.

There are times when the NOT..IN predicate may seem to more easily describe the desired outcome or may be used for a set difference. As a simple example, consider the following query:

```
SELECT sname
FROM  Student
WHERE class IN (1,3,4);
```

This produces the following output:

```
SNAME
-----------
Lineas
Mary
Richard
Kelly
Lujack
Elainie
Donald
Chris
Lynette
Susan
Monica

SNAME
-----------
Hillary
Phoebe
Holly
Steve
Brad
Rachel
George
```

```
Jerry
Cramer
Fraiser
Harrison

SNAME
----------
Francis
Jake
Losmith
Lindsay
Benny
Gus

28 rows selected.
```

Contrast this to the following query:

```
SELECT sname
FROM   Student
WHERE class NOT IN (2);
```

This produces the following output:

```
SNAME
----------
Lineas
Mary
Richard
Kelly
Lujack
Elainie
Donald
Chris
Lynette
Susan
Monica

SNAME
----------
Hillary
Phoebe
Holly
Steve
Brad
Rachel
George
```

```
Jerry
Cramer
Fraiser
Harrison

SNAME
----------
Francis
Jake
Losmith
Lindsay
Benny
Gus

28 rows selected.
```

In this case, you get the same output as the previous query because the Student table only has classes 1, 2, 3, and 4. You would expect the same result provided all classes are 1, 2, 3, or 4. If counts did not match, this would indicate that some value of class were not 1, 2, 3, or 4.

As another example, suppose you want the name of students who are not computer science (COSC) or math majors. The command would be the following:

```
SELECT sname
FROM   Student
WHERE major NOT IN ('COSC','MATH');
```

You must be very careful with the NOT..IN predicate for two reasons:

1. The logic of "NOT something" may not be what you think it is (we'll look at this in more detail in Exercise 6-7 at the end of the chapter).

If nulls are present in the data, you get odd answers with NOT..IN (particularly prior to Oracle 8).

Consider the following table:

Stumajor

Name	Major
Mary	Biology
Sam	Chemistry
Alice	Art
Tom	

If you perform the following query:

```
SELECT *
FROM Stumajor
WHERE major IN ('Chemistry','Biology');
```

It produces the following output:

```
NAME          MAJOR
----------    ----------
Mary          Biology
Sam           Chemistry

2 rows selected.
```

If you perform the following query:

```
SELECT *
FROM Stumajor
WHERE major NOT IN ('Chemistry','Biology');
```

It produces the following output:

```
NAME          MAJOR
----------    ----------
Alice         Art

1 rows selected.
```

The value, null, is not equal to anything. You might expect that NOT..IN would give you <Tom,null>, but it does not. Why? Because nulls in the selection field (here, `major`) are ignored or do not return a "True" test.

The Difference Operation

To illustrate the difference operation, suppose set A is the set of students in classes 2, 3, or 4 and that set B is a set of students in class = 2. We could use the NOT..IN predicate to remove the students in set B from set A (thereby using a difference operation). For example, suppose we use the following query:

```
SELECT sname
FROM   Student
WHERE  class IN (2,3,4)
 AND NOT class IN (2);
```

This produces the following output:

```
SNAME
_____

Mary
Kelly
Donald
Chris
Susan
Monica
Phoebe
Holly
Rachel
Jerry
Cramer

SNAME
_____

Harrison
Francis
Jake
Losmith
Benny
Gus

17 rows selected.
```

> This output is actually the same as the output you get when you use the following query:

```
SELECT sname
FROM Student
WHERE class IN (3,4);
```

In Oracle, you can also use the MINUS predicate as follows:

```
SELECT sname
FROM   Student
WHERE class IN (2,3,4)
       MINUS
SELECT sname
FROM   Student
WHERE class IN (2);
```

This produces the following output:

```
    SNAME
    ----------
    Benny
    Chris
    Cramer
    Donald
    Francis
    Gus
    Harrison
    Holly
    Jerry
    Kelly
    Losmith

    SNAME
    ----------
    Mary
    Monica
    Phoebe
    Rachel
    Susan

    16 rows selected.
```

A more interesting, less obvious example of "difference" is a situation in which sets are created on the fly. Suppose you want to find the names of students who are not majoring in COSC or MATH but you want to delete from that set those who have made an A in some course. Finding the names of students who are not COSC or MATH majors is completed as before:

```
SELECT sname
FROM   Student
WHERE major NOT IN ('COSC','MATH');
```

This produces the following output:

```
    SNAME
    ----------
    Lineas
    Richard
    Harley
    Donald
    Chris
    Lynette
    Susan
    Bill
```

```
Phoebe
Holly
Jessica

SNAME
----------
Steve
Cedric
Rachel
George
Cramer
Fraiser
Harrison
Francis
Smithly
Sebastian
Losmith

SNAME
----------
Genevieve
Lindsay
Benny
Gus
Romona
Ken

28 rows selected.
```

The set of students who have earned A's can be found as follows:

```
SELECT Student.sname
FROM   Student
WHERE Student.stno IN
  (SELECT g.student_number
  FROM   Grade_report g
  WHERE g.grade = 'A');
```

This produces the following output:

```
SNAME
----------
Lineas
Mary
Brenda
Richard
Lujack
```

```
Donald
Lynette
Susan
Holly
Sadie
Jessica

SNAME
----------
Steve
Cedric
Jerry

14 rows selected.
```

Therefore, the difference operation would be to find the difference of the two sets as follows:

```
SELECT sname
FROM  Student
WHERE NOT major IN ('COSC','MATH')
 MINUS
SELECT Student.sname
FROM  Student
WHERE Student.stno IN
 (SELECT gr.student_number
 FROM  Grade_report gr
 WHERE gr.grade = 'A');
```

This produces the following output:

```
SNAME
----------
Benny
Bill
Chris
Cramer
Fraiser
Francis
Genevieve
George
Gus
Harley
Harrison
```

```
SNAME
_____

Ken
Lindsay
Losmith
Phoebe
Rachel
Romona
Sebastian
Smithly

19 rows selected.
```

CHAPTER 6 EXERCISES

1. In this exercise, you'll test the UNION statement. Having seen how the union statement works, demonstrate some permutations to see what will work "legally" and what won't. First, create two tables as follows:

Table1

A	B
x1	y1
r1	s1

Table2

A	B	C	D
x2	y2	z2	w2
r2	s2	T2	u2

Let the type of A's and B's be CHAR(2). Let the type of C in Table2 be VARCHAR2(2) and D in Table2 be VARCHAR2(3).

Try the following statements and note the results:

```
SELECT * FROM Table1 UNION SELECT * FROM Table2;
SELECT * FROM Table1 UNION SELECT A,B FROM Table2;
SELECT * FROM Table1 UNION SELECT B,A FROM Table1;
SELECT * FROM Table1 UNION SELECT A,C FROM Table2;
SELECT * FROM Table1 UNION SELECT A,D FROM Table2;
CREATE OR REPLACE VIEW viewx AS
SELECT A,B
FROM Table2;
SELECT *
FROM Table1
  UNION
SELECT *
FROM viewx;
```

Feel free to experiment with any other combinations that you deem appropriate or that you wonder about.

2. Create and print the result of a query that generates the name, class, and course numbers of students who have earned B's in computer science courses. Store this query as Q61. (Be sure to store the result too.) Then, revise Q61 to delete from the result set those students who are sophomores (class = 2) using NOT..IN to SELECT out sophomores. Repeat this exercise using MINUS instead of NOT..IN.

3. Find the student names, grades, and course numbers of students who have earned A's in computer science or math courses. Create a join of the `Section` and `Grade_report` tables (be careful to not create the Cartesian product), then UNION the set of "course numbers COSC____ and A" with the set of "course number MATH____ and A."

   Hint: Start with the query to get names, grades, and course numbers for COSC____ and A, then turn this into a view. Do the same for MATH____ and A, then execute the UNION statement as follows (using your view names):

   ```
   SELECT *
   FROM view1a
     UNION
   SELECT *
   FROM view1b;
   ```

4. Find the names and majors of students who have earned a C in any course. Make the section "who have earned a C in any course" a subquery for which you use IN.

5. A less obvious example of a difference query would be to find a difference that is not based on simple, easy-to-get sets. Suppose that set A is the set of students who have earned A's and B's in computer science (COSC) courses. Suppose further that set B is the set of students who have taken math courses (regardless of what grade they earned).

   Then, set A minus set B would contain names of students who have earned A's or B's in computer science courses, less those who have taken math courses. Similarly, set B minus set A would be the set of students who took math courses, less those who took COSC courses and earned an A or a B in COSCxxxx.

   Build these queries into set difference queries as views based on student numbers and execute them.

   a. First, run a query that gives the student number, name, course, and grade for each set. Save each query as Q65a and Q65b.

   b. After saving each query, reconstruct it into a view of just student numbers, verify that it works, and then use create view to create set A and set B. Verify that you have the same number of tuples in set A as you have in Q65a and in set B as in Q65b.

c. Then, display the student numbers of students in each set difference—show (set A minus set B) and (set B minus set A). Look at the original queries, Q65a and Q65b, to verify your result.

6. Create two tables, T1 and T2, that contain a `name` and a `salary`. In the first table, order the attributes as `name, salary`. In the second table, order the attributes as `salary, name`. Use the same types for each—VARCHAR2(20), NUMBER(2), for example. Populate the tables with two tuples each.

Can you UNION these two tables with SELECT * FROM T1 UNION SELECT * FROM T2? Why or why not? If not, can you force the union of the two tables? Illustrate how. Be sure to DROP the tables when you are finished.

Optional Exercise

7. (De Morgan's Theorem) Find the result set for all sections that are offered in building 13 and call this set A. Find the result set for all sections that are offered in bldg. 36 and call this set B. Construct the SQL to find the following result sets:

a. The result of set A or set B (use WHERE bldg = 13 or bldg = 36).

b. The result of the complement of (a): NOT(set A or set B).

c. The result of NOT(A) and NOT(B).

d. The COUNT of all rows in the `Section` table.

Is the count in d = a + b? Is the result of c the same as the result of b? Explain why or why not in each case.

Joins versus Subqueries

The purpose of this chapter is to demonstrate how you can use subqueries as alternatives to joins. There are two main issues to consider in choosing between subqueries and joins (and other techniques as well).

You must consider how you get information, which is often subjective. By understanding the limitations of joins and subqueries (and sets and other techniques, for that matter), you will broaden your choices as to how to get information from the database.

You must consider performance. You usually have choices related to how to get information—joins, sets, subqueries, views, and so on. On a large database, you need to be flexible and consider other choices if a query performs poorly and is done often.

> Although set operations are also viable choices for retrieving data from multiple tables, they are less common and usually less efficient than joins and subqueries.

The IN Subquery

Suppose a query states that we list the names of students who have earned A's or B's in any course. This query can be completed as either a subquery or as a join. As a subquery, it would take the following form:

```
SELECT Student.sname
FROM   Student
WHERE  "link to Grade_report "
 IN ("link to Student" - subquery involving Grade_report)
```

The link between the Student table and the Grade_report table is the student number. In the Student table, the appropriate attribute is stno, and in the Grade_report table, it is student_number. When using a link between tables with the IN subquery, only the linking attributes can be mentioned in the WHERE .. IN and in the result set of the subquery. Thus, the statement with a subquery is as follows:

> The part of the query *before* the IN is called the *outer query*. The part of the query *after* the IN is called the *inner query*.

```
SELECT  Student.sname
FROM    Student
WHERE   Student.stno
  IN    (SELECT gr.student_number
  FROM   Grade_report gr
  WHERE  gr.grade = 'B' OR gr.grade = 'A');
```

This produces the following output:

```
SNAME
----------
Lineas
Mary
Zelda
Ken
Mario
Brenda
Richard
Kelly
Lujack
Reva
Harley

SNAME
----------
Donald
Chris
Lynette
Susan
Hillary
Phoebe
Holly
Sadie
Jessica
Steve
Cedric
```

```
SNAME
----------
George
Jerry
Cramer
Fraiser
Francis
Smithly
Sebastian
Lindsay
Stephanie

31 rows selected.
```

The Subquery as a Join

An alternative way to perform the preceding query would be to form a joined relation, and not use a subquery, as follows:

```
SELECT  Student.sname
FROM    Student, Grade_report gr
WHERE   Student.stno = gr.student_number
 AND    (gr.grade = 'B' OR gr.grade = 'A');
```

Whether it is the join or the subquery that is more efficient depends on which SQL you are using. Database systems such as Oracle parse queries and execute them according to a plan, much like a programming language compiles source code and generates an object module for execution. The program that creates the execution plan in Oracle is called the *optimizer*. Even if you write a query as a subquery, the Oracle optimizer may indeed internally convert your query to a join (or vice versa).

If you use the join version, then any Student-Grade_report tuple (row) that has equal student numbers and a grade of A or B is SELECTed. Thus, you should expect many duplicate names in the output. To get the desired result without duplicates, you must add the qualifier DISTINCT to the join query as follows:

```
SELECT DISTINCT Student.sname
FROM Student, Grade_report gr
WHERE ...
```

In the subquery version of the query, no duplication of names in the output will occur as you are setting up a set (the subquery) from which you will choose names—a given name is either in the subquery set or it is not.

As we have seen earlier, using DISTINCT is not performance-efficient because of the internal sorting that occurs. So, when using a query that uses a join and DISTINCT versus using one that uses a subquery, the Oracle optimizer is confronted with an interesting internal problem: Internally, when joining with DISTINCT, the Oracle optimizer must choose between joining and then sorting versus creating a result set for the subquery and actually doing the query with the subquery result set. For small tables, no difference is likely to be noted. For large tables on production databases, you would have to test each type of query to see how it performed.

When the Join Cannot Be Turned into a Subquery

If the original query had been one that asked for output from the Grade_report table, such as "list the names and grades of all students who have earned A's or B's in any course," the query would be asking for information from both the Student and Grade_report tables. In this case, you must join the two tables to get the information. Refer again to the first query example in which you were asked to list the names of students who have earned A's or B's in any course. That query only asked for information from the Student table. In the first query example, the query used the Grade_report table; however, nothing from the Grade_report table was in the outer result set. The answer to the question posed here (a result set that lists the names and grades of all students who have earned A's or B's in any course) would be:

```
SELECT  DISTINCT Student.sname, gr.grade
FROM    Student, Grade_report gr
WHERE   Student.stno = gr.student_number    -- join condition
 AND    (gr.grade = 'B' OR gr.grade = 'A');
```

This produces the following output:

```
SNAME        G
-----------  -
Brenda       A
Brenda       B
Cedric       A
Cedric       B
Chris        B
Cramer       B
Donald       A
Fraiser      B
Francis      B
George       B
Harley       B


SNAME        G
-----------  -
Hillary      B
Holly        A
Holly        B
Jerry        A
Jessica      A
Jessica      B
Kelly        B
Ken          B
Lindsay      B
Lineas       A
Lineas       B


SNAME        G
-----------  -
Lujack       A
Lujack       B
Lynette      A
Lynette      B
Mario        B
Mary         A
Mary         B
Phoebe       B
Reva         B
Richard      A
Sadie        A


SNAME        G
-----------  -
Sadie        B
Sebastian    B
Smithly      B
Stephanie    B
```

```
Steve      A
Steve      B
Susan      A
Zelda      B

41 rows selected.
```

If information from a table is needed in a result set, then that table cannot be buried in a subquery—it must be in the outer query.

More Examples Involving Joins and IN

The purpose of this section is to show several queries that will and will not allow the use of the subquery. As we have discussed, some joins can be expressed as subqueries, while others cannot. In addition, all subqueries with the IN predicate can be re-formed as a join. How do you know whether you can use a subquery? It depends on the final, outer result set. Some examples will help clarify this point.

Example 1

In this example, we will find the names of all departments that offer a course with "INTRO" in the title. In order to create an appropriate query, we need the Course table (to find the course information) and the Department_to_major table (to find the names of the departments). It's usually a good idea to look at the tables first with DESC to be sure the information can be found in them. Thus, we begin by showing the Course and Department_to_major tables using DESC as follows:

```
SQL> DESC Course;
```

This produces the following output:

```
Name                Null?      Type
----------------    ----       --
COURSE_NAME                    CHAR(20)
COURSE_NUMBER       NOT NULL   CHAR(8)
CREDIT_HOURS                   NUMBER(2)
OFFERING_DEPT                  CHAR(4)
```

```
SQL> DESC Department_to_major;
```

This produces the following output:

```
Name        Type
_____  ___
DCODE       CHAR(4)
DNAME       CHAR(20)
```

Note that the query only asks for department names, not the names of
the INTRO courses. This is because we did not ask for the names of the
courses, just that they have INTRO in the title. We can find this result
using a subquery because all the information in the result set is contained in the outer query, which uses the Department_to_major table as
follows:

```
SELECT d2m.dname
FROM   Department_to_major d2m
WHERE  d2m.dcode
   IN   (SELECT Course.offering_dept
   FROM   Course
   WHERE Course.course_name LIKE '%INTRO%');
```

This produces the following output:

```
DNAME
_____
Chemistry
Computer Science
Political Science
```

Note that this query can also be completed as a join as follows:

```
SELECT d2m.dname
FROM   Department_to_major d2m, Course c
WHERE  d2m.dcode=c.offering_dept
AND    c.course_name LIKE '%INTRO%';
```

When done as a join, the query produces the following output:

```
DNAME
_____
Chemistry
Computer Science
Computer Science
Political Science
```

> Since DISTINCT
was not used for
the result set, all
occurrences of
matching rows in
the join are report-
ed. This further illus-
trates a subtle differ-
ence between using
joins and sub-
queries.

Example 2

In this example, we will list the student name, student major code, and section identifier of students who earned C's in courses taught by Professor Jones (JONES).

The first question we must ask ourselves is: *Which tables are needed?* By looking at the information we need to collect, we can see we will need the Student, Grade_report, and Section tables. As noted above, it's usually a good idea to look at the tables first with DESC to be sure the information can be found in them. Thus, we begin by showing the Student, Grade_report, and Section tables using DESC as follows:

```
SQL>DESC Student;
```

This produces the following output:

```
Name       Null?        Type
_____    _____   _____
STNO       NOT NULL     NUMBER(3)
SNAME                   VARCHAR2(20)
MAJOR                   CHAR(4)
CLASS                   NUMBER(1)
```

```
SQL>DESC Grade_report;
```

This produces the following output:

```
Name             Null?       Type
_____         _____   _____
STUDENT_NUMBER   NOT NULL    NUMBER(3)
SECTION_ID       NOT NULL    NUMBER(6)
GRADE                        CHAR(1)
```

```
SQL>DESC Section;
```

This produces the following output:

```
Name          Null?        Type
_____    _____   __
SECTION_ID    NOT NULL     NUMBER(6)
COURSE_NUM                 CHAR(8)
SEMESTER                   VARCHAR2(6)
YEAR                       CHAR(2)
INSTRUCTOR                 CHAR(10)
BLDG                       NUMBER(3)
ROOM                       NUMBER(3)
```

The next question we must ask ourselves is: *Where are the columns that are needed in the result set?* We need to get the names and major codes from the Student table, and we can get the section identifiers from the Grade_report table. Thus, the result set part of the query—that is, the outer query—must contain the Student and Grade_report tables. The rest of the query can contain any other tables we need to answer the question. The resulting query may look like this:

```
SELECT s.sname, s.major, g.section_id
FROM   Student s, Grade_report g
WHERE  g.student_number = s.stno    /* join condition Student-
                                       Grade_report */

AND    g.grade = 'C'
AND    g.section_id IN
 (SELECT t.section_id
  FROM Section t
  WHERE t.instructor like '%JONES%');
```

This produces the following output:

SNAME	MAJO	SECTION_ID
Richard	ENGI	145

In this case, the query could also have been done as a three-table join as shown below:

```
SELECT s.sname, s.major, t.section_id
FROM   Student s, Grade_report g, Section t
WHERE  s.stno = g.student_number
AND g.section_id=t.section_id
AND g.grade='C'
AND t.instructor LIKE '%JONES%';
```

Example 3

In this example, we'll list the student name and student major code of students who earned C's in courses taught by Professor Jones (JONES).

Again, the first question we must ask ourselves is: *Which tables are needed?* By looking at the information we need to collect, we can see we will need the Student, Grade_report, and Section tables. (Since we have already used DESC to view these tables in the previous example, we will not do so again here.) Next, we must ask ourselves: *Where are the columns*

> This is very similar to Example 2, but only that in this example we are not looking for the section identifier.

that are needed in the result set? As we can see, they are all in the Student table. Thus, because the only table needed in the outer query is the Student table, the query can be done in a number of ways. The options include:

1. Student Join Grade_report Join Section   [three-table join]

2. Student Sub (Grade_report Join Section)   [Student outer, join in subquery]

3. Student Join Grade_report Sub (Section)   [Done like example 2 (above) with section_id removed from the result set]

4. Student (Sub Grade_report (Sub Section)) [A three-level subquery]

Each of these queries could produce the same result with different efficiencies. We'll study them in detail in the exercises at the end of the chapter.

Subqueries with Operators

In previous chapters, we have seen SELECTs with conditions like the following:

```
SELECT *
FROM Room
WHERE capacity = 25;
```

In this example, the 25 is a constant and the = is an operator. The constant can be replaced by a subquery, while the operator can be any logical comparison operator (such as =, <>, <, >, <=, >=). For example, we could devise a query to tell us which classrooms have a below-average capacity as follows:

```
SELECT *
FROM Room
WHERE capacity <
  (SELECT AVG(capacity)
  FROM Room);
```

This produces the following output:

```
  BLDG    ROOM    CAPACITY   O
  _____   _____   _____   _
  36      123     35         N
  79      179     35         Y
  79      174     22         Y
  36      122     25         N
  36      121     25         N
  36      120     25         N

  6 rows selected.
```

This result set produces below-average capacity rooms. The only danger in using subqueries in this fashion is that *the subquery must return only one row*. If an aggregate function is applied to a table in the subquery in this fashion, you will always get only one row; even if there is a WHERE clause that excludes all rows, the subquery returns one row with a null value. For example, if we changed the preceding query to:

```
SELECT *
FROM Room
WHERE capacity <
  (SELECT AVG(capacity)
   FROM    Room
   WHERE   bldg = 99);
```

The query would run (without producing any errors), but the result would be "no rows selected." If we changed the query to:

```
SELECT *
FROM Room
WHERE bldg =
  (SELECT bldg
   FROM    Room
   WHERE   capacity > 10);
```

We would get:

```
  ERROR: single-row subquery returns more than one row
```

When using operators, only single values are acceptable from the subquery. Again, to ensure we get only one row in the subquery and hence ensure a workable query, we can use an aggregate with no GROUP BY or HAVING (which we'll discuss in Chapter 8).

> As with other queries that include derived results, the caveat to audit the result is always applicable.

CHAPTER 7 EXERCISES

Use the techniques we discussed in this chapter to construct and execute the following queries:

1. Find the student numbers of students who have earned A's or B's in courses taught in the fall semester. Do this in two ways: once using a subquery and once using a join.

2. Find all students who took a course offered by the accounting department. List the student name and student number, the course taken (course name), and the grade the student earned in that course. Hint: Begin with the `Department_to_major` table and use an appropriate WHERE. Note that this cannot be done with a multi-level subquery. Why?

3. Find the names of students who are sophomores (`class = 2`) as well as the name of their department (based on their `major`).

4. Find the names of departments that offer courses at the junior or senior levels (either one) but *not* at the freshman level. (The course level is the first digit after the prefix. Therefore, AAAA3yyy is a junior course, and so on.)

    Hint: Begin by creating the outer query—the names of departments that offer courses at the junior or senior levels. Save this query as q74. Then, construct the subquery—a list of departments that offer courses at the freshman level. "Save" the subquery as a view. Examine both lists of departments. When you have the outer query and the subquery results, recall the original query that you saved (q74) and add the subquery. Check your result with the department lists you just generated. Re-do the last part of the experiment with your view. You should get the same result.

5. Find the names of courses that are prerequisites for other courses. List the course number and name, and the number and name of the prerequisite course.

6. List the names of instructors who teach courses that have other than three-hour credits. Do this in two ways: once with IN and once with NOT..IN.

7. Create a table called `Secretary` with the attributes "dcode CHAR(4)" (for department code) and "name VARCHAR2 (20)" (for the secretary name). Populate the table as follows:

Secretary

dCode	name
ACCT	Sally
COSC	Chris
ENGL	Maria

a. Create a query that lists the names of departments that have secretaries (use IN and the `Secretary` table in a subquery with the `Department_to_major` table in the outer query). Save this query as q77a.

b. Create a query that lists the names of departments that do not have secretaries (use NOT..IN). Save this query as q77b.

c. Add one more row to the `Secretary` table that contains <null, 'Brenda'> (This could be a situation in which you have hired Brenda but have not yet assigned her to a department.)

d. Recall q77a and re-run it.

Recall q77b and re-run it.

The behavior of NOT..IN when nulls exist may surprise you. If nulls may exist in the subquery, then NOT..IN should either:

(i) not be used (we will see how to use another predicate, NOT EXISTS, in Chapter 9, which is a workaround to this problem) or

(ii) should include AND whatever IS NOT NULL.

If you use NOT..IN in a subquery, you must ensure that nulls will not occur in the subquery or you must use some other predicate (such as NOT EXISTS). Perhaps the best solution is to avoid NOT..IN unless you can't figure out another way to solve a problem.

e. To see a correct answer, add the phrase "WHERE dcode IS NOT NULL" to the subquery in the IN and NOT..IN cases and run them again.

Do *not* delete the `Secretary` table because we will revisit this problem in Chapter 9.

8. Devise a list of course names that are offered in the fall semester in rooms where the capacity is equal to or above the average room size.

Optional Exercise

9. Set the autotrace facility on with this command:

```
SQL>SET AUTOTRACE ON EXPLAIN
```

Note that AUTOTRACE will only work if the user already owns a proper PLAN_TABLE, and the user has sufficient privileges to run AUTOTRACE (that is, the PLUSTRACE role or equivalent privileges).

Then, write and run each of the queries (these are the same queries that were listed in the "Example 3" section earlier in the chapter):

a. `Student Join Grade_report Join Section` [three table join]

b. `Student Sub (Grade_report Join Section)` [Student outer, join in subquery]

c. `Student Join Grade_report Sub (Section)` [Done like example 2 (above) with section_id removed from the result set]

d. `Student (Sub Grade_report (Sub Section))` [A three-level subquery]

You can modify the queries in the exercise to return only a count of what would be the result set (that is, start with SELECT * FROM ...). Use the Cost= result in the Execution Plan output to rank order the four queries from least to most efficient.

GROUP BY and HAVING

In this chapter, we'll discuss how to use aggregation, grouping, and the HAVING clause in a SELECT. By using these added features, you can group data of a particular type, filter the output with HAVING, and do combinations of aggregate calculations (such as sums, averages, and counts). We'll also take a brief look at nulls.

Aggregates/Column Functions

As we discussed in Chapter 4, an aggregate (or group) function is one that extracts information—such as a count of tuples or an average, minimum, or maximum—by operating on multiple rows. Some examples follow:

```
SELECT COUNT(*)    -- count(*) counts rows
FROM Student;

SELECT AVG(credit_hours), MAX(credit_hours)  /* two aggre-
                                                gates on the
                                                same set of
                                                data */
FROM Course
WHERE course_number LIKE 'COSC____';

SELECT COUNT(stno) "Student Numbers"  /* an alias is used for
                                         count of non-null
                                         student numbers */
FROM Student;
```

In the next sections, we'll expand the use of aggregation in queries.

The GROUP BY Clause

GROUP BY is a clause in a SELECT statement that is designed to be used in conjunction with aggregate functions. GROUP BY will return one row for each *value* of the column(s) that is grouped. For example, you can extract COUNTs of class groups from the Student table with a statement like the following:

```
SELECT class, COUNT(*)
FROM Student
GROUP BY class;
```

This will produce the following output:

CLASS	COUNT(*)
1	11
2	10
3	7
4	10
	10

This type of statement gives you a new way to retrieve and organize aggregate data. To use the statement, you must GROUP BY *at least* what you are aggregating. A statement like the following will cause a syntax error because it implies that you are to COUNT both class and major, but GROUP BY class only:

```
SELECT class, major, COUNT(*)
FROM Student
GROUP BY class;
```

To be syntactically and logically correct, you must have all of the non-aggregate columns in the GROUP BY clause.

The following is the correct COUNT of class and major:

```
SELECT class, major, COUNT(*)
FROM Student
GROUP BY class, major;
```

This produces the following output:

```
CLASS     MAJO    COUNT(*)
_____    ___     _____
   1      COSC    4
   1      ENGL    3
   1      POLY    3
   1      UNKN    1
   2      ACCT    1
   2      COSC    2
   2      ENGL    2
   2      MATH    3
   2      POLY    2
   3      ART     1
   3      CHEM    1

CLASS     MAJO    COUNT(*)
_____    ___     _____
   3      ENGL    4
   3      MATH    1
   4      ACCT    4
   4      CHEM    1
   4      COSC    3
   4      MATH    1
   4      POLY    1
          COSC    1
          ENGL    1
          MATH    2
          POLY    2

CLASS     MAJO    COUNT(*)
_____    ___     _____
  UNKN     1
           3

24 rows selected.
```

In a similar vein, the following query would be improper because you must GROUP BY ohead to SUM capacities for each ohead value:

> ohead, an attribute in the Room table, is short for rooms with overhead projectors.

```
SELECT ohead, SUM(capacity)
FROM Room;
```

If you SELECT attributes *and* use an aggregate function, you must GROUP BY the non-aggregate attributes.

The correct version of this statement is as follows:

```
SELECT ohead, SUM(capacity)
FROM   Room
GROUP  BY ohead;
```

This produces the following output:

```
O   SUM(CAPACITY)
-   -------
N   110
Y   142
    100
```

This is the sum of room capacities for rooms that have no overhead projectors (N), rooms that do have overhead projectors (Y), and rooms in which the overhead projector capacity is unknown (null).

Observe that in the Room table that follows, some rooms have null values for ohead. Those rows are summed and grouped along with the non-null rows:

```
BLDG   ROOM   CAPACITY  O
-----  -----  -----     -
  13   101    85        Y
  36   123    35        N
  58   114    60
  79   179    35        Y
  79   174    22        Y
  58   112    40
  58   110              Y
  36   122    25        N
  36   121    25        N
  36   120    25        N
```

GROUP BY and ORDER BY

To enhance the display of a GROUP BY clause, you can combine it with an ORDER BY clause. Consider the following example:

```
SELECT class, major, COUNT(*)
FROM   Student
GROUP  BY class, major;
```

This produces the following output:

```
CLASS   MAJO   COUNT(*)
_____   __     _____
    1   COSC   4
    1   ENGL   3
    1   POLY   3
    1   UNKN   1
    2   ACCT   1
    2   COSC   2
    2   ENGL   2
    2   MATH   3
    2   POLY   2
    3   ART    1
    3   CHEM   1
    3   ENGL   4
    3   MATH   1
    4   ACCT   4
    4   CHEM   1
    4   COSC   3
    4   MATH   1
    4   POLY   1
        COSC   1
        ENGL   1
        MATH   2

CLASS   MAJO   COUNT(*)
_____   __     _____
        POLY   2
        UNKN   1
               3

24 rows selected.
```

The result set will be ordered by the class and then by major because of the internal sorting required to do the grouping. Ordering of the result set on any other column(s) including the aggregate can also be used. Consider the following example, which orders by COUNT(*) in descending order (DESC here stands for descending order):

```
SELECT    class, major, COUNT(*)
FROM      Student
GROUP BY class, major
ORDER BY COUNT(*) DESC;
```

This produces the following output:

```
CLASS    MAJO    COUNT(*)
-----    --      -----
    1    COSC    4
    3    ENGL    4
    4    ACCT    4
    1    ENGL    3
    4    COSC    3
                 3
    2    MATH    3
    1    POLY    3
    2    COSC    2
    2    POLY    2
         POLY    2
         MATH    2
    2    ENGL    2
    1    UNKN    1
    3    ART     1
    3    MATH    1
    4    POLY    1
         UNKN    1
         ENGL    1
         COSC    1
    4    MATH    1

CLASS    MAJO    COUNT(*)
-----    --      -----
    4    CHEM    1
    3    CHEM    1
    2    ACCT    1

24 rows selected.
```

The HAVING Clause

The HAVING clause is used as a final filter on a SELECT. The HAVING clause filters the result set by a condition *after* the grouping functions have been applied. Consider the following statement:

```
SELECT   class, COUNT(*)
FROM     Student
GROUP BY class;
```

This displays the count of students in various classes (classes of students = 1, 2, 3, 4, which correspond to freshman, sophomore, and so on). If you are only interested in classes that have more than a certain number of students in them, you could use the following statement:

```
SELECT   class, COUNT(*)
FROM     Student
GROUP BY class
HAVING COUNT(*) > 9;
```

This would produce the following output:

CLASS	COUNT(*)
1	11
2	10
4	10
	10

HAVING and WHERE

As we just mentioned, HAVING is a final filter rather than a conditional filter in a SELECT statement. The conditional filter is the WHERE clause, which excludes rows from a result set. Note that the following two queries would give the same result:

```
SELECT   class, COUNT(*)
FROM     Student
GROUP BY class
HAVING   class = 3;

SELECT   class, COUNT(*)
FROM     Student
WHERE    class = 3
GROUP BY class;
```

Both queries would produce the following output:

CLASS	COUNT(*)
3	7

The first of these two queries (the one using HAVING) is less efficient because the query engine must complete the query before removing rows WHERE class = 3 from the result. In the second version (the one using WHERE instead of HAVING), the rows WHERE class = 3 are removed before grouping takes place. WHERE is not always a substitute for HAVING, but when it can be used instead of HAVING, it should be.

Consider the following query, its meaning, and the processing that is required to finalize the result set:

```
SELECT    class, major, COUNT(*)
FROM      Student
WHERE     major = 'COSC'
GROUP BY class, major
HAVING COUNT(*) > 2;
```

This produces the following output:

CLASS	MAJO	COUNT(*)
1	COSC	4
4	COSC	3

In this example, all computer science (COSC) majors (per the WHERE clause) will be grouped and counted and then displayed only if COUNT(*) > 2. The query might erroneously be interpreted as "Group and count all 'COSC' majors by class, but only if there are two in a class." This interpretation is wrong because SQL applies the WHERE, then the GROUP BY, and, finally, filters with the HAVING criterion.

GROUP BY and HAVING: Aggregates of Aggregates

A "usual" GROUP BY has an aggregate and a column that are grouped as shown below:

```
SELECT COUNT(stno), class
FROM Student
GROUP BY class;
```

This produces a result set of counts by class, as follows:

COUNT(STNO)	CLASS
11	1
10	2
7	3
10	4
10	

While you must have `class` or some other attribute in the GROUP BY, you don't have to have the `class` in the result set. Consider the following query:

```
SELECT COUNT(stno)
FROM Student
GROUP BY class;
```

This produces the following output:

```
COUNT(STNO)
-------
    11
    10
     7
    10
    10
```

This query generates the same information as the former query, but the `class` is not reported in the result set. This latter type of query is useful when you want to determine aggregates of aggregates.

Suppose you wanted to find the `class` with the minimum number of students. You might try the following query:

```
SELECT MIN(COUNT(stno)), class
FROM Student
GROUP BY class;
```

However, this query will not work. The MIN function is an aggregate, and aggregates operate on tables that contain rows. In this case, you are asking MIN to operate on a table of counted classes that have not yet been calculated. The point is that SQL cannot handle this mismatch of aggregation and grouping. The way to find the `class` with the minimum number of students is to first display the counts of classes, grouped by `class`, as follows:

```
SELECT COUNT(stno)
FROM Student
GROUP BY class;
```

You then find the minimum students in a class as follows:

```
SELECT MIN(COUNT(stno))
FROM Student
GROUP BY class;
```

This produces the following output:

MIN(COUNT(STNO))
7

You then use this information in a subquery with a HAVING clause as follows:

```
SELECT COUNT(stno), class
FROM Student
GROUP BY class
HAVING COUNT(stno) =
    (SELECT MIN(COUNT(stno))
    FROM Student
    GROUP BY class);
```

This produces the following output:

COUNT(STNO)	CLASS
7	3

Auditing IN Subqueries

In this section, we consider a potential problem of using aggregation with subqueries. As with Cartesian products and joins, aggregation hides detail and should always be audited. Consider the following two tables:

> This table, Table GG, has not been created for you. You will have to create it in order to run the queries that follow.

Table GG (a table like the Grade_report table, which contains student numbers (num), grades (gd), and student names (sname)):

NUM	GD	SNAME
100	A	BRENDA
110	B	BRENDA
120	A	BRENDA
200	A	BRENDA
210	A	BRENDA

```
220     B       BRENDA
100     A       RICHARD
100     B       DOUG
200     A       RICHARD
110     B       MORRIS
```

Table SS (a table like the `Section` table, which contains a section identifier (`sec`) and an instructor name (`iname`)):

```
SEC     INAME
---     -----
100     JONES
110     SMITH
120     JONES
200     ADAMS
210     JONES
```

> This table, `Table` SS, has not been created for you. You will have to create it in order to run the queries that follow.

Suppose you want to find out how many A's each instructor awarded. You might start with a join of the table like the `Grade_report` table, table GG, and the table like the `Section` table, table SS. A normal equi-join would be as follows:

```
SELECT *
FROM   GG, SS
WHERE  GG.num = SS.sec -- join condition
;
```

This produces the following output:

```
SEC   INAME   NUM   GD   SNAME
---   -----   ---   --   -----
100   JONES   100   A    BRENDA
100   JONES   100   A    RICHARD
100   JONES   100   B    DOUG
110   SMITH   110   B    MORRIS
110   SMITH   110   B    BRENDA
120   JONES   120   A    BRENDA
200   ADAMS   200   A    BRENDA
200   ADAMS   200   A    RICHARD
210   JONES   210   A    BRENDA
```

In addition, the following query tells you that there are six A's in the GG table:

```
SELECT COUNT(*)
FROM GG
WHERE gd = 'A';
```

Now, if you try the following query:

```
SELECT SS.iname
FROM   SS, GG
WHERE  SS.sec = GG.num -- join condition
 AND   GG.gd = 'A';
```

You get the following output:

```
INAME
─────
JONES
JONES
ADAMS
JONES
JONES
ADAMS
```

With a COUNT and GROUP BY as follows:

```
SELECT    SS.iname, COUNT(*)
FROM      SS, GG
WHERE     SS.sec = GG.num        -- join condition GG to SS
 AND      GG.gd = 'A'
GROUP BY SS.iname;
```

You get the following output:

INAME	COUNT(EXPRESSION 1)
ADAMS	2
JONES	4

So far, so good, and everything appears normal. You may note that the final count/grouping has the same number of A's as the original tables—the sum of the counts equals 6. Now, if you had devised a count query with a sub-SELECT, you could get an answer that looks correct but in fact is not. For example, consider the following subquery version of the preceding join query:

```
SELECT SS.iname, COUNT(*)
FROM    SS
WHERE   SS.sec IN
 (SELECT  GG.num
 FROM     GG
 WHERE    GG.gd = 'A')
 GROUP BY SS.iname;
```

This produces the following output:

INAME	COUNT(EXPRESSION 1)
ADAMS	1
JONES	3

Why did you get this output? The answer is that the second query is counting names of instructors and whether an A is present in the set of courses that this instructor teaches—not how many A's are in the set, just whether there are any. The join query gives you all of the A's in the joined table and hence gives the correct answer to the question, "How many A's did each instructor award?" The sub-SELECTed query answers a different question: "In how many sections did the instructor award an A?"

The point in this example is that if you are SELECTing and COUNTing, *it is a very good idea to audit your results often.* If you want to count the number of A's by instructor, begin by first counting how many A's there are. Then, you can construct a query to join and count. You should be able to total and reconcile the number of A's to the number of A's by instructor.

Nulls Revisited

Nulls present a complication with regard to aggregate functions and other queries. This is because nulls are never equal, less than, greater than, or not equal to any value. Using aggregates by themselves on

> This table, Sal, has not been created for you. You will have to create it in order to run the queries that follow.

columns that contain nulls will ignore the null values. For example, suppose you had the following table (call it Sal):

```
NAME        SALARY
-----       ------
Joe         1000
Sam         2000
Bill        3000
Dave
```

Consider the result of the following query:

```
SELECT  COUNT(*), AVG(salary), SUM(salary), MAX(salary),
MIN     (salary)
FROM    Sal;
```

This would produce the following output:

COUNT(*)	AVG(SALARY)	SUM(SALARY)	MIN(SALARY)	MAX(SALARY)
4	2000	6000	1000	3000

COUNT(*) counts all rows, but the AVERAGE, SUM, and so on ignore the nulled salary row in computing the aggregate. Counting columns indicates the presence of nulls. If you count with SELECT COUNT(column name) FROM Sal, you get:

COUNT(NAME)
4

Or, with the "salary" column, you get

COUNT(SALARY)
3

This indicates you have a null salary. If you want to include nulls in the aggregate, you can use the NVL function, which we have discussed in previous chapters. NVL returns a value if the value is null. NVL has the form NVL (column name, value if null), which is used in place of the column name. For example, if you type:

```
SELECT name, NVL(salary, 0)
FROM Sal;
```

This produces the following output:

```
NAME          NVL(SALARY,0)
_____        _____
Joe           1000
Sam           2000
Bill          3000
Dave          0
```

If you type:

```
SELECT COUNT(NVL(salary,0))
FROM Sal;
```

This produces the following output:

```
COUNT(NVL(SALARY,0))
_____
    4
```

If you type:

```
SELECT AVG(NVL(salary, 0))
FROM Sal;
```

This produces the following output:

```
AVG(NVL(SALARY,0))
_____
    1500
```

What seems almost contradictory to these examples is that when grouping is added to the query, nulls in the grouped column are included in the result set. So, if you had another column in your table like this:

```
NAME     SALARY   JOB
_____    _____    ___
Joe      1000     Programmer
Sam      2000
Bill     3000     Plumber
Dave              Programmer
```

And if you ran a query like the following:

```
SELECT SUM(salary), job
FROM Sal
GROUP BY job;
```

You would get the following result:

SUM(SALARY)	JOB
3000	Plumber
1000	Programmer
2000	

Thus, the aggregate will ignore values that are null, but grouping will compute a value for the nulled column value.

CHAPTER 8 EXERCISES

1. Display a list of courses (course names) that have prerequisites and the number of prerequisites for each course. Order the list by the number of prerequisites.

2. How many juniors (class = 3) are there in the Student table?

3. Group and count all MATH majors by class and display the count if there are two or more in a class. (Remember that class here refers to freshman, sophomore, and so on and is recorded as 1, 2, 3, and so on).

4. Print the counts of A's, B's, and so on from the Grade_report table.

5. Print the counts of course numbers offered in descending order by count. Use the Section table only.

6. Create a table with names and number-of-children (NOC). Populate the table with five or six tuples. Use COUNT, SUM, AVG, MIN, and MAX on the NOC attribute in one query and check that the numbers you get are what you expect.

7. Create a table of names, salaries, and job locations. Populate the table with at least 10 tuples and no fewer than three job locations. (There will be several employees at each location.) Find the average salary for each job location with one SELECT.

8. Print an ordered list of instructors and the number of A's they assigned to students. Order the output by number of A's (lowest to

greatest). You can (and probably will) ignore instructors who assign no A's.

9. Create a table called `Employees` with a name, a salary, and a job title field. Include exactly six tuples. Make the salary null in one tuple, the job title null in another, and both the salary and the job title null in another. Use this data:

Name	Salary	Title
Mary	1000	Programmer
Brenda	3000	
Stephanie		Artist
Alice		
Lindsay	2000	Artist
Christina	500	Programmer

    a. Display the table.

    b. Display count, sum, maximum, minimum, and average salary.

    c. Display count, sum, maximum, minimum, and average salary, counting salary as 0 if no salary is listed.

    d. Display the average salary grouped by job title on the table.

    e. Display the average salary grouped by job title when null salary is counted as 0.

    f. Display the average salary grouped by job title when salary is counted as 0 if it is null and include a value for "no job title."

10. Find the instructor and the course where the maximum number of A's were awarded.

Optional Exercise

11. Find the COUNT of the number of students by `class` who are taking classes offered by the computer science (COSC) department. Turn on autotrace (SET AUTOTRACE ON EXPLAIN). Perform the query in two ways: once using a condition in the WHERE clause and once filtering with a HAVING clause. Which is more efficient, WHERE or HAVING? Hint: These queries need a five-table join.

Delete (DROP) all of your "scratch" tables (the ones you created just for this exercise, including `Employees`, `NOC`, and any others you may have created).

Correlated Subqueries

A correlated subquery is one in which:
• there is a subquery (and hence a main, outer query), and
• the information in the subquery is referenced by the outer, main query such that the inner query may be thought of as being executed repeatedly.

In this chapter, we'll take a look at correlated subqueries. We'll discuss existence queries and correlation as well as NOT EXISTS. We'll also take a look at SQL's universal and existential qualifiers. Before discussing correlated subqueries in detail, however, let's make sure we understand what a non-correlated subquery is.

Non-Correlated Subqueries

A non-correlated subquery is a subquery that is independent of the outer query. The subquery could be executed on its own. The following is an example of a query that is not correlated:

```
SELECT  s.sname
FROM    Student s
WHERE   s.stno IN
   (SELECT gr.student_number
    FROM   Grade_report gr
    WHERE  gr.grade = 'A');
```

> The part of the query in parentheses is the subquery (also referred to as a *nested query* or *embedded query*). Note that the subquery is an independent entity—it would work by itself if run as a stand-alone query.

We have seen previously (in earlier chapters) that Oracle rearranges queries to gain efficiency. Rearrangement aside, the following subquery can be *thought* of as being evaluated first, creating the set of student numbers who have A's:

```
(SELECT  gr.student_number
FROM     Grade_report gr
WHERE    gr.grade = 'A');
```

The subquery result set is then used to determine which tuples (rows) in the main query will be SELECTed. The outer query uses the IN predicate to test whether a row should appear in the result set. IN what? In the result set of the subquery. Consider the following:

```
SELECT  s.sname                       -- outer
FROM    Student s                      -- outer
WHERE   s.stno IN                      -- outer
   (SELECT gr.student_number           -- inner
    FROM    Grade_report gr            -- inner
    WHERE   gr.grade = 'A')            -- inner
;
```

This produces the following output:

```
SNAME
----------
Lineas
Mary
Brenda
Richard
Lujack
Donald
Lynette
Susan
Holly
Sadie
Jessica

SNAME
----------
Steve
Cedric
Jerry

14 rows selected.
```

Correlated Subqueries

In the beginning of the chapter we stated that correlated subqueries are subqueries in which there is a subquery (and hence a main, outer query), and the information in the subquery is referenced by the outer, main query.

Correlated queries present a different execution scenario to the database manipulation language (DML) than do ordinary, non-correlated subqueries. The correlated subquery cannot stand alone, as it depends on the outer query; therefore, completing the subquery prior to execution of the outer query is not an option. The efficiency of the correlated subquery varies; in Oracle it may be worthwhile to test the efficiency of correlated queries versus joins or sets.

> One situation in which you can't avoid correlation is the "for all" query, which we'll discuss later in this chapter.

The following is an example of a correlated query:

```
SELECT  s.sname
FROM    Student s
WHERE   s.stno IN
        (SELECT gr.student_number
        FROM    Grade_report gr
        WHERE   gr.student_number = s.stno  /*s.stno refer-
                                            ences outer
                                            query  */

        AND     gr.grade = 'B');
```

This produces the following output:

```
SNAME
-----------
Lineas
Mary
Brenda
Kelly
Lujack
Reva
Harley
Chris
Lynette
Hillary
Phoebe
```

```
SNAME
----------
Holly
Sadie
Jessica
Steve
Cedric
George
Cramer
Fraiser
Francis
Smithly
Sebastian

SNAME
----------
Lindsay
Stephanie
Zelda
Mario
Ken

27 rows selected.
```

Here, the inner query references the outer one—observe the use of s.stno in the WHERE clause of the inner query. Rather than thinking of this query as creating a set of student numbers that have B's, each tuple (row) from the outer query is SELECTed individually and tested against all rows of the inner query one at a time until it is determined whether a given student number is in the inner set and whether that student earned a B.

This situation is like a nested DO loop in a programming language, where the first tuple from the Student table is SELECTed and tested against all tuples from the Grade_report table. Then, the second tuple from the Student table is SELECTed and tested against all tuples from the Grade_report table. The following is the DO loop in pseudo-code:

```
LOOP1: For each tuple in Student s DO
   LOOP2: For each tuple in Grade_report gr DO
     IF (gr.student_number = s.stno) then
     IF (gr.grade = 'B') THEN TRUE
   END LOOP2;
   if TRUE, then Student tuple is SELECTed
END LOOP1;
```

This query also could have been done without correlation in a manner similar to our first example in this chapter.

You might think that a correlated query is less efficient than doing a simple subquery because the simple subquery is done once and the correlated subquery is done once for each outer tuple (row). However, the internal handling of how the query executes depends on the SQL and the optimizer for that database engine. In Oracle, the database engine is designed so that queries containing correlation are quite efficient.

Existence Queries and Correlation

Correlated subqueries are often written so that the question in the inner query is one of existence. For example, assume we want to find the names of students who have taken a computer science (COSC) class and have earned a grade of B in that course. This query can be written in several ways. For example, we can use a non-correlated subquery as follows:

```
SELECT s.sname
FROM  Student s
WHERE s.stno IN
  (SELECT gr.student_number FROM Grade_report gr, Section
  WHERE   Section.section_id = gr.section_id  /* join condi-
                                                  tion
                                                Grade_report
                                                -Section */
  AND     Section.course_num LIKE 'COSC____'
  AND     gr.grade = 'B');
```

This would produce the following output:

```
SNAME
----------
Lineas
Mary
Brenda
Lujack
Reva
Harley
Chris
Lynette
Hillary
Phoebe
Holly
```

```
SNAME
----------
George
Cramer
Fraiser
Francis
Lindsay
Stephanie

17 rows selected.
```

> This query could also be done by creating a double-nested subquery containing two INs, or it could be written using a three-table join.

Since this query is non-correlated, we can think of this query as forming the set of student numbers of students who have earned B's in COSC courses—the inner query result set. In the inner query, we must have both the Grade_report and the Section tables because the course numbers are in the Section table and the grades are in the Grade_report table. Once we form this set of student numbers (that is, once we complete the inner query), the outer query looks through the Student table and SELECTs only those students who are in the inner query result set.

Had we chosen to write the query with an unnecessary correlation, it might look like this:

```
SELECT  s.sname
FROM    Student s
WHERE   s.stno IN
  (SELECT gr.student_number
   FROM   Grade_report gr, Section
   WHERE  Section.section_id = gr.section_id/* join condition
                                               Grade_report-
                                               Section */
   AND    Section.course_num LIKE 'COSC____'/*correlation */
   AND    gr.student_number = s.stno
   AND    gr.grade = 'B');
```

The final result of this query would be the same as the previous query. In this case, using the Student table in the subquery *is* unnecessary. Although correlation is unnecessary, we have provided this example for several reasons:

• to show when correlation is necessary,

• to show how to untangle unnecessarily correlated queries, and

• to show how you might migrate your thought process toward correlation, should it be necessary.

First, let's look at situations in which correlation *is* necessary, and, in particular, introduce a new predicate: EXISTS.

EXISTS

As noted earlier, there will be situations in which the correlation of a subquery *is* necessary. Another way to write the correlated query is with the EXISTS predicate, which looks like this:

```
SELECT s.sname
FROM Student s
WHERE EXISTS
 (SELECT 1 FROM Grade_report gr, Section
 WHERE Section.section_id = gr.section_id   /* join condition
                                               Grade_report-
                                               Section */

 AND Section.course_num like 'COSC____'
 AND gr.student_number = s.stno             /*  correlation */
 AND gr.grade = 'B');
```

This query produces the same output (17 rows) as both of the previous queries. Let's dissect this query.

The EXISTS predicate says, "Choose the row from the Student table in the outer query if the subquery is TRUE (that is, if a row in the subquery *exists* that satisfies the condition in the subquery WHERE clause)." Since no actual result set is formed, "SELECT 1" is used as a "dummy" result set to indicate that the subquery is TRUE (1 is returned) or FALSE (no rows are returned). In the non-correlated case, we tied the student number in the Student table to the inner query by the IN predicate as follows:

```
SELECT s.stno
FROM    Student s
WHERE   s.stno IN
 (SELECT "student number...)
```

When using the EXISTS predicate, we do not use any attribute of the Student table, but rather we are seeking only to find whether the subquery WHERE can be satisfied.

We have indicated that we are using EXISTS with (SELECT 1...). Using the EXISTS predicate, the subquery does not form a result set per se, but rather returns TRUE or FALSE. The use of SELECT * in the inner query is common among SQL programmers. However, from an "internal" standpoint, SELECT * causes the SQL engine to check the data dictionary unnecessarily. Because the actual result of the inner query is not important, it is strongly suggested that you use SELECT 'X' (or SELECT 1)... instead of SELECT *... so that a constant is SELECTed instead of some "sensible" entry. The SELECT 'X'... or (SELECT 1...) is simply more efficient.

In the EXISTS case, we do not specify what attributes need be SELECTed in the inner query's result set; rather, we use SELECT 1 to select something (a 1) if the subquery WHERE is satisfied (that is, TRUE) and to select nothing (no rows would give FALSE) if the condition in the subquery WHERE is not met. The EXISTS predicate forces us to correlate the query. To illustrate that correlation is usually necessary with EXISTS, consider the following query:

```
SELECT s.sname                           /* exists-uncorrelated */
FROM  Student s
WHERE EXISTS
 (SELECT 'X' FROM Grade_report gr, Section t
  WHERE    t.section_id = gr.section_id      /* join condition
                                                Grade_report-
                                                Section */
  AND      t.course_num like 'COSC____'
  AND      gr.grade = 'B');
```

This produces the following output:

```
SNAME
----------
Lineas
Mary
Brenda
Richard
Kelly
Lujack
Reva
Elainie
Harley
Donald
Chris
Lynette
Susan
Monica
Bill
Hillary
Phoebe
Holly
```

```
Sadie
Jessica
Steve
 .
 .
 .

SNAME
_____
Zelda
Mario
Romona
Ken
Smith
Jake

48 rows selected.
```

This query uses EXISTS, but has no correlation. This syntax infers that for each student tuple, we test the joined the `Grade_report` and `Section` tables to see whether there is a course number like COSC and a grade of B (which, of course, there is). We unnecessarily ask the subquery question over and over again. The result from this latter, uncorrelated EXISTS query is the same as:

```
SELECT  s.sname
FROM    Student s;
```

The point is that the correlation is necessary when we use EXISTS.

Consider another example in which a correlation could be used. Suppose we want to find the names of all students who have three or more B's. A first pass at a query might be something like this:

```
SELECT  s.sname
FROM    Student s WHERE "something" IN
 (SELECT "something"
  FROM    Grade_report
  WHERE   "count of grade = 'B'" > 2);
```

This query can be done with a HAVING clause as we saw previously, but we want to show how to do this in yet another way. Suppose we arrange the subquery to use the student number from the `Student` table as a filter and count in the subquery only when a row in the `Grade_report` table correlates to that student. The query looks like this:

```
SELECT  s.sname
FROM    Student s
WHERE   2 < (SELECT COUNT(*)
 FROM   Grade_report gr
 WHERE  gr.student_number = s.stno
 AND    gr.grade = 'B');
```

This results in the following output:

```
SNAME
───────────
Lineas
Mary
Lujack
Reva
Chris
Hillary
Phoebe
Holly

8 rows selected.
```

Although there is no EXISTS in the query, it is implied. The syntax of the query doesn't allow an EXISTS, but the sense of the query is "WHERE EXISTS a COUNT OF 2 WHICH IS LESS THAN...". In this correlated query, we must examine the Grade_report table for each member of the Student table to see whether the student has two B's. We test the entire Grade_report table for each student tuple in the outer query.

If it were possible, a subquery without the correlation would be more desirable. The overall query might be:

```
SELECT  s.sname
FROM    Student s
WHERE   s.stno in
```

We might attempt to write the following query:

```
SELECT  s.sname
FROM    Student s
WHERE   s.stno IN
 (SELECT gr.student_number
 FROM   Grade_report gr
 WHERE  gr.grade = 'B');
```

However, this would give us only students who had made at *least* one B, as seen in the following output:

```
SNAME
----------
Lineas
Mary
Brenda
Kelly
Lujack
Reva
Harley
Chris
Lynette
Hillary
Phoebe

SNAME
----------
Holly
Sadie
Jessica
Steve
Cedric
George
Cramer
Fraiser
Francis
Smithly
Sebastian

SNAME
----------
Lindsay
Stephanie
Zelda
Mario
Ken

27 rows selected.
```

To get students who have earned three B's, we could try the following query:

```
SELECT  s.sname
FROM    Student s
WHERE   s.stno IN
 (SELECT  gr.student_number, COUNT(*)
 FROM     Grade_report gr
 WHERE    gr.grade = 'B'
 GROUP BY gr.student_number
 HAVING COUNT(*) > 2);
```

However, this will not work because the subquery cannot have two attributes in its result set unless the main query has two attributes in the WHERE .. IN. Here, the subquery must have only gr.student_number to match s.stno. We might then construct an inline view as with the following query:

```
SELECT  s.sname
FROM    Student s
WHERE   s.stno IN
 (SELECT student_number
 FROM    (SELECT   student_number, COUNT(*)
         FROM      Grade_report gr
         WHERE     gr.grade = 'B'
         GROUP BY student_number
         HAVING COUNT(*) > 2));
```

This succeeds in Oracle but fails in some other SQLs. The output of this query would be:

```
SNAME
---------
Lineas
Mary
Lujack
Reva
Chris
Hillary
Phoebe
Holly

8 rows selected.
```

As you can see, we can query the database using various methods with SQL. In this case, the correlated query may be the easiest to see and perhaps the most efficient.

From IN to EXISTS

A simple example of converting from IN to EXISTS, or from uncorrelated to correlated queries (or vice versa), would be to move the set test in the WHERE .. IN of the uncorrelated query to the WHERE of the EXISTS in the correlated query. For example, note the placement of the set test in the following uncorrelated query:

```
SELECT *
FROM    Student s
WHERE   s.stno IN
 (SELECT g.student_number
  FROM    Grade_report g
  WHERE   grade = 'B');
```

Now note the placement of the set test in the following correlated query:

```
SELECT *
FROM    Student s
WHERE   EXISTS
 (SELECT g.student_number
  FROM    Grade_report g
  WHERE   grade = 'B'
  AND     s.stno = g.student_number);
```

This produces the following output:

STNO	SNAME	MAJO	CLASS	BDATE
2	Lineas	ENGL	1	15-APR-80
3	Mary	COSC	4	16-JUL-78
8	Brenda	COSC	2	13-AUG-77
13	Kelly	MATH	4	12-AUG-80
14	Lujack	COSC	1	12-FEB-77
15	Reva	MATH	2	10-JUN-80
19	Harley	POLY	2	16-APR-81
24	Chris	ACCT	4	12-FEB-78
34	Lynette	POLY	1	16-JUL-81
121	Hillary	COSC	1	16-JUL-77
122	Phoebe	ENGL	3	15-APR-80

```
STNO    SNAME        MAJO   CLASS  BDATE
_____   _____   __     _____  _____
123     Holly        POLY   4      15-JAN-81
125     Sadie        MATH   2      12-AUG-80
126     Jessica      POLY   2      16-JUL-81
127     Steve        ENGL   1      11-MAR-80
129     Cedric       ENGL   2      15-APR-80
132     George       POLY   1      16-APR-81
143     Cramer       ENGL   3      15-APR-80
144     Fraiser      POLY   1      16-JUL-81
146     Francis      ACCT   4      11-JUN-77
147     Smithly      ENGL   2      13-MAY-80
148     Sebastian    ACCT   2      14-OCT-76

STNO    SNAME        MAJO   CLASS  BDATE
_____   _____   __     _____  _____
155     Lindsay      UNKN   1      15-OCT-79
157     Stephanie    MATH          16-APR-81
5       Zelda        COSC          12-FEB-78
7       Mario        MATH          12-AUG-80
6       Ken          POLY          15-JUL-80

27 rows selected.
```

This example gives us a pattern to move from one kind of query to the other and to test the efficiency of both kinds of queries.

NOT EXISTS

There are some situations in which the EXISTS and NOT EXISTS predicates are necessary. For example, if we ask a "for all" question, it must be answered by "existence" (actually, the lack thereof [that is, "not existence"]). In logic, the statement "find x for all y" is logically equivalent to "do not find x where there does not exist a y." In SQL, there is no "for all" predicate. Instead, SQL uses the idea of "for all" logic with NOT EXISTS. (A word of caution, however: SQL is not simply a logic exercise, as we will see.) We will first see how EXISTS and NOT EXISTS work in SQL, and then tackle the "for all" problem. Consider the following query:

```
SELECT  s.sname
FROM    Student s
WHERE   EXISTS
 (SELECT 'X'
 FROM    Grade_report gr
 WHERE   s.stno = gr.student_number
 AND     gr.grade = 'C');
```

This produces the following output:

```
SNAME
-----------
Brenda
Richard
Reva
Donald
Susan
Monica
Bill
Sadie
Jessica
Steve
Alan

SNAME
-----------
Rachel
Smithly
Sebastian
Jake
Losmith
Genevieve
Thornton
Lionel
Benny
Gus
Zelda

SNAME
-----------
Mario
Ken

24 rows selected.
```

For this correlated query, "student names" are SELECTed when:

(a) the student is enrolled in a section (WHERE s.stno = gr.student_number), and

(b) the same student has a grade of C.

Both (a) and (b) must be TRUE for the student tuple to be SELECTed. Recall that we use SELECT 1 or SELECT 'X' in our inner query because we want the subquery to return something if the subquery is TRUE. Therefore, SELECT .. EXISTS "says" SELECT .. WHERE TRUE, and the inner query is TRUE if any row (tuple) is SELECTed in the inner query. Now consider the following query, which contains a NOT EXISTS:

```
SELECT  s.sname
FROM    Student s
WHERE NOT EXISTS
  (SELECT 'X'
  FROM    Grade_report gr
  WHERE   s.stno = gr.student_number
  AND     gr.grade = 'C');
```

This produces the following output:

```
SNAME
----------
Lineas
Mary
Kelly
Lujack
Elainie
Harley
Chris
Lynette
Hillary
Phoebe
Holly

SNAME
----------
Brad
Cedric
George
Jerry
Cramer
Fraiser
Harrison
Francis
Lindsay
Stephanie
Romona

SNAME
----------
Smith
Jake

24 rows selected.
```

In this query, we are still SELECTing with the pattern SELECT .. WHERE TRUE because all SELECTs with EXISTS work that way. However, the twist is that the subquery must be FALSE to be SELECTed with NOT EXISTS. If the subquery is FALSE, then NOT EXISTS is TRUE and the outer row (tuple) is SELECTed.

Now, logic implies that if either (a) s.stno <> gr.student_number or (b) gr.grade <> 'C', then the subquery "fails"—that is, it is FALSE for that student tuple. Because the subquery is FALSE, the NOT EXISTS would return a TRUE for that row. Unfortunately, this logic is not quite what happens. Recall that we characterized the correlated query as follows:

```
LOOP1: For each tuple in Student s DO
    LOOP2: For each tuple in Grade_report DO
      IF (gr.student_number = s.stno) THEN
      IF (gr.grade = 'C') THEN TRUE
    END LOOP2;
    if TRUE, then student tuple is SELECTed
END LOOP1;
```

Note that LOOP2 is completed before the next student is tested. In other words, just because a student number exists that is not equal, it will not cause the subquery to be FALSE. Rather, the entire subquery table is parsed.

For the case EXISTS WHERE s.stno = gr.student_number..., is there a gr.grade = 'C'? If, when the student numbers are equal, no C can be found, then the subquery *fails*—it is FALSE for that outer student tuple. So with NOT EXISTS, we will SELECT students who have student numbers equal in Grade_report and Student tables but who have no 'C' in the Grade_report table. The point about "no C in the Grade_report table" can only be answered TRUE by looking at all the rows in the inner query.

SQL Universal and Existential Qualifiers: The "For All" Query

In SQL, "for all" or "for each" are the universal qualifiers, while "there exists" is the existential qualifier. As we mentioned above, SQL does not have a "for all" predicate; however, logically, the following relationship exists:

For all x, WHERE P(x) is true

This is logically the same as:

There does not exist an x, WHERE P(x) is not true.

A "for all" type SQL query is less straightforward than the other queries we have used. The "for all" type SQL query involves a double-nested, correlated query using the NOT EXISTS predicate. The next section shows an example.

Example 1

To show a "for all" type SQL query, we will need to use a database other than our student records. We have created a table called Cap (for "capability"). This table has names of students who have multiple foreign-language capabilities. We begin by looking at the table by typing the following query:

```
SELECT *
FROM Cap
ORDER BY name;
```

This produces the following output:

NAME	LANGU
BRENDA	FRENCH
BRENDA	CHINESE
BRENDA	SPANISH
JOE	CHINESE
KENT	CHINESE
LUJACK	FRENCH
LUJACK	GERMAN
LUJACK	CHINESE
LUJACK	SPANISH
MARY JO	GERMAN
MARY JO	CHINESE
MARY JO	FRENCH
MELANIE	FRENCH
MELANIE	CHINESE
RICHARD	GERMAN
RICHARD	SPANISH
RICHARD	CHINESE
RICHARD	FRENCH

18 rows selected.

Suppose we want to find out which languages are spoken by all students. Although this manual exercise would be very difficult for a large table, for our practice table, we can answer the question by

(a) displaying and studying the table ordered by name

(b) displaying and studying the table ordered by language

To see how to answer a question of this type for a much larger table where sorting and examining the result would be tedious, we will construct a query. We will show the query and then dissect the result. The query to answer our question of which languages are spoken by all students looks like this:

```
SELECT name, langu
FROM  Cap x
WHERE NOT EXISTS
     (SELECT 'X'
      FROM Cap y
      WHERE NOT EXISTS
              (SELECT 'X'
               FROM Cap z
               WHERE x.langu =z.langu
                              AND y.name=z.name));
```

As you will see, all of the "for all/for each" questions follow this double-nested, correlated NOT EXISTS pattern. It is convenient to use the table aliases (x, y, and z) here for the three instances of Cap.

The output for this query will be:

```
NAME       LANGU
_____     ____

BRENDA     CHINESE
RICHARD    CHINESE
LUJACK     CHINESE
MARY JO    CHINESE
MELANIE    CHINESE
JOE        CHINESE
KENT       CHINESE

7 rows selected.
```

To SELECT a "language" spoken by all students, the query proceeds as follows:

a. SELECT a row in Cap (x) (outer query).

b. For that row, begin SELECTing each row again in Cap (y) (middle query).

c. For each of the middle query rows, we want the inner query (Cap (z)) to be TRUE for all cases of the middle query (remember that TRUE is translated to FALSE by the NOT EXISTS). As each inner query is satisfied (it is TRUE), it forces the middle query to continue looking for a match—to look at all cases and eventually conclude FALSE (evaluate to FALSE overall). If the middle query is FALSE, the outer query sees TRUE because of its NOT EXISTS.

To make the middle query (y) find FALSE, all of the inner query (z) occurrences must be TRUE (that is, the languages from the outer query must exist with all names from the middle one [y] in the inner one [z]). For an eventual "match," every row in the middle query for an outer query row must be FALSE (that is, every row in the inner query is TRUE).

These steps are explained in further detail in the next example where we used a smaller table, Cap1 (so it will be easier to understand the explanation).

Example 2

> Note that this table, Cap1, does not exist. You will have to create it. Keep the attribute names and types similar to the table, Cap.

Suppose we had this simpler table, Cap1, as shown below:

NAME	LANGU
Joe	Spanish
Mary	Spanish
Mary	French

Let's now look at how we can answer the same question, which languages are spoken by all students, using this smaller table, Cap1.

The query will be similar to the one used in Example 1:

```
SELECT name, langu
FROM  Cap1 x
WHERE NOT EXISTS
      (SELECT 'X'
      FROM Cap1 y
      WHERE NOT EXISTS
      (SELECT 'X'
              FROM    Cap1 z
              WHERE x.langu = z.langu
              AND     y.name = z.name))
ORDER BY langu;
```

The output for this query will be:

```
NAME           LANGU
_____    _____

JOE            SPANISH
MARY           SPANISH
```

How This Query Works

The following is a step-by-step explanation of how this query would work in the Cap1 table:

1. The tuple <Joe, Spanish> is SELECTed by the outer query (x).

2. The tuple <Joe, Spanish> is SELECTed by the middle query (y).

3. The tuple <Joe, Spanish> is SELECTed by the inner query (z).

4. The inner query is TRUE:

X.LANGU = Spanish
Z.LANGU = Spanish
Y.NAME = Joe
Z.NAME = Joe

5. Because the inner query is TRUE, the NOT EXISTS of the middle query translates this to FALSE and continues with the next row in the middle query. The middle query SELECTs <Mary, Spanish> and the inner query begins again with <Joe, Spanish> seeing:

X.LANGU = Spanish
Z.LANGU = Spanish
Y.NAME = Mary
Z.NAME = Joe

This is FALSE, so the inner query SELECTs a second row <Mary, Spanish>:

X.LANGU = Spanish
Z.LANGU = Spanish
Y.NAME = Mary
Z.NAME = Mary

This is TRUE, so the inner query is TRUE. (Notice that the X.LANGU has not changed yet; the outer query (X) is still on the first row.)

6. Because the inner query is TRUE, the "NOT EXISTS" of the middle query translates this to FALSE and continues with the next row in the middle query.

The middle query now SELECTs <Mary, French> and the inner query begins again with <Joe, Spanish> seeing:

X.LANGU = Spanish
Z.LANGU = Spanish
Y.NAME   = Mary
Z.NAME   = Joe

This is FALSE, so the inner query SELECTs a second row <Mary, Spanish>:

X.LANGU = Spanish
Z.LANGU = Spanish
Y.NAME   = Mary
Z.NAME   = Mary

This is TRUE, so the inner query is TRUE.

7. Because the inner query is TRUE, the NOT EXISTS of the middle query again converts this TRUE to FALSE and wants to continue, but the middle query is out of tuples. This means that the middle query is FALSE.

8. Because the middle query is FALSE, and because we are testing

"SELECT distinct name, language
 FROM Cap1 x
 WHERE NOT EXISTS
    (SELECT 'X' FROM Cap1 y ...",

the FALSE from the middle query is translated to TRUE for the outer query and the tuple <Joe,Spanish> is SELECTed for the result set. Note that "Spanish" occurs with both "Joe" and "Mary."

9. The second row in the outer query will repeat the steps FROM above for <Mary, Spanish>. The value "Spanish" will be seen to occur with both "Joe" and "Mary" as <Mary, Spanish> is added to the result set.

10. The third tuple in the outer query begins with <Mary, French>. The middle query SELECTs <Joe, Spanish> and the inner query SELECTs <Joe, Spanish>. The inner query sees:

    X.LANGU = French
    Z.LANGU = Spanish
    Y.NAME = Joe
    Z.NAME = Mary

This is FALSE, so the inner query SELECTs a second row, <Mary, Spanish>:

    X.LANGU = French
    Z.LANGU = Spanish
    Y.NAME = Joe
    Z.NAME = Mary

This is FALSE, so the inner query SELECTs a third row, <Mary, French>:

    X.LANGU = French
    Z.LANGU = French
    Y.NAME = Joe
    Z.NAME = Mary

This is also FALSE. The inner query fails. The inner query evaluates to FALSE, which causes the middle query to see TRUE because of the NOT EXISTS. Because the middle query sees TRUE, it is finished and evaluated to TRUE. Because the middle query evaluates to TRUE, the NOT EXISTS in the outer query changes this to FALSE and "X.LANGU = French" fails. It failed because X.LANGU = French did not occur with all a values of NAME.

The "For All" Query as a Relational Division

Consider again the "for all" query we have presented:

```
SELECT name, langu
FROM  Cap1 x
WHERE NOT EXISTS
      (SELECT 'X'
      FROM Cap1 y
      WHERE NOT EXISTS
      (SELECT 'X'
            FROM  Cap1 z
            WHERE x.langu = z.langu
            AND   y.name = z.name))
ORDER BY langu;
```

The tip-off of what a query of this kind means can be found in the innermost query. You will find a phrase that says "WHERE *x.langu* = *z.langu*…". The *x.langu* is where the query is testing which *language* occurs *for all* names.

This query is a SQL realization of a relational division exercise. Relational division is a "for all" operation just like that which we have illustrated above. In relational algebra, the query must be set up into a divisor, dividend, and quotient in this pattern:

Quotient (B) ➡ Dividend (A, B) divided by Divisor (A).

If the question is "What language for *all* names?" then the Divisor, A, is names, and the quotient, B, is language. It is most prudent to set up SQL like relational algebra with a two-column table (like Cap or Cap1) for the Dividend and then treat the Divisor and the Quotient appropriately. Our query will have the attribute for language, x.langu, in the inner query, as langu will be the quotient. We have chosen to also report name in the result set.

Example 3

Note that the preceding query is completely different from the following one, which asks, "Which *students* speak all languages?":

```
SELECT DISTINCT name, langu
FROM   Cap1 x
WHERE NOT EXISTS
        (SELECT 'X'
        FROM Cap1 y
        WHERE NOT EXISTS
                (SELECT 'X'
                FROM    Cap1 z
                WHERE   y.langu = z.langu
                AND     x.name = z.name))
ORDER BY langu;
```

This would produce the following output:

NAME	LANGU
MARY	FRENCH
MARY	SPANISH

2 rows selected.

Note the phraseology, "for all languages," which infers that x.name will occur in the WHERE of the inner query.

Using the table Cap, the following query:

```
SELECT DISTINCT name, langu
FROM  Cap x
WHERE NOT EXISTS
        (SELECT 'X'
        FROM Cap y
        WHERE NOT EXISTS
                (SELECT 'X'
                FROM    Cap z
                WHERE   y.langu = z.langu
                AND     x.name = z.name))
ORDER BY langu;
```

Would produce:

```
NAME        LANGU
_____      ____
LUJACK      CHINESE
RICHARD     CHINESE
LUJACK      FRENCH
RICHARD     FRENCH
LUJACK      GERMAN
RICHARD     GERMAN
LUJACK      SPANISH
RICHARD     SPANISH

8 rows selected.
```

Here note that the inner query contains x.name, which means the question was "Which names occur for *all* languages?" or, put another way, "Which students speak all languages?" The "all" goes with languages for x.name.

CHAPTER 9 EXERCISES

1. List the names of students who have received C's. Do this in three ways: (a) as a *join*, (b) as an *uncorrelated* subquery, and (c) as a *correlated* subquery. Show both results and account for any differences.

2. In the section "Existence Queries and Correlation," we were asked to find the names of students who have taken a computer science class

and earned a grade of B. We noted that this could be done in several ways. One query could look like the following:

```
SELECT  s.sname
FROM    Student s
WHERE   s.stno IN
  (SELECT gr.student_number
  FROM    Grade_report gr, Section
  WHERE   Section.section_id = gr.section_id /* join con-
                                                dition
                                                Grade_repo
                                                rt-Section
                                                */

  AND     Section.course_num LIKE 'COSC____'
  AND     gr.grade = 'B');
```

Re-do this query putting the finding of the COSC course in a correlated subquery. The query should be:

The Student table uncorrelated subquery to the Grade_report table correlated EXISTS to the Section table.

3.   In the section "SQL Universal and Existential Qualifiers," we illustrated an existence query:

```
SELECT  s.sname
FROM    Student s
WHERE EXISTS
  (SELECT 'X'
  FROM    Grade_report gr
  WHERE   s.stno = gr.student_number
  AND     gr.grade = 'C');
```

and a NOT EXISTS version:

```
SELECT  s.sname
FROM    Student s
WHERE NOT EXISTS
  (SELECT 'X'
  FROM    Grade_report gr
  WHERE   s.stno = gr.student_number
  AND     gr.grade = 'C');
```

Show that the EXISTS version is the complement of the NOT EXISTS version—count the tuples in the EXISTS result, the tuples in the NOT EXISTS result, and the tuples in the Student table. Also, devise a query to test the compliment with IN and NOT..IN.

4.   a.   Discover whether all students take courses by counting the students, then count those students whose student numbers are in

the Grade_report table and those who are not. Use IN and then NOT..IN and then use EXISTS and NOT EXISTS. How many students take courses and how many students do not?

b. Find out which students have taken courses but who have not taken COSC courses. Create a set of student names and courses from the Student, Grade_report, and Section tables (use the prefix COSC to indicate COSC courses). Then use NOT..IN to "subtract" from that set another set of student names where students (who take courses) have taken COSC courses. For this set difference, use NOT..IN.

c. Change NOT..IN to NOT EXISTS (with other appropriate changes) and explain the result. The "other appropriate changes" include adding the correlation and the change of the result attribute in the subquery set.

5. There exists a table called Plants. List the table and then find out what company or companies have plants in all cities. Verify your result manually. Note: if you are having trouble finding Plants, ask yourself who owns the table Plants?

6. **a.** Run the following query and print the result:

```
SELECT distinct name, langu
FROM    Cap x
WHERE NOT EXISTS
  (SELECT 'X'
  FROM    Cap y
  WHERE NOT EXISTS
    (SELECT 'X'
    FROM    Cap z
    WHERE   X.langu =Z.langu
    AND     Y.name=Z.name));
```

Save the query (e.g., save forall) and hand in the result.

b. Re-create the Cap table under your account number (that is, call it some other name such as LANG1). To do this, first create the table and then use the INSERT statement with the subselect option (INSERT INTO LANG1 AS SELECT * FROM Cap;).

c. Add a new person to your table who speaks only BENGALI.

d. Recall your SELECT from above (get forall).

e. CHANGE the table from CAP to LANG1 (for all occurrences use CHANGE/Cap/lang1/ repeatedly, assuming that you called your table LANG1).

f. Start the new query (the one you just created with LANG1 in it).

g. How is this result different from the situation when "Newperson" was not in LANG1? Provide an explanation of why the query did what it did.

7. (Refer to Exercise 7 in Chapter 7) The D2M table is a list of four-letter department codes with the department names. In Exercise 7-7, we created a table called Secretary, which should now have data like this:

Secretary

dCode	Name
ACCT	Sally
COSC	Chris
ENGL	Maria
null	Brenda

In Exercise 7-7, we did the following:

a. Create a query that lists the names of departments that have secretaries (use IN and the Secretary table in a subquery with the Department_to_major table in the outer query). Save this query as q77a.

b. Create a query that lists the names of departments that do not have secretaries (use NOT..IN). Save this query as q77b.

c. Add one more row to the Secretary table that contains <null,'Brenda'>. (This could be a situation in which we have hired Brenda but have not yet assigned her to a department.)

d. Recall q77a and re-run it.

e. Recall q77b and re-run it.

We remarked in Exercise 7-7 that the NOT..IN predicate has problems with nulls: The behavior of NOT..IN when nulls exist may surprise you. If nulls may exist in the subquery, then NOT..IN should not be used. If you use NOT..IN in a subquery, you must ensure that nulls will not occur in the subquery or you must use some other predicate (such as NOT EXISTS). Perhaps the best solution is to avoid NOT..IN.

Here, we repeat Exercise 7-7 using NOT EXISTS:

a. Re-word query q77a to use EXIST. You will have to correlate the inner and outer queries. Save this query as q99a.

b. Re-word query q77b to use NOT EXISTS. You will have to correlate the inner and outer queries. Save this query as q99b. You should *not* have a phrase "IS NOT NULL" in your NOT EXISTS query.

c. Re-run q99a with and without <null, Brenda>.

d. Re-run q99b with and without <null, Brenda>.

Note the difference in behavior versus the original question. List the names of those departments that have/do not have secretaries. The point here is to encourage you to use NOT EXISTS in a correlated query rather than NOT..IN.

REFERENCE

Earp, R., & Bagui, S. (2001). *An In-Depth Look at Oracle's Correlated Subqueries*, Oracle Internals, Vol. 3(4), 2–8.

CREATE TABLEs and SQLLOADER

In previous chapters, we concentrated primarily on retrieving information from an existing database. This chapter revisits the creation and loading of tables and shows some of the CONSTRAINTs that we can place on table definition. In particular, we'll review the "simple" CREATE TABLE and discuss the NOT NULL constraint as well as PRIMARY KEY constraints. We'll also discuss the UNIQUE and CHECK constraints and referential integrity. Finally, we'll examine the SQLLOADER and a couple of examples of it in use.

The "Simple" CREATE TABLE

You have seen a "simple" CREATE TABLE statement in earlier chapters. To refresh your memory, consider the following example:

```
CREATE TABLE Test1
    (name            VARCHAR2(20),
     ssn             CHAR(9),
     dept_number     INTEGER,
     acct_balance    NUMBER (9,2));
```

In this example, we create a table called Test1.

- Name is a variable character string with a maximum length of 20,

- ssn (social security number) is a fixed-length character string of 9,

- `dept_number` is an integer (which in Oracle simply means no decimals are allowed), and

- `acct_balance` is an attribute that can have 9 digits with the last two assumed after the decimal (similar to a COBOL 9(7)V99 field).

Some notes:

1. Oracle does not use a plethora of data types. For numeric values there is NUMBER, INTEGER, SMALLINT, or FLOAT. For numeric values with decimals, you should use NUMBER with values like NUMBER(9,2) or NUMBER(3,1). INTEGER(INT) is the same as NUMBER except that it doesn't accept decimal digits as an argument. If we define an attribute to be of type INTEGER and insert a value with decimal parts, the decimal parts will be truncated. Note that SMALLINT or FLOAT can be used like NUMBER, but the SMALLINT data type will also truncate any decimal places. SMALLINT, INTEGER, and FLOAT data types are ANSI SQL data types. Oracle will automatically convert them to an equivalent NUMBER data type with appropriate scale and precision. You can also specify DOUBLE PRECISION, REAL, or DECIMAL which are also ANSI standard, and will convert to NUMBER with appropriate scale and precision.

2. VARCHAR2 is preferred by Oracle and is in line with the correct SQL standard.

3. Beyond choosing types for attributes, you may need to make other choices to create an effective database. Some of these "add-ons" are called CONSTRAINTs because they make you enter *good* data and hence maintain the integrity of the database. In the following sections, we will explore these CONSTRAINTs, including NOT NULL, PRIMARY KEY, UNIQUE, CHECK, and referential CONSTRAINTs.

When you are finished with the *test* table, Test1, it is appropriate to delete (DROP) it with the following statement:

```
SQL> DROP TABLE Test1;
```

The NOT NULL Constraint

The NOT NULL constraint is an attribute integrity CONSTRAINT that allows the database creator to deny the creation of a tuple (row) where an attribute would have a null value. Usually, a null signifies a missing data item. As we have mentioned in previous chapters, nulls in databases present an interpretation problem—do they mean not applicable, not

> We will re-create Test1 and similar tables with other options in the following sections, so if you are doing the exercises as they are presented, delete (DROP) the tables when you are finished with them.

available, unknown, or what? If a situation in which a null is present could affect the integrity of the database, then the table creator can deny anyone the ability to insert nulls into the table for that attribute. To deny nulls, we create a table with the NOT NULL constraint on an attribute(s). For example, the dept_number attribute with NOT NULL would look like this:

```
CREATE TABLE Test1
 (name            VARCHAR2(20),
  ssn             CHAR(9),
  dept_number     INTEGER NOT NULL,
  acct_balance    NUMBER (9,2));
```

This produces the following output:

```
Table created.
```

The NOT NULL constraint can also be added to the attribute after the fact. To add a NOT NULL constraint to an existing table, an ALTER TABLE command is used. For example, consider the following:

```
ALTER TABLE Test1
MODIFY name NOT NULL;
```

This produces the following output:

```
Table altered.
```

This ALTER TABLE command placed the NOT NULL constraint on the attribute, name. To view the constraints on Test1, we could now type:

```
DESC Test1
```

This would produce:

Name	Null?	Type
NAME	NOT NULL	VARCHAR2(20)
SSN		CHAR(9)
DEPT_NUMBER	NOT NULL	NUMBER(38)
ACCT_BALANCE		NUMBER(9,2)

Note the NOT NULL constraints placed on the `name` and `dept_number` attributes in the above output. The NOT NULL constraint was placed on the `dept_number` attribute during the CREATE TABLE.

PRIMARY KEY Constraints

When creating a table, a PRIMARY KEY constraint will prevent duplicate attribute values for the attribute(s) defined as a primary key. Internally, the designation of a PRIMARY KEY also creates a primary key index. Designation of a PRIMARY KEY will be necessary for the referential integrity constraints that follow. The designation of a PRIMARY KEY also automatically puts the NOT NULL constraint in the definition of the attribute(s). A fundamental rule of relational database is that primary keys cannot be null.

Creating the PRIMARY KEY Constraint

There are several ways to create a primary key:

1. The first way to create a primary key is to add the PRIMARY KEY constraint to the attribute upon creation as follows:

```
CREATE TABLE xxx
    (ssn    CHAR(9)        CONSTRAINT ssn_pk PRIMARY KEY,
    name    VARCHAR2(20), etc.
```

This technique is called adding the constraint at the "column level." ssn_pk is the name of the PRIMARY KEY constraint for `ssn`. It is conventional to name all CONSTRAINTs (although most people don't bother to name NOT NULL constraints). If we don't give a CONSTRAINT a name, the system will define one; however, it's much better if we know what the name is (or should be) so that we can manipulate the CONSTRAINT (using ENABLE, DISABLE, or DROP).

2. The second way to create a primary key is at the table level. In this method, the CREATE TABLE looks like this:

```
CREATE TABLE xxx
  (ssn              CHAR(9),
  blah blah...,
  acct_balance      NUMBER,
  CONSTRAINT ssn_pk PRIMARY KEY (ssn))
```

3. The third way to create a primary key is at the table level by adding the stipulation of the PRIMARY KEY *post hoc*. This can be done by using the ALTER TABLE command as follows:

```
ALTER TABLE xxx
ADD CONSTRAINT ssn_pk PRIMARY KEY (SSN);
```

Adding a Concatenated Primary Key

The second and third ways of creating a primary key at the table level are the only ways to designate a concatenated PRIMARY KEY. A statement like this is syntactically incorrect:

```
CREATE TABLE xxx
  (ssn              CHAR(9)      PRIMARY KEY,
   salary           NUMBER(9,2)  PRIMARY KEY);
```

However, we can add the primary key at the table level in the following way:

```
CREATE TABLE xxx
  (ssn                  CHAR(9),
   salary               NUMBER(9,2),
   CONSTRAINT ssn_salary_pk    PRIMARY KEY (ssn, salary));
```

We can also add our PRIMARY KEY in two separate statements with a CREATE TABLE and then an ALTER TABLE. First the CREATE TABLE:

```
CREATE TABLE xxx
  (ssn                  CHAR(9),
   salary    NUMBER(9,2));
```

Then the ALTER TABLE command can be used to add the primary key constraint, as shown below:

```
ALTER TABLE xxx
ADD CONSTRAINT ssn_salary_pk PRIMARY KEY (ssn, salary);
```

> If the primary key is a single column primary key, then it can be added at the column level when the table is created. If the primary key is a concatenated key, it must be added at the table level (either at creation or later). If the primary key is added after the table is created, it must be added at the table level, regardless of the number of columns in the key.

Another Example of Adding a Concatenated Primary Key

In our `Grade_report` table, a grade cannot be determined by either student number or section_id alone; it requires both attributes to uniquely identify a grade. The CREATE/ALTER TABLE for the `Grade_report` table is shown below. First we create the `Grade_report` table as shown below:

```
CREATE TABLE      Grade_report
 (student_number CHAR(9),
 section_id       CHAR(9),
 grade            CHAR(1));
```

Then we add a primary key constraint using the ALTER TABLE command, as shown below:

```
ALTER TABLE     Grade_report
ADD CONSTRAINT  snum_section_pk
PRIMARY KEY     (student_number, section_id);
```

The UNIQUE Constraint

Like PRIMARY KEY, UNIQUE is another attribute integrity CONSTRAINT. UNIQUE will disallow duplicate entries for an attribute even though the attribute is not a PRIMARY KEY. The UNIQUE constraint is different from the PRIMARY KEY constraint in three ways:

1. UNIQUE keys can exist in addition to (or without) the PRIMARY KEY.

2. UNIQUE does *not* necessitate NOT NULL, whereas PRIMARY KEY does.

3. There can be more than one UNIQUE key, but only one PRIMARY KEY.

As an example of the UNIQUE constraint, suppose that we created a table of names and occupational titles in which everyone was supposed to have a unique title. Suppose further that the table had an employee number as a PRIMARY KEY. The CREATE TABLE might look like this:

```
CREATE TABLE Emp
 (empno   NUMBER(3),
```

```
name        VARCHAR2(20),
title       VARCHAR2(20)
CONSTRAINT  empno_pk    PRIMARY KEY (empno),
CONSTRAINT  title_uk    UNIQUE (title));
```

When adding a UNIQUE constraint, an index will be built automatically for those attributes included in the unique key.

The CHECK Constraint

In addition to the PRIMARY KEY and the UNIQUE constraints, we can put a CHECK constraint on our attribute definition in Oracle. A CHECK constraint will disallow a value that is outside the bounds of the CHECK. Consider the following example:

```
CREATE TABLE StudentA
  (ssn      CHAR(9),
   class    NUMBER(1)   CONSTRAINT class_ck CHECK (class
                        BETWEEN 1 AND 4),
   name     VARCHAR(2));
```

Here we could not, for example, successfully execute INSERT INTO StudentA VALUES ('123456789',5,'Smith'). We could, however, enter a null value for class, which technically does not violate the integrity CONSTRAINT (unless we so specify by making class also NOT NULL).

> Technically speaking, NOT NULL is also a form of a CHECK constraint.

Referential Integrity

Relationships in relational database are logical connections between tables. Relationships are realized via foreign key–primary key constraints. Not only do we make a logical connection by defining the constraint, but also we can enforce a referential integrity CONSTRAINT, a foreign key–primary key constraint. A referential integrity CONSTRAINT is one in which a row in one table cannot exist if a value in that table refers to a value in another table that does not exist. To clarify the idea of referential integrity, suppose we have the following two tables:

Department

deptno	deptname
1	Accounting
2	Personnel
3	Development

Employee

empno	empname	dept
100	Jones	2
101	Smith	1
102	Adams	1
104	Harris	3

And suppose that `deptno` is the primary key of the `Department` table, and `dept` is the foreign key in the `Employee` table. If we were trying to perform a join, the `deptno` field of the `Department` table would be joined to the `dept` field of the `Employee` table. The relationship between the `Department` and `Employee` tables is through the primary key of the `Department` table (deptno), and the foreign key of the `Employee` table (dept).

To maintain referential integrity, it would be inappropriate to enter a tuple (row) in the `Employee` table that did not have a department number defined in the `Department` table. To try to insert the tuple

    <105,'Walsh',4>

in the `Employee` table would be a violation of the integrity of the database because department number 4 does not exist (that is, it has no integrity).

It would likewise be invalid to try to change a value in an existing tuple (that is, perform an UPDATE) to make it equal to a value that did not exist. If, for example, we tried to change

    <100,'Jones',2>

to

    <100,'Jones',5>

it would be an operation that violated database integrity because there was no department 5.

While `deptno` in the `Department` table cannot be null due to the Entity Integrity Constraint, `dept` in the `Employee` table can be null. It is acceptable for dept to be undefined, but it is not acceptable for dept to point to a non-existent deptno. If the Employee table were created with dept as NOT NULL, this would constitute a mandatory relationship. If dept could be null, then the relationship would be optional.

Finally, it would be invalid to DELETE a tuple in the Department table that contained a value for department number that was already in the Employee table. For example, if

```
<2,'Personnel'>
```

were deleted from the Department table, then the tuple

```
<100,'Jones',2>
```

would refer to a non-existent department. It would therefore be a reference or relationship with no integrity.

In each case (INSERT, UPDATE, and DELETE), we say that there needs to be a referential integrity CONSTRAINT on the dept attribute in the Employee table referencing deptno in the Department table. When this primary key (deptno in the Department table)–foreign key (dept in the Employee table) is defined, we have defined the relationship of the Employee table to the Department table.

In the INSERT and UPDATE cases from earlier, we would expect (correctly) that the usual action of the system would be to deny the action. In the case of the DELETE, there are options we will explore that allow us to either disallow (RESTRICT) the DELETE or CASCADE the delete operation. Some versions of SQL, including later versions of Oracle, also have a DELETE option to set newly unreferenced foreign keys to null.

> A foreign key constraint must point to the primary key of another table (or the same table), or it must be null. If a NOT NULL constraint is placed on the foreign key column, it enforces a mandatory relationship between parent and child entities, while allowing null values allows an optional relationship.

Defining the Referential Integrity CONSTRAINT

To enable a referential integrity CONSTRAINT, it is necessary for the attribute that is being referenced to be first defined as a PRIMARY KEY. In the Employee-Department example above, we have to first create the

Department table with a PRIMARY KEY. The creation statement for the Department table (the *referenced* table) could look like this:

```
CREATE TABLE Department
  (deptno                      NUMBER(3),
  deptname                     VARCHAR2(20),
  CONSTRAINT      deptno_pk    PRIMARY KEY (deptno));
```

The Employee table (the *referencing* table) would then be created using the following statement:

```
CREATE TABLE Employee
  (empno   NUMBER(4)
          CONSTRAINT empno_pk PRIMARY KEY,
  empname VARCHAR2(20),
  dept    NUMBER(3) CONSTRAINT dept_fk
          REFERENCES Department(deptno));
```

The CREATE TABLE Employee… statement defines an attribute, dept, to be of type NUMBER(3), but the statement goes further in defining dept to be a *foreign* key that references another table, Department. Within the Department table, the referenced attribute, deptno, must be an already defined PRIMARY KEY.

Also note that the Department CREATE TABLE must be executed first. If we use CREATE TABLE as illustrated for the Employee table before the Department table was created we would be trying to reference a non-existent table and we would get an error.

Adding the Foreign Key After Tables Are Created

As we have seen with other constraints, the foreign key can be added after tables are created. To do so, we must have set up the primary key of the referenced table. The syntax of the ALTER TABLE command would look like this:

```
ALTER TABLE xxx
  ADD CONSTRAINT dept_fk
  FOREIGN KEY (dept)
  REFERENCES Department(deptno);
```

The (optional) name of the CONSTRAINT is dept_fk. Note that the column names must match exactly, so it would be prudent to do a DESC *tablename* before actually writing the ALTER TABLE command so that you can be sure of the column names.

> However, if both CREATE TABLE statements were enclosed within a CREATE SCHEMA statement, you can create the Employee table before the Department table.

Using Delete and the Referential Constraint

There are three possibilities in the DELETE subcategory of foreign key referential CONSTRAINT enforcement in Oracle—RESTRICT, CASCADE, and SET NULL. RESTRICT will not allow you to delete a referenced key in the referenced table at all. CASCADE will not only allow the deletion, it will delete all dependent references to the table. SET NULL will delete the entry in the primary key table and then set the dependent values to null.

ON DELETE RESTRICT

ON DELETE RESTRICT is the default referential integrity delete option and is not explicitly allowed in Oracle. In the previous CREATE TABLE Employee... example, the delete defaults to being a RESTRICT. Because of this constraint, we cannot violate the referential CONSTRAINT; we will get an error message if we try to do so.

After the two tables are created, it is necessary to populate the Department table first so that when employees are added to the database, valid department numbers can be used. This population ordering can be overcome by using ALTER TABLE .. DISABLE and disabling the CONSTRAINT by name. However, this is not advisable unless a great number of tuples must be loaded at once.

ON DELETE CASCADE

The referential integrity delete option of ON DELETE CASCADE is more dangerous than the other options in that it tells us to delete the tuples in the "dependent table" (in this case, the Employee table) that are affected by the deletion of the tuple in the referenced table (in this case, the Department table). Suppose, for example, we had a deptno = 3 in the Department table. Also suppose we had the Employee table referencing the Department table, and we had employees in department 3. If we deleted department 3 in the Department table, then with CASCADE we would also delete all employees in the Employee table with dept = 3.

When adding the ON DELETE CASCADE option, the option is added after the REFERENCES clause of CREATE TABLE as shown below:

```
CREATE TABLE Employee
 (empno      NUMBER(3)    CONSTRAINT empno_pk PRIMARY KEY,
 empname     VARCHAR2(20),
 dept        NUMBER(3)    REFERENCES department(deptno)
                          ON DELETE CASCADE);
```

> There is no warning in Oracle that you have deleted rows in the dependent table when CASCADE is in effect—the dependent rows just disappear. Thus, you should audit your database before and after issuing a DELETE command that involves referential CASCADEs.

ON DELETE SET NULL

In later versions of Oracle, the SET NULL option for referential integrity was added. Remember that a foreign key, if allowed to be null, indicates an optional relationship. If the relationship is mandatory, a foreign key cannot be null. If the relationship is optional, then the ON DELETE SET NULL may be appropriate for the referential constraint. The syntax for the CREATE TABLE is similar to our previous examples except for the REFERENCES clause:

```
CREATE TABLE Employee
  (empno      NUMBER(3)      CONSTRAINT empno_pk PRIMARY KEY,
  empname     VARCHAR2(20),
  dept        NUMBER(3)      REFERENCES department(deptno)
                            ON DELETE SET NULL);
```

If a department in the Department table is deleted and if there are dependent rows from the Employee table, then the dependent rows will have their values for the dept field set to null.

More on CONSTRAINT Names

The table user_constraints contains the CONSTRAINT information we have placed on your table(s). The following is the DESC of user_constraints:

Name	Null?	Type
OWNER	NOT NULL	VARCHAR2(30)
CONSTRAINT_NAME	NOT NULL	VARCHAR2(30)
CONSTRAINT_TYPE		VARCHAR2(1)
TABLE_NAME	NOT NULL	VARCHAR2(30)
SEARCH_CONDITION		LONG
R_OWNER		VARCHAR2(30)
R_CONSTRAINT_NAME		VARCHAR2(30)
DELETE_RULE		VARCHAR2(9)
STATUS		VARCHAR2(8)

Thus, if we had created a table called `Test1` with an unnamed CON-STRAINT (for example, an unnamed PRIMARY KEY) in it, we could see the CONSTRAINTs with a query like the following:

```
SELECT table_name, constraint_name, constraint_type
FROM user_constraints;
```

This would produce the following output:

TABLE_NAME	CONSTRAINT_NAME	C
TEST1	SYS_C001930	P

`Test1` is the name of the table on which the constraint was created. The SYS_C001930 is a system-allocated CONSTRAINT name. This is what happens when you don't name the CONSTRAINT yourself. The P tells us that this is a PRIMARY KEY constraint. The C in the previous output stands for CONSTRAINT_TYPE. The values for the available constraint types are as follows:

P is a primary key
U is unique
R is a foreign key
C is a check constraint
V is a WITH CHECK OPTION for views

In an earlier chapter, you learned how to create a view in Oracle. As we discussed, a view can provide restrictions on what can be viewed (selected). When a view is created, we can specify a WITH CHECK OPTION, which would also disallow INSERTs or UPDATEs to the original table.

SQLLOADER

As discussed in earlier chapters, to load (populate) SQL tables, we can use "INSERT INTO xxx VALUES..." (xxx being a pre-created table) or "INSERT INTO xxx SELECT...," but neither of these commands is particularly appropriate for larger tables. For larger tables, Oracle has a utility called a SQLLOADER. Oracle uses the utility called SQLLOADER (called SQLLDR in some systems) to populate existing tables (in Oracle) from a host file. There are two important caveats about SQLLOADER:

1. The SQL table must be created first within SQLPLUS.

2. The SQLLOADER facility is fussy about format and stingy on error elucidation.

Next we will take a look at a couple of examples using the SQLLOADER.

SQLLOADER Example 1

1. The first step would be to create a table in SQL as follows:

```
CREATE TABLE Auto
    (vin        NUMBER(3) CONSTRAINT vin_pk PRIMARY KEY,
    make        VARCHAR2(15),
    model       VARCHAR2(15));
```

2. Once the table has been created in SQL, we can then exit (or HOST) to the host system by typing:

```
SQL> HOST
```

3. Then, in the host, we need to use the editor to create a file. So, at the host prompt type:

```
F:\Oracle\Ora81\BIN> EDIT auto.ctl
```

This will open up an editor in your host and you can type in the following script (as shown in Figure 10.1):

```
LOAD DATA
INFILE *
    REPLACE
    INTO TABLE Auto
 (vin       POSITION (01:03)      INTEGER EXTERNAL,
    make    POSITION (05:11)      CHAR(7),
    model   POSITION (12:20)      CAHR(9))
BEGINDATA
111 Chevy Lumina
222 Honda Accord
333 Ford  Mustang
444 Volks Bug
```

4. Save your file.

5. Now you are ready to load the data from the host to the SQL files. Suppose your sql-user-id is xxxxx and your password is yyy. You would then execute the following command:

> In the host, the file can be named anything you want. We named our file auto.ctl. The file extension is conventionally "ctl," as in "auto.ctl." Other file extensions are allowable but it is suggested that you stay with the convention.

FIGURE 10.1 Using the DOS Editor

    SQLLOADER xxxxx/yyy auto.ctl

or

    SQLLDR xxxxx/yyy auto.ctl

You would then see the screen shown in Figure 10.2.

You have now loaded 4 records into your SQL table Auto.

The file auto.ctl contains one SQLLOADER scenario for loading a file. There are other scenarios, but the one we are demonstrating should work well for us. We used a load scenario where data is input from the auto.ctl file, but this could be done with another file instead of the one

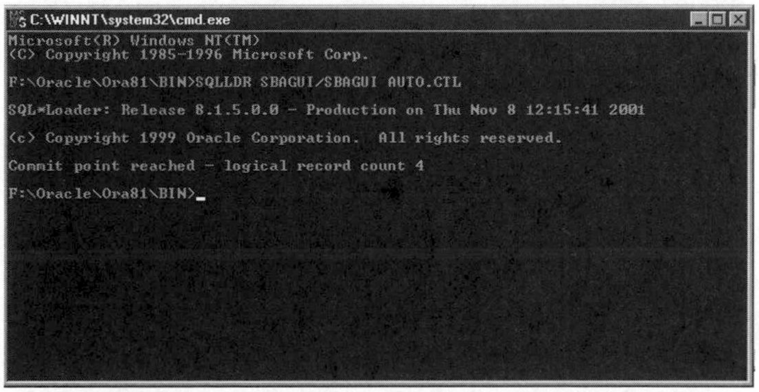

FIGURE 10.2 Using SQLLDR

designated by "INFILE * ... BEGINDATA." If data were loaded from a file, the first few lines would be:

```
LOAD DATA
INFILE *
 REPLACE
 INTO TABLE Auto
```

BEGINDATA would not be appropriate (we'll look at an example shortly). Note that the REPLACE option can be used instead of APPEND or INSERT. REPLACE replaces whatever is in the Auto table with the data provided, so be careful if you really mean to "append" rather than "replace." Note that you can also INSERT into an empty table.

The phrase "INTO TABLE Auto" implies that the Auto table has been defined in SQL. The attribute names vin, make, and model must match *exactly* the names you used to create the Auto table. The information after POSITION describes the *incoming* data in the *.ctl file. It does not have to match the defined Auto table, but it does have to match the data after BEGINDATA if you enter any data description (or it must match your file if you use the file option—see the following example). The file ends when you run out of data to input.

The SQLLOADER xxxxx/yyy auto.ctl statement can also be done in a variety of ways. Again, the xxxxx is your user-id (the one you currently use to sign onto Oracle). The yyy is your password. So for "rsmith" with a password of "frog," the statement would be SQLLOADER rsmith/frog auto.ctl.

When you re-enter SQL, and type:

```
SELECT *
FROM Auto;
```

The result will be:

VIN	MAKE	MODEL
111	Chevy	Lumina
222	Honda	Accord
333	Ford	Mustang
444	Volks	Bug

If you get an error, you have most likely done one of the following:

• You named the load file with an extension other than ".ctl."

- You did not create the Auto table in SQL first.

- You used a different column (attribute) name in the .ctl file than in the table you created under SQL.

- You are a column off in describing the data.

If the loader doesn't work, look for a "—.bad" file in the operating system to help with error elucidation (in this case, it would be "auto.bad".)

Another SQLLOADER Example

Often it is easier to load data from a file rather than "in line." If loading from a file, the "INFILE * " is replaced with the file name. You may also prefer to delimit the input fields with commas (or another character) and you may want to enclose text in quotes. The following is an alternative example of an SQLLOADER:

```
LOAD DATA
INFILE 'site.dat'
 REPLACE INTO TABLE site
FIELDS TERMINATED BY ',' OPTIONALLY ENCLOSED BY "'"
(site_id, location)
```

where site.dat looks like this:

```
1, 'PARIS'
2, 'BOSTON'
3, 'LONDON'
4, 'STOCKHOLM'
5, 'OTTAWA'
6, 'WASHINGTON'
7, 'LA'
8, 'TORONTO'
```

CHAPTER 10 EXERCISES

Note: Unless otherwise directed, name all CONSTRAINTs except NOT NULL.

1. To test choices of type, create a table with various types like this:

```
CREATE TABLE Test1
  (name              VARCHAR2(20),
   ssn               CHAR(9),
   dept_number       INTEGER,
   acct_balance      NUMBER (9,2));
```

Then, INSERT values into the table to see what will and will not be accepted. The following data may or may not be acceptable. You are welcome to try other choices:

```
'xx','yy',2,5
'xx','yyy',2000000000,5
'xx','yyyy',2,1234567.89
```

2. To test the errors generated when NOT NULL is used, create a table called Test2, which looks like this:

```
CREATE TABLE Test2
        (a      CHAR(2)         NOT NULL,
         b      CHAR(3));
```

INPUT some data and try to enter a null value for A. Acceptable input data for a null is "null."

3. a. Create or re-create if necessary, Test1 from Exercise 1, which does not specify the PRIMARY KEY. Populate the table with at least one duplicate ssn. Then, try to impose the PRIMARY KEY constraint with an ALTER TABLE command. What happens?

   b. Re-create the table Test1 from Exercise 1, but this time add a PRIMARY KEY of ssn. If you still have Test1 from Exercise 3a above, you may be able to delete *offending* rows and add the PRIMARY KEY constraint. Enter two more tuples to your table—one containing a new ssn and one with a duplicate ssn. What happens?

4. Create the Department and Employee tables as per the examples in the chapter with all the CONSTRAINTs (PRIMARY KEYs, referential and UNIQUE constraints, CHECK constraints). You can add the CONSTRAINTs at create time or you can use ALTER TABLE to add the CONSTRAINTs. Populate the Department table first with departments 1, 2, and 3. Then populate the Employee table.

   Note: Before doing the next few exercises, it is prudent to create two tables called Deptbak and Empbak, which will contain the data you load. This is because you will be deleting, inserting, dropping, re-creating, and so on. You can create the Deptbak and Empbak tables with the data we have been using with a command like this:

```
CREATE TABLE Deptbak
AS SELECT *
FROM Dept;
```

   Then, when you have added, deleted, updated, and so on and you want the original table from the start of this problem, you simply run the commands:

```
DROP TABLE Deptbak;
CREATE TABLE Deptbak
AS SELECT *
FROM Dept;
```

a. Create a violation of insertion integrity by adding an employee to a nonexistent department. What happens?

b. Create an UPDATE violation by trying to change

(i) an existing employee to a nonexistent department, and

(ii) a referenced department number.

c. Try to DELETE a department for which there is an employee. What happens? What happens if you try to DELETE a department where no employee has yet to be assigned to it?

d. Re-do this entire experiment (starting with Exercise 4a) except when you create the Employee table, specify the DELETE constraint as CASCADE.

5. In the chapter, we used the phrase ON DELETE CASCADE in an example where the Employee table was referenced to (depended on) the Department table.

a. Create the Employee and Department tables as shown in the chapter and use SQLLOADER (or SQLLDR) to populate them with three or four tuples each (the Department table first). Show the resulting tables and show the user_constraint table entries.

b. Suppose that there were another table that depended on the Employee table, such as Dependent, where the Dependent table contained the attributes name and empnum. Create the Dependent table. Then add the referential constraint where empnum references the Employee table, with ON DELETE CASCADE (and note that the Employee table also has an ON DELETE CASCADE). You are creating a situation in which the Dependent table references the Employee table, which references the Department table. Will the system let you do this? If so, and if you delete a tuple from the Department table, will it cascade through the Employee table and on to the Dependent table?

6. a. Create a table (your choice) with a PRIMARY KEY, a UNIQUE constraint, and a CHECK option. INSERT data into the table and as you do, enter a *good* row and a *bad* row (the *bad* row violates a constraint). Demonstrate a violation of each of your constraints one at a time. Show the successes and the errors as you receive them.

b. Display the dictionary view `user_constraints` and explain the output.

c. Display the dictionary view `all_constraints` and list the CONSTRAINTs that are contained in the `Student` table that you can see.

d. Display the dictionary view `all_cons_columns` and list the CONSTRAINTs that are contained in the `Student` table that you can see.

Multiple Commands, START Files, and Reports in SQLPLUS

It is sometimes prudent to create a set of commands that you would like to execute as one. In a programming language such as C, you usually do this by creating a procedure (module). In SQLPLUS, this "proceduration" can be accomplished in several ways. There are two general paths:

1. You can write a script that is run with a START command.
2. You can write a procedure or function that is compiled and used appropriately.

In this chapter, we'll discuss the first general path, writing a script that is run with a START command. We'll then discuss the DECODE, GREATEST, and LEAST functions, which have many useful purposes. In addition, we'll look at adding reporting features to a START file, as well as using the ACCEPT and PROMPT commands with these files. We'll discuss the second general path, writing a procedure or function, in subsequent chapters.

Creating a File (a START Table) and STARTing It

We have already seen a simple version of a "START file" in Chapter 3. To create and store such a START file, we begin by using the editor as follows:

```
SQL> EDIT twocomm <enter>
```

This will create a text file called "twocomm.sql." (The .sql extension is automatically added.) Now suppose we want to display the Student table and then the Prereq table in one script. We type the following in the editor:

```
SELECT * FROM Student  /* can use semicolons or slashes, but
                          in scripts, slashes are more read-
                          able */
/
SELECT * FROM Prereq
/
```

We then save the file, exit the editor and return to the SQL prompt. This saves the file as "twocomm.sql." To START the file, we type:

```
SQL> START twocomm
```

The two commands in the file are then executed one after the other.

An alternative, quicker way to START a command is to use the "@" symbol like this:

```
SQL> @twocomm
```

> Although the file name is "twocomm.sql," we START "twocomm" (without the .sql extension).

A START File with Editing Features

As a preliminary exercise, suppose we executed a simple SELECT as follows:

```
SELECT stno, sname, class, major
FROM Student;
```

When we do this, we get the default headings and column widths in our output. In this case, we get an output that looks like this:

```
STNO  SNAME       CLASS  MAJO
----- ----------  -----  ----
    2 BURNS       1      ENGL
    3 DAVENPORT   4      COSC
    8 BROWN       2      COSC
   10 ADAMS       1      ENGL
etc.
```

A first embellishment might be to give the headings meaningful descriptors using column aliases as follows:

```
SELECT     stno      "Student #",
           sname     "Student Name",
           class     "Class",
           major     "Major"
FROM       Student;
```

This would produce the following output:

```
Student #   Student Name Class Majo
---------   ------------ ----- --
        2   BURNS            1  ENGL
        3   DAVENPORT        4  COSC
        8   BROWN            2  COSC
etc.
```

This is better, but we still can't see all of the Major column (the r is cut off), so we would want to format the output a bit more. To embellish the Major column, we can execute the following column formatting statement:

```
SQL> COLUMN major FORMAT a8
```

When we re-run the SELECT, we get the following output:

```
Student #   Student Name Class Major
---------   - ---------- ----- --
        2   BURNS            1  ENGL
        3   DAVENPORT        4  COSC
        8   BROWN            2  COSC
etc.
```

The major column now has a FORMAT length of 8 characters. Having formatted major, the major column will be formatted until we change it—that is, until we CLEAR it, or we sign off from SQL (terminate the session). For simple reports, we will create formats just as we did here and then run the SELECT, all in one script. The following is an example of a beginning "report START file" that edits the attributes produced in a SQL SELECT:

```
REM Student Report .. April 17, 2006
REM by A. Mozart
REM
COLUMN stno    HEADING 'Student Number'    FORMAT A14
COLUMN sname   HEADING 'Student name'      FORMAT A20
COLUMN class   HEADING 'Class code'
COLUMN major   HEADING 'Major code'        FORMAT A6
SELECT stno, sname, class, major
FROM           Student
ORDER BY class
/
```

Suppose we call this script "first.sql." As before, we run the script with:

```
SQL>@first
```

The REM in the script is a non-executable remark. As illustrated, there are other options for formatting columns. Here, we used a heading and a width. Numeric columns use a 999 COBOL-like format. The following tabular listing gives some examples of formats and their effects.

Suppose that we had a table like Payroll (amount NUMBER(6,2)) and we had the following format and value combinations:

SQL> COLUMN amount FORMAT (see table below)

format	value in amount	resulting output
9999.99	0.00	.00
9999.99	1.00	1.00
9999.99	1000.00	1000.00
9990.00	0.00	0.00
9990.00	1.00	1000.00
9990.00	1000.00	10.00
90.00	5555.55	#######
999,990.00	5555.55	5,555,55
$99,990.00	5555.55	$5,555.55
$99,990.00	7.77	$7.77

> The ####### in the output occurs because the value is too large for the format available.

Using the DECODE, GREATEST, and LEAST Functions

Let's now turn our attention to three functions: DECODE, GREATEST, and LEAST. These three functions will allow us to enhance our display of results.

DECODE

If we want, we can also affect our output by using the DECODE function, which is exclusively an Oracle function.

The very useful DECODE function allows us to insert an IF-THEN-ELSE-IF logic into a SELECT command. For example, the following statement fragment:

```
DECODE(class,1,'Freshman',2,'Soph',3,'Junior',4,'Senior',
'Unknown')
```

says:

```
IF class = 1 THEN RETURN 'Freshman'
ELSE IF class = 2 THEN RETURN 'Soph'
ELSE IF class = 3 THEN RETURN 'Junior'
ELSE IF class = 4 THEN RETURN 'Senior'
ELSE RETURN 'Unknown'
```

> Oracle also offers a version of the standard (SQL 92) CASE statement in Oracle 8i and later Oracle versions. We will illustrate both the DECODE and CASE statements in this section.

Thus, if we type:

```
SELECT sname, major, DECODE (class, 1, 'Freshman','Other')
FROM    Student
WHERE   rownum < 5;
```

We get the following output:

```
SNAME       MAJO DECODE(C
----------  ---- --------
Lineas      ENGL Freshman
Mary        COSC Other
Brenda      COSC Other
Richard     ENGL Freshman
```

> The CASE statement, which was added to Oracle 8i, is an alternative to DECODE. The equivalent Oracle 8.1.6 CASE syntax of the above query would be:

```
SELECT sname, major,
     CASE WHEN class = 1
             THEN 'Freshman'
     ELSE 'Other'
     END
FROM Student
WHERE rownum < 5;
```

In general, in the DECODE function DECODE (a,b,c,d,e,f...), first a is compared to b and c is returned if true (that is, return c if a = b). Then a is compared to d, and e is returned if true (that is, return e if a = d); Then a is compared to f, and so on.

The comparison of a is to b,d,f... and every other second entry in the function. If the number of values in the DECODE is even, the last entry is the "catchall" entry, which is triggered if all other entries compare as not equal. If the number of values in the DECODE is odd, and nothing in the b,d,f... stream matches, then a null is returned. The following are some illustrations:

```
DECODE (a,b,c,d,e,f) says:
  IF a = b THEN c
  ELSE IF a=d THEN e
  ELSE f (the "catchall")
DECODE (a,b,c,d,e) says:
  IF a = b THEN c
  ELSE IF a=d THEN e
  ELSE NULL
```

The problem with the second example (which includes five values, a,b,c,d,e) is that the statement presumes that everyone knows that a null will be returned in such a DECODE *and* that Oracle will continue to have the function work in this way. Both are dangerous programming practices. It would be much better to adopt a convention that *one never allows an odd number of arguments in a DECODE*, hence always furnishing a "catchall" category. One never knows what data lurks in databases.

GREATEST and LEAST

DECODE only compares for equal, so if we want to "decode" ranges such as:

```
IF         a < 1000 THEN x
ELSE IF    a >= 1000 AND a < 2000 THEN y
ELSE IF    a >= 2000 AND a < 3000 THEN z
ELSE w,
```

we must use the GREATEST or LEAST functions. The LEAST function works like this:

```
LEAST(attribute1, attribute2, attribute3, …)
```

This returns the LEAST value of all attributes in the list. The previous IF-statement coded as a DECODE with the LEAST could then be done as follows:

```
DECODE (a,     LEAST(a,999), x,
               LEAST(a,1999), y,
               LEAST(a,2999), z, w)
```

In this example, if the value of a were 45, then LEAST(a,999) would return the lower of the two numbers, hence returning 45, hence returning x from the DECODE function. If the value of a were 1300, then LEAST(a,999) would return 999, which is not equal to a. The DECODE would then look at the value of LEAST(a,1999) and return a, 1300, (the least of 1300 and 1999). It would then compare this 1300 to the first a and find them equal. The overall DECODE would then return y.

The easiest way to *play* with the DECODE function is to use the dual table. You can write statements like this:

```
SELECT DECODE (10,11,2,3) FROM dual;
```

This returns a 3 because 10 is not equal to 11.

You can then continue to experiment with statements like:

```
SELECT DECODE (10,10,2,3)        FROM dual;
SELECT DECODE (10,11,2,3,10,4)   FROM dual;
SELECT DECODE (10,11,2)          FROM dual;
SELECT GREATEST (1,3)            FROM dual;
```

> The logic of DECODE can be inverted to use GREATEST. We'll look at this in more detail in the Exercises section at the end of the chapter.

Adding Reporting Commands to a START File

We can obtain a bit more embellished report by using the following editing commands in the START file:

• **_SET ECHO ON:_** This command lists each of the commands in a file when the file is run with a START command.

• **_SET FEEDBACK OFF:_** This command prevents messages like '7 rows selected' from appearing.

• **_SET HEADSEP:_** The punctuation that follows the heading separator SET HEADSEP indicates where we want to break a page title or a column heading that runs longer than one line.

• **_SET LINESIZE:_** This command governs the numbers of characters that will appear on a single line.

• **_SET NEWPAGE:_** This command prints blank lines before the top line (date, page number) of each page in the report. For example, if we type:

```
SET PAGESIZE 65
SET NEWPAGE 8
```

This will leave eight blank lines at the top of the page, and each page will have 57 lines. If we increase the size of NEWPAGE, fewer rows of information will be on each page.

• **_SET PAGESIZE:_** This command sets the total number of lines that will be allowed on each page.

• **_TTITLE:_** This command puts the title on the top of each page. The title should be enclosed in single quotation marks. If a heading separator (as explained above) is used in the TTITLE, it produces a split title (that is, it runs on more than one line).

• **_BTITLE:_** This command works just like TTITLE except that the title is placed on the bottom of the page.

• **_BREAK ON:_** This feature causes the report to be segmented by some attribute and gives a page break when the value of the attribute changes. We must BREAK on the attribute we are ORDERing by or the BREAK makes no sense. We can have only one BREAK in a script. If we use two BREAKs, the second supercedes the first.

• *COMPUTE:* This feature allows us to sum, count, average (and so on) attributes and include them with the BREAK. For example, for a "BREAK ON class," we might add a COMPUTE that looks like this:

```
COMPUTE COUNT OF stno ON class;
```

This would cause the COUNT of student numbers to be displayed when the report is "broken on class." Note that we can only use COMPUTE with BREAK.

A New and Improved Script

A *new* and *improved* script follows. The report file is in three parts:

1. The format part

2. The query part

3. The reset part

Each of the parts are set off by comments, as shown below:

```
REM ... first SET your parameters
SET FEEDBACK OFF
SET ECHO OFF
SET VERIFY OFF
REM report1.sql - a sample report file     -- format part
REM by R. Earp
SET HEADSEP #
TTITLE     'Student report#List of students'
BTITLE     'From the student file for COP 4710'
COLUMN stno      HEADING 'Student Number' FORMAT 999 /* 999 is
                              used for numeric formatting */
COLUMN sname     HEADING 'Student Name'   FORMAT A20 /* A is
                              used for character formatting */
COLUMN cla       HEADING 'Class'          FORMAT A10 /* refs
                                       column alias */
COLUMN major     HEADING 'Major'          FORMAT A6
BREAK ON cla SKIP 2 -
      ON REPORT                  /* again, refs column alias */
COMPUTE COUNT OF stno ON cla
COMPUTE COUNT OF stno ON report
SET LINESIZE 60
SET PAGESIZE 20       /* intentionally SET small to illustrate
                                       what happens */
SET NEWPAGE 0
SPOOL out.x           /* This writes all the output to a file
                                       called out.x */
```

```
SELECT stno, sname, major      -- query part

   DECODE(class,1,'Freshman',2,'Soph',3,'Junior',4,'Senior',
'Unknown')                                      /* see below */
  cla,   /* note the column alias, cla, for the DECODE ... */
FROM Student
ORDER BY class
/

REM  query is over ...
REM now reSET all the parameters you SET above  -- reset part
SPOOL OFF
TTITLE OFF
BTITLE OFF
CLEAR COLUMNS
CLEAR BREAKS
CLEAR COMPUTES
SET FEEDBACK ON
SET VERIFY ON
SET ECHO ON
```

At the end of the report file it is a good idea to SET SPOOL OFF, TTITLE OFF, BTITLE OFF, CLEAR the columns, and CLEAR all breaks. It is also a good idea to SET the FEEDBACK, VERIFY, and ECHO back on. This will reset the system for this session.

The output of the preceding report file will look like this:

```
Fri Nov 21          page    1

    Student report
    List of students
Student Number        Student Name   Class     Major
--------              ----------     -----     ---
       2              BURNS          Freshman  ENGL
      10              ADAMS                    ENGL
      17              SMITH                    COSC
      34              FRAZIER                  POLY
     121              HENNESSY                 COSC
     128              ALLENBEE                 COSC
     144              COLBY                    POLY
     132              APPLEGATE                POLY
     127              ZEBRIN                   ENGL
      70              EARP                     POLY
      14              HARPER                   COSC
--------              **********
      11              count
```

```
     From the student file for COP 4710


Fri Nov 21        page    2
    Student report
    List of students
Student Number       Student Name   Class    Major
_____              _____    _____    ____
       8             BROWN          Soph     COSC
      19             MCDONALD                POLY
     147             OSWALD                  ENGL
     130             SMITHSON                COSC
     129             WEATHERBY               ENGL
     126             ZORRO                   POLY
     125             HORNADY                 MATH
      15             WILLIAMSON              MATH
_____              **********
       8             count


     From the student file for COP 4710


Fri Nov 21        page    3
    Student report
    List of students
Student Number       Student Name   Class    Major
_____              _____    _____    ____
      49             HUGHES         Junior   ENGL
     122             SIMPSON, B              ENGL
     131             LOSMITH                 ENGL
     148             MITTERAND               ACCT
     143             BURNSIDE                ENGL
      62             HAIRE                   MATH
_____              **********
       6             count


       3             DAVENPORT      Senior   COSC
      20             JONES                   ACCT


     From the student file for COP 4710
Fri Nov 21        page    4
    Student report
    List of students
Student Number       Student Name   Class    Major
_____              _____    _____    ____
     145             SWENSON        Senior   ACCT
      31             HANEY                   COSC
```

```
     146              FRANCIS              ACCT
     142              MILLER               COSC
      24              TAYLOR               ACCT
     123              SMYTHE               POLY
      13              SIMPSON, A           MATH
 _____             **********
       9              count


 _____
      34

       From the student file for COP 4710
```

As before, if the file were named "report1.sql," it would be invoked like this:

```
START report1
```

or

```
@report1
```

> We can have only one BREAK in a script, but we can have several "ON ...'s". In the following example, the "cla" is a column alias, but it could be a column name. "ON REPORT" gives us a BREAK on the whole report:

```
BREAK ON cla SKIP 2 -
     ON REPORT         /* again, references column alias */
```

BREAKs work in conjunction with COMPUTEs. We may have a "COMPUTE" for each "ON ... " in the break, such as:

```
COMPUTE COUNT OF stno ON cla
COMPUTE COUNT OF stno ON report
```

The following part of the previous output was the result of the "COMPUTE COUNT OF stno ON cla":

```
 _____     **********
     11      count
```

We can sum, average, find the min, max, standard deviation, and variance if we wish with "computes on breaks."

> It is a very good idea to reset all the COLUMNs, BREAKs, SETs, and so on after we finish the report because these values persist until we sign off, unless we reset the parameters.

Using START Files with ACCEPT and PROMPT

We can create a script that contains the commands ACCEPT and PROMPT. ACCEPT tells SQLPLUS to accept input from the keyboard, and PROMPT allows us to display a message or prompt on the screen. For example, we may want to create a script that allows the user to SELECT * from *whatever*, where *whatever* is any table name that will be typed in by the user. Such a script could look like this (bold added for emphasis):

```
REM        This file uses ACCEPT and PROMPT
SET ECHO OFF
SET VERIFY OFF
ACCEPT tab1 PROMPT ' Enter table name --> '
SELECT * FROM &tab1;
SET VERIFY ON
SET ECHO ON
```

Once you run this above script, the PROMPT command will display the following on the screen for you (the cursor will be blinking where you are supposed to type in a table name):

Enter table name --> _

This dialog looks like a programming language dialog where you enter the table name. You can now type in Student, or any other table name. Let's type in Student, as shown below:

Enter table name --> Student

Student will now be assigned to tab1 (this is done by the use of the ACCEPT command).

So, the next statement in our script,

```
SELECT * FROM &tab1;
```

will now be executed as SELECT * FROM Student, displaying the Student table.

If we did not use the SET ECHO OFF in our script, then the whole script (in our case the line, SELECT * FROM &tab1;) will be again displayed on our screen before the execution of the output. To see the full effect of SET

ECHO ON/OFF try the script again with SET ECHO ON on top of the script instead of SET ECHO OFF and see what happens.

Using START Files with Positional Input

We can also use positional input with &1, &2, and so on with START files. A useful primitive version of a script for looking up information in the data dictionary would be the following (name the script look.sql):

```
COLUMN tname FORMAT A20
COLUMN notes FORMAT A50
SELECT table_name tname, SUBSTR (comments,1,50) notes
FROM Dict
WHERE UPPER (comments) LIKE UPPER ('%&1%')
/
```

Now, when looking for something in the dictionary, such as all entries having something to do with privileges, we can execute the following command:

```
@LOOK
```

We will then get the prompt:

```
Enter value for 1:
```

Now type in priv, to view all comments in the Dict table that have something to do with privileges, as shown below:

```
Enter value for 1: priv
```

You will now get:

```
old    3: WHERE UPPER (comments) LIKE UPPER ('%&1%')
new    3: WHERE UPPER (comments) LIKE UPPER ('%priv%')
TNAME                    NOTES
_____    _____
ALL_POLICIES             All policies for objects if the user has
                         system pr
ALL_REPGROUP_PRIVILE  Information about users who are regis-
                         tered for obj
GES

DBA_PRIV_AUDIT_OPTS   Describes current system privileges
                         being audited
```

```
DBA_REPGROUP_PRIVILE    Information about users who are regis-
                        tered for obj

DBA_RSRC_CONSUMER_GR    Switch privileges for consumer groups

DBA_RSRC_MANAGER_SYS    system privileges for the resource man-
                        ager

DBA_SYS_PRIVS           System privileges granted to users and
                        roles
USER_REPGROUP_PRIVIL    Information about users who are regis-
                        tered for obj

USER_RSRC_CONSUMER_G    Switch privileges for consumer groups
                        for the user
TNAME                   NOTES
---------------         ---------------------------

USER_RSRC_MANAGER_SY    system privileges for the resource man-
                        ager for the

USER_SYNONYMS           The user's private synonyms
USER_SYS_PRIVS          System privileges granted to current
                        user
ROLE_SYS_PRIVS          System privileges granted to roles
ROLE_TAB_PRIVS          Table privileges granted to roles
SESSION_PRIVS           Privileges which the user currently has
                        set
GV$ENABLEDPRIVS         Synonym for GV_$ENABLEDPRIVS
V$ENABLEDPRIVS          Synonym for V_$ENABLEDPRIVS

17 rows selected.
```

This output gives all tables that have "PRIV" (uppercased) anywhere in the comments attribute (also uppercased) in the dictionary table (Dict).

Note the first two lines at the beginning of this output:

```
old  3: WHERE UPPER (comments) LIKE UPPER ('%&1%')
new  3: WHERE UPPER (comments) LIKE UPPER ('%priv%')
```

We got these two lines because the look.sql script did not include a SET ECHO OFF command at the beginning of the script.

CHAPTER 11 EXERCISES

1. Create two START files, one called `seton`, the other called `setoff`, where `setoff` contains the SET .. OFF commands and `seton` the SET .. ON commands.

    ```
    setoff:
    SET VERIFY OFF
    SET ECHO OFF
    seton:
    SET VERIFY OFF
    SET ECHO ON
    ```

    Then, create a simple script (called simple.sql) that calls these two scripts:

    ```
    REM Simple script - name is simple.sql
    START SEToff
    ACCEPT whatever PROMPT 'Enter table name - '
    SELECT * FROM &whatever;
    START seton
    ```

    When you get this working, try these variations:

    a. What happens if you do not use `setoff` in the latter script?

    b. What happened if you do not use `seton`?

    c. Try other SET commands (set them OFF, then back ON) such as ECHO, VERIFY, and FEEDBACK.

    (To see current values of SET parameters, use SHOW, as in SHOW ECHO. To see all SET parameters, you can use SHOW ALL, but you will probably have to spool the output and look at it offline because the listing produced by SHOW ALL is too long for one page.)

2. Create a script to display the section number, instructor name, and course title for the `Student` table. Use variants of the following commands in your script:

    ```
    SET commands: WRAP, PAGESIZE, LINESIZE, NEWPAGE
    ```

    Use TTITLE, BTITLE, column formatting, COMPUTE (used only with break), and number pages with SQL.PNO. Use COL, TAB, LEFT, RIGHT, CENTER, SKIP, SKIP<n>, and FORMAT.

3. Write a script that inputs several positional parameters so that you could say something like:

    ```
    START showstudent student 3
    ```

    which would translate into "SELECT * FROM Student WHERE class = 3"

4.   Create a temporary table with the following data in it:

employee	salary
Alice	35000
Bob	33000
Sam	55500
Sally	45000
Brenda	88900

Then, display the table like this:

employee	salary
Alice	Low
Bob	Low
Sam	Medium
Sally	Medium
Brenda	High

Use the cutoff of 45,000 to differentiate between Low and Medium and 66,000 between Medium and High. Do not use LEAST in the command—use GREATEST.

Beginning PL/SQL Examples: Anonymous Blocks, Procedures, Functions, and Packages

PL/SQL stands for Procedural Language SQL (also called Programming Language SQL, although the consensus seems to be "Procedural"). PL/SQL is a limited programming language that allows you to go beyond the relational database/SQL bounds by performing procedural (row-by-row) commands. SQL is a set-at-a-time operation—you SELECT from a table, create a table, and so on. You can address sets of rows with SQL, but you do not ordinarily address individual rows with SQL. With PL/SQL, you can treat a table as a flat file that is accessed one row at a time.

PL/SQL is used in anonymous blocks, procedures, functions, and packages, all of which are compiled at runtime. If the action taken by a procedure or function has to be done repeatedly, the compiled procedure (or function or package) can be distributed to users, providing some security and information hiding.

In a nutshell, **procedures** are used for performing a set of SQL commands or operations, **functions** are operations that return a value, and **packages** are an umbrella under which we can group related procedures and functions into one unit. Procedures cannot be used in SQL SELECT statements, whereas functions can be. **Anonymous blocks** are a good way to begin learning PL/SQL, but they have limited applicability.

> In Chapter 11 we introduced the notion that SQLPLUS can execute multiple commands for us with one script or block. This chapter presumes that you have covered the idea of START files or blocks.

> Triggers also use PL/SQL. We'll cover them in the next chapter.

This chapter is not meant to be a complete primer on PL/SQL; rather, it is intended to introduce the concepts and usefulness of PL/SQL and hopefully will provoke further inquiry.

Anonymous Blocks

An *anonymous block* is a set of PL/SQL statements that may be used to perform a series of tasks using the PL/SQL language. *PL/SQL blocks* are divided into three parts: a declaration section, a program body, and an exceptions section. PL/SQL blocks are often depicted as follows:

```
DECLARE
... declarations
BEGIN
... procedural statements
EXCEPTIONS
... exception commands
END
```

Consider the following example:

```
DECLARE
 amount NUMBER := 0;
BEGIN
 SELECT COUNT(*)
 INTO amount
 FROM Student
 WHERE Student.class = 3;
 DBMS_OUTPUT.PUT_LINE(amount);
END;
```

Only the executable section (the BEGIN..END) of the block is required. The DECLARE and EXCEPTIONS parts are optional.

You can create an anonymous block called block1 with a SQL extension and execute it with a command such as @block1. For example, if the preceding query were saved as "whatever.sql," it would be executed with @whatever from the SQL prompt. To see output from a procedure or anonymous block, you can use the dbms_output package, as illustrated in the preceding example. To see the output, you must execute the following command before executing the PL/SQL block:

```
SET SERVEROUTPUT ON
```

If you then run the @whatever script, you would get the following output:

```
7

PL/SQL procedure successfully completed.
```

Using blocks like those illustrated above is unusual but serves to introduce the look and feel of PL/SQL. The dbms_output package, as used above, is cumbersome and limited in its display. PL/SQL is not usually used to display values as in the preceding example, but rather it is used with procedures and functions to perform tasks.

Elementary Procedures with Sequence Structures

Procedures in SQLPLUS use PL/SQL commands—not SQL commands *per se*. A procedure may also use some Data Manipulation Language (DML) commands (such as INSERT INTO .. VALUES), but not Data Definition Language (DDL) commands (such as CREATE TABLE). In this section we'll study some examples of procedures to see how they look and act.

Suppose we wanted to create a procedure to INSERT values into a table. We could, of course, use a single INSERT INTO .. VALUES command. We will look at a variant on this theme. A simplified syntax for procedure definition is the following:

```
CREATE OR REPLACE PROCEDURE procedure-name
(parameter list—with types, without lengths)
AS
     Local variable declarations (if any); /* if no locals,
                                   then no semicolon */
BEGIN
  Statement;
  Statement;
  Statement;
END procedure-name;
```

As with anonymous blocks, there is a declaration section and a procedure body. (There could have been an EXCEPTIONS section, but this procedure does not illustrate that feature.) The CREATE PROCEDURE includes a procedure-name followed by a parameter list (if any), which is where data is passed into the procedure when it is executed. The word AS is a necessary syntax marker; IS can also be used. If there are local variables, they are declared after the AS and followed by a semicolon. If there are no local variables, then there is no semicolon. Comments follow the /* ... */ format as in SQL (and C and other languages), and the body of the procedure is surrounded by a BEGIN .. END pair. END can be labeled (and should be). Statements in the body of the procedure involve local variables, INSERT, DELETE, or UPDATE SQL statements, SELECT SQL statements with an INTO option, or other special-purpose PL/SQL statements (like EXIT) as well as assignment and program-control statements.

A Simple Example of a Procedure

Let us now look at a step-by-step example of creating a simple PL/SQL procedure.

Suppose we have a table named Worker with attributes name, state, salary, and dept. The steps to create a simple PL/SQL procedure to INSERT a value into a table would be as follows:

1. Create a script file called testp1.sql. Type in the following script:

```
CREATE OR REPLACE PROCEDURE testp1
AS
BEGIN
    INSERT INTO Worker VALUES ('Pradeep', 'TX', 25000, 2);
END testp1;
```

2. Save the script file.

3. Compile the procedure by typing:

```
SQL> @testp1
```

You should get:

```
Procedure created.
```

If errors occur, they are displayed with the following statement:

```
SQL> SHOW ERRORS
```

4. To execute this procedure, type:

```
SQL> EXECUTE testp1
```

> If you get errors while running the above script, copy the Worker table to another table, for example, Worker1 (with CREATE TABLE Worker1 AS SELECT * FROM Worker), and then use Worker1 instead of Worker. Then remember to use Worker1 instead of Worker in all the scripts and SELECT statements that follow.

You will get:

```
PL/SQL procedure successfully completed.
```

Now if you type:

```
SELECT *
FROM Worker;
```

You will get:

NAME	ST	SALARY	DEPT
Sikha	FL	55000	2
Richard	AL	53000	1
George	TX	45000	2
Pradeep	TX	25000	2

4 rows selected.

Re-Using a Procedure

Procedures are stored in compiled form in Oracle. So once the procedure has been compiled (as shown in step 3 above), the next time you want to use the procedure you do not have to re-compile it; you can just re-execute it (that is, just do step 4 over again to re-execute the procedure).

However, the previous example does not use a parameter list or local variables and is, of course, an essentially useless procedure that always inserts the same value into the table.

Deleting a Procedure

A procedure will be saved unless you specifically delete the procedure.

To delete the procedure type:

```
DROP PROCEDURE testp1;
```

You will get:

```
Procedure dropped.
```

> If you delete the script file called testp1.sql at this point, you will not have deleted the procedure because the procedure is compiled and saved as testp1. "Testp1.sql" was just the script file that was used to create and compile the procedure.

Adding a Parameter List to a Procedure

In order to make the above procedure more meaningful, we would need to pass a parameter list to the procedure so that we would be able to insert different values for name, state, salary, and dept into the Worker table. The following procedure is an example of how a parameter list can be passed into a procedure to insert values:

```
CREATE OR REPLACE PROCEDURE testp1
(namein          VARCHAR2,
 statein         CHAR,
 salaryin        NUMBER,
 deptin          NUMBER)
AS
BEGIN
    INSERT INTO Worker VALUES (namein, statein, salaryin,
                                          deptin);

END testp1;
```

Save and compile this procedure (as shown in steps 1–3 of the previous example). Since this procedure has a parameter list, this procedure will have to be executed slightly differently from the previous example. Here you will have to include the parameter list while trying to execute the procedure. To execute this procedure you would type:

```
SQL> EXECUTE testp1 ('Pradeep','AL',18000,3);
```

You can also use it as an anonymous PL/SQL block, as follows:

```
BEGIN
testp1 ('Pradeep','AL',18000,3);
END;
/
```

Performing More than One Action in a Procedure

So far, in the above example, we were only performing one action with the procedure—inserting values into a table, Worker. Procedures can perform more than one action. The following is a procedure that inserts a worker's name, state, and department number but lets the procedure compute the salary to pay the worker. In the procedure, the first three values are passed into the procedure through the parameter list (name, state, and department number). The salary for the new worker will be the average salary of all workers minus 20 percent. Here is the procedure:

```
CREATE OR REPLACE PROCEDURE testp2
  (namein            VARCHAR2,
   statein           CHAR,
   deptin            NUMBER)
  AS
  avg_salary         NUMBER;              /* local variable */
  new_salary         NUMBER DEFAULT  0;       /* zero is the
                                                 default salary */

  BEGIN
  SELECT AVG(salary) INTO avg_salary FROM Worker;
  new_salary := avg_salary - (avg_salary*0.20);  /* assignment
                                      is by the := operator */
  INSERT INTO Worker VALUES (namein, statein, new_salary,
                             deptin);
  END testp2;
```

To execute this procedure, if you type:

```
SQL> EXECUTE testp2 ('Pradeep','OH',3);
```

And then if you type:

```
SELECT *
FROM Worker;
```

You will get:

NAME	ST	SALARY	DEPT
Sikha	FL	55000	2
Richard	AL	53000	1
George	TX	45000	2
Pradeep	OH	40800	3

4 rows selected.

This example illustrates the use of the PL/SQL SELECT..INTO statement. The usual action is to SELECT..INTO a local variable, which is then evaluated or used. This procedure also illustrates the control structure of sequence. The SELECT is executed first, followed by the assignment statement for new_salary and the INSERT. Because there are no statement sequence altering structures, the statements are executed in a sequential manner.

Procedures with Selection and Iteration

As with other procedural programming languages, PL/SQL has both selection and iteration in addition to the sequence control structure. Selection is performed by using an IF statement, and iteration is performed by a LOOP. Each repetition in a loop can be considered an iteration.

Example of a Procedure with Selection

An example of selection could be one in which the salary of the worker in the previous example was computed based on the average salary of the department; if no one were in the department, then a default salary of 15,000 could be used. This version of the salary procedure would look like this:

```
CREATE OR REPLACE PROCEDURE testp3
  (namein          VARCHAR2,
   statein         CHAR,
   deptin          NUMBER)
  AS
  avg_salary       NUMBER := 0;          /* default may also be
                                             entered this way  */
  new_salary       NUMBER;
  BEGIN
  SELECT AVG(e.salary) INTO avg_salary
  FROM Worker e WHERE e.dept = deptin; /* note the table alias
                                                              */
  IF avg_salary > 0 THEN
     new_salary := avg_salary - (avg_salary*0.20);
  ELSE
     new_salary := 15000;
  END IF;
  INSERT INTO Worker VALUES (namein, statein, new_salary,
                                 deptin);
  END testp3;
```

Example of a Procedure with Iteration

The LOOP control structure in Oracle's PL/SQL is usually used with a cursor. A *cursor* is a pointer that is declared in a procedure; it allows the programmer to access each row of a table, one at a time. Suppose in this example we wanted to assign our newest worker a salary that was equal to the average salary of everybody in the company except Tom. The procedure could look like this:

```
CREATE OR REPLACE PROCEDURE testp4
  (namein                   VARCHAR2,
   statein                  CHAR,
   deptin                   NUMBER)
  AS
  avg_salary                NUMBER := 0;
  sumsal                    NUMBER;
  total_emps_less_Tom       NUMBER;
  new_salary                NUMBER;
  CURSOR sal_cursor IS
  SELECT salary, name FROM Worker;
BEGIN
  sumsal := 0;    /* initialize the sum of salaries to zero */
    total_emps_less_Tom := 0;          /* initialize counter */
  FOR row IN sal_cursor LOOP
    IF row.name <> 'Tom' THEN
       sumsal := sumsal + row.salary;
       total_emps_less_Tom := total_emps_less_Tom + 1;
    END IF;
  END LOOP;
  new_salary := sumsal/total_emps_less_Tom;
  INSERT INTO Worker VALUES (namein, statein, new_salary,
                             deptin);
  END testp4;
```

Some points about this example:

1. The declaration of the CURSOR is done in a similar way to other variables. The syntax assigns a name for the CURSOR (here, it is "sal_cursor").

2. The LOOP (or iteration) illustrated is a FOR loop, which is common in PL/SQL. There are other loops, but the FOR loop hides some loop complexity and is used in a similar way to the FOR (or DO) in C, C++, and other languages.

3. IFs require END IF; LOOPs require END LOOP.

4. The variable, row, is not declared! This construction is clearly a language oddity, but that is the way the FOR loop is handled. "row" is the local pointer that points to the CURSOR, which points to values in a cursor-table.

5. The PL/SQL keyword EXIT can be used in a loop and has the same meaning as in C—that is, it branches to the statement just beyond the loop. EXIT is usually used in an IF as in IF such-and-such THEN EXIT; EXIT can also be used in a statement that says, "EXIT WHEN such-and-such"; EXITs can only be used inside of LOOPs.

IN PL/SQL, there are LOOP loops (also called *simple loops*), which almost always use an EXIT command. These are similar to the preceding example in testp4 without the FOR or the cursor. There is also a WHILE LOOP structure.

Functions

A *function* is similar in form to a procedure, but has a different use. A function returns a value, which may be used virtually anywhere—in command-line SQL statements, in PL/SQL code, and in procedures and other functions.

The syntax for a function is similar to that of a procedure except that it has a RETURN data type declared and a RETURN statement as follows:

```
CREATE OR REPLACE FUNCTION function-name
(parameter list–with types, without lengths)
RETURN datatype
IS  /* or AS * /  local variable definitions
BEGIN
    Statement;
    Statement;
    Statement;
    Return (local variable);
END function-name;
```

Example of a Function

We can create a function called Howmany, which counts the number of rows in the Student table as follows:

```
CREATE OR REPLACE FUNCTION howmany
RETURN NUMBER
IS num NUMBER;
BEGIN
    SELECT COUNT(*) INTO num FROM Student;
    RETURN (num);
END howmany;
```

As before, we might save this script as "howmany.sql." Once we run the script:

```
SQL> @howmany
```

We will get:

```
Function created.
```

Note that a function is different from a procedure in that a function must return a value, whereas procedures cannot return values. You can test the function with the `Dual` table as shown below:

```
SQL>SELECT howmany FROM Dual;
```

This will give:

```
HOWMANY
-------
     48
```

One use of a function is in a PL/SQL procedure or package in which a repetitive operation is performed. As with procedures, functions can have parameter lists.

Deleting a Function

Just like a procedure, the compiled version of the function will be saved unless you delete it. To delete a function, type:

```
DROP FUNCTION function_name;
```

Packages

A *package* is a group of procedures and functions that are combined into one entity. For example, if a programmer wanted to create a personnel package, it might contain procedures that added workers, deleted workers, or updated some information for some worker(s). The package might also contain useful functions that would enhance the ability to write procedures. Some information hiding can be accomplished using packages because all of the procedures and functions contained in the package don't have to be visible. Packages are modeled after the Ada language with a specification and body part. The specification has to be created before you can add information to the body.

Creating a Package

Suppose we create part of the aforementioned personnel package. We will create a procedure to add a worker and a function called average_sal that computes the average salary of workers, which will be used in the procedure.

1. The first step would be to create a function as follows:

```
CREATE OR REPLACE FUNCTION average_sal
RETURN          NUMBER
IS   num        NUMBER;   /* IS or AS—either one works */
BEGIN
    SELECT AVG(salary)  INTO num FROM Worker;
    RETURN (num);
END average_sal;
```

Save and compile the function, and make sure that the function works before proceeding.

2. We then incorporate the function into a procedure like testp3 as follows:

```
CREATE OR REPLACE PROCEDURE testp3
                (namein          VARCHAR2,
                 statein         CHAR,
                 deptin          NUMBER)
AS
BEGIN
    INSERT INTO Worker VALUES (namein, statein, average_sal,
                                        deptin);
END testp3;
```

> Once again, if you get errors, you may have to use the Worker1 table instead of the Worker table.

Once again, save and compile the procedure (and make sure there are no errors in the procedure) before proceeding.

3. After testing the function and the procedure, both the function, average_sal, and the procedure, testp3, could be put into a package. Suppose we call the package pack1. Packages are created in a two-step process: first the package specification, and then the package body.

3a. A package specification can be created as follows:

```
CREATE OR REPLACE PACKAGE pack1
AS
 PROCEDURE testp3 (namein VARCHAR2, statein CHAR,
                        deptin NUMBER);
END pack1;
```

Create this package specification as a script file so that you can save and compile it before proceeding.

The specification contains the procedure and/or function headings that will be the interfaces for the package. Note that we did not include the function `average_sal` in the specification. `average_sal` will be kept inside the package (that is, it will be hidden), used by the procedures in the package (`testp3`), and unknown and inaccessible outside of the package.

3b. Next, the package body has to be created. The format for the package body containing the function, `average_sal`, and the procedure, `testp3`, is created as follows:

```
CREATE OR REPLACE PACKAGE BODY pack1
AS
 PROCEDURE testp3 … details from above      -- heading must
                          match specification
END pack1;
```

The CREATE OR REPLACE parts of the procedure have been stripped off and the debugged version is put inside the package.

This is shown in the script that you would type in, shown below:

```
CREATE OR REPLACE PACKAGE BODY pack1
AS
PROCEDURE testp3
 (namein VARCHAR2, statein CHAR, deptin NUMBER)
AS
BEGIN
 INSERT INTO Worker VALUES (namein, statein, avg_sal,
                             deptin);
END testp3;
END pack1;
```

3c. Save this above script file as pack_body. Compile the script by typing:

```
@pack_body
```

You will get:

```
Package body created.
```

4. Now that we have created the package, we are ready to use it. Invocation of the procedure is a little different than before because the package name now must be used to qualify the procedure as follows:

```
SQL>EXECUTE pack1.testp3 ('Pradeep','OH',3);
```

Now if you type:

```
SELECT *
FROM Worker;
```

You will get:

```
NAME                ST    SALARY      DEPT
_____         _    _____     _____
Sikha               FL    55000        2
Richard             AL    53000        1
George              TX    45000        2
Pradeep             OH    51000        3

4 rows selected.
```

Note the newly inserted last line in the above output.

Another Approach to Creating This Package

If we were not concerned about information hiding, we could also create the package specification as:

```
CREATE OR REPLACE PACKAGE pack1
AS
    FUNCTION average_sal RETURN NUMBER;
    PROCEDURE testp3 (namein VARCHAR2, statein CHAR, deptin
                        NUMBER);
END pack1;
```

In this case, the package body would be compiled as:

```
CREATE OR REPLACE PACKAGE BODY pack1
AS
    FUNCTION average_sal … details from above
    PROCEDURE testp3 … details from above  -- heading must
match specification
END pack1;
```

Although this method would work perfectly, it would not achieve any information hiding.

Chapter Twelve

> A RETURN *type* has to be included for functions.

Deleting a Package

A package will also be saved until it is deleted. To delete a package type:

```
DROP PACKAGE package_name;
```

Defining a PL/SQL INDEX BY Table

A PL/SQL INDEX BY table is like an array of values, indexed by a number. Oracle 8.1.5 contains another table structure called a ***nested table***. A useful extension of the previous procedures might be to examine, update, and transfer (INSERT) values in tables, much like we would with a programming language with an array. In the current version of PL/SQL, the array, the PL/SQL table, may contain only one attribute from an existing table. The following is an example of a simple PL/SQL CREATE TABLE:

```
CREATE OR REPLACE PROCEDURE testtab2 AS
    TYPE inttab IS TABLE OF AA.x%type   /* the x%type says use
                                 whatever AA.x's type is */
    INDEX BY binary_integer;       /* You first DEFINE a type */
    Itt     inttab;     /* Then, you DECLARE a variable of that
                                        type, inttab */
    N        binary_integer;
BEGIN
  n := 0;
  FOR AArec IN (SELECT * FROM AA) LOOP
  n := n + 1;
  itt(n) := AArec.x;
  END LOOP;
END  testtab2;
```

In this example, we have the CREATE OR REPLACE PROCEDURE statement as before except that this one does not have parameters. We define a type for our table and then declare a variable of that type as follows:

```
    TYPE  inttab ...    (defines the type)
    int inttab;   (declares a variable of that type)
```

The PL/SQL table will contain values from the AA table, the column named x:

```
type inttab is table of AA.x%type
```

The "%type" means that the internal PL/SQL table will have the same type as whatever x's type is. The phrase "INDEX BY binary_integer" is required in all INDEX BY tables definitions. In this procedure, we have also declared a variable called n, which is of type binary_integer to be used as an index for our table. After the DECLARE, we have the procedure block (BEGIN .. END), which defines what the procedure will do. In the example, we select one value into our internal table, itt, from the table AA, column x, for every row in AA as follows:

```
BEGIN
 n := 0;
 FOR AArec IN (SELECT * FROM AA) LOOP /* note the inline cur-
                                         sor */
                                      /* AArec assumed as
                                         record type of AA it
                                         is not necessary to
                                         declare AArec Note
                                         the multi line com-
                                         ment .... */
 n := n + 1;
 itt(n) := AArec.x;
 END LOOP;
END;
```

As before, the FOR LOOP has the syntax:

```
FOR condition loop
...
END loop;
```

The condition in this case is that there are rows in AA; hence, the way this is written is "while there are rows in AA, do this loop...". Rather than have a BEGIN..END block for the loop or define a cursor, the syntax of PL/SQL may use "FOR .. LOOP" ... "END LOOP." Within the loop, values from AA, column x are assigned to itt (our table variable) with a statement:

```
itt(n) := AArec.x
```

Again, as before, to execute testtab2, we type:

```
SQL> EXECUTE testtab2;
```

As before, if we were to make a mistake in compiling the procedure, the errors can be viewed with SHOW ERRORS.

Using a PL/SQL Table

Here is a more complex example of a PL/SQL CREATE TABLE:

```
CREATE OR REPLACE PROCEDURE testtab3 AS
    TYPE inttab is table of AA.x%type
    INDEX BY   binary_integer;
         itt  inttab;
         n    binary_integer;
         sumx binary_integer;
         nmax binary_integer;
BEGIN
   n := 0;
   sumx := 0;
   nmax := 0;
FOR AArec IN (SELECT * FROM AA)
LOOP
/* AArec assumed as record type of AA */
n := n + 1;
itt(n) := AArec.x;
sumx := sumx + AArec.x;
IF nmax < itt(n)
   THEN nmax := itt(n);
END IF;
END LOOP;
INSERT INTO Result VALUES (n);
INSERT INTO Result VALUES (nmax);
INSERT INTO Result VALUES (sumx);
END testtab3;
```

> The table called
> Result has not
> been created for
> you. You must cre-
> ate it (with one
> attribute of type
> NUMBER) before
> you can compile
> this script without
> errors.

This is essentially the same example as before, but in this example, we have created two more variables, sumx and nmax. Sumx will sum the x-values from AA and nmax will tell us what the maximum value of x was. The FOR loop goes through the table creating our PL/SQL table, itt. In addition, the values of AA.x are tested and summed.

Selection is performed in the procedure with the following IF statement:

```
IF nmax < itt(n)
THEN nmax := itt(n);
END IF;
```

This uses the syntax "IF condition, action, END IF."

We mentioned before that this process doesn't have an output procedure such as write or display or print. To make the procedure do something, we inserted the values for n, nmax, and sumx into a table called Result, which contains only one attribute, a number. We also inserted our results into three rows. We could have used the dbms_output package as we did earlier in the exercise.

Arrays and PL/SQL tables are for situations in which you must go through the data and collect some information, and then go through the data again for some reason, such as to determine the median value of a set of values.

CHAPTER 12 EXERCISES

1. Create a test table called Emp2 that is similar to the Worker table in the chapter. (Use CREATE TABLE Emp2 AS SELECT * FROM WORKER.) Write a procedure called add_any_emp to INSERT values into your Emp2 table. If a salary is greater than 20000, then set that salary to 20000. Insert at least three rows into your table with your procedure. In furnishing values for the procedure, include a salary greater than 20000 for one of those rows. Display your populated table.

2. Write a procedure called new_emp to access the Emp2 table created in Exercise 1. In your procedure, insert a new worker named Madison from WI into the department that has the highest department number. Make the salary equal to the average of all other workers less 15%. Pass the name and state through the parameter list. Save the script you use to create this procedure.

3. Write a function called avg_emp that returns the average salary of workers in your Emp2 table. Do not include the lowest salary in the average. Display the average salary using the Dual table.

4. Retrieve the script used to create the procedure in Exercise 2 and use the function created in Exercise 3 in the procedure to add another worker to the table. The parameter list should include name, state, and department number.

5. Create a package called Salary that contains both the procedure, new_emp, and the function, avg_emp, but rename the function avg_emp1 for the package. Test new_emp by adding another worker to the EMP2 table and show the table after your addition. Do not put the function in the package specification (you are hiding the function in the package). Try to use avg_emp1 in a SELECT (SELECT Salary.evg_emp1 FROM Dual). Does it work?

REFERENCE

Feuerstein, S. *Oracle PL/SQL*, O'Reilly & Associates, Inc., Cambridge, 1995.

Introduction to Triggers

This chapter introduces and discusses triggers. We'll look at what triggers are, how to create triggers, the difference between row level and statement level triggers, enabling and disabling triggers, and deleting triggers. We'll also look at triggers in which one table affects another trigger, and we'll discuss the issue of mutating tables.

What Is a Trigger?

A *trigger* is a PL/SQL procedure that executes when a table-modifying event (such as an insert, delete, or update) occurs. Triggers may be fired for each *row* affected (FOR ANY ROW [WHEN]...), or at the *statement* level for an insert, update, or delete operation. Triggers may be fired *before* or *after* an event (a triggering action) takes place. There are therefore 12 categories of triggers (BEFORE/AFTER, row/statement, UPDATE/INSERT/DELETE):

```
BEFORE UPDATE row-level
BEFORE UPDATE statement-level
AFTER  UPDATE row-level
AFTER  UPDATE statement-level
BEFORE INSERT row-level
BEFORE INSERT statement-level
AFTER  INSERT row-level
AFTER  INSERT statement-level
```

> Oracle 8 and higher versions now also have another type of trigger, the INSTEAD OF triggers. Because this chapter is an introductory chapter on triggers, we won't cover INSTEAD OF triggers.

```
BEFORE DELETE row-level
BEFORE DELETE statement-level
AFTER  DELETE row-level
AFTER  DELETE statement-level
```

There are four general uses for triggers:

1. To enforce complex business rules (rules that are more complex than may be ordinarily available with a SQL constraint or command).

2. To compute a value that is based on other values or circumstances.

3. To "audit" an insert, delete, or update action (Oracle provides auditing features, but triggers are a less formal approach to auditing).

4. To implement security measures.

A few well-placed database triggers, written in the correct way, can reduce application coding and testing times. On the other hand, poorly written database triggers can destroy an application.

A Simple Trigger Example

Triggers are written in special syntax using PL/SQL. Suppose you want to create a trigger such that when you UPDATE the Student table, if there is a change in the major attribute from any major to a Master's in computer science (MACS), then you want to set the value of the class attribute to 6. This can be done by creating a BEFORE UPDATE trigger.

A script file would have to be created such that a trigger would fire every time there is an update of the Student table. This would have to be done with a CREATE TRIGGER command in a PL/SQL block (BEGIN..END). A stepwise approach to creating such a trigger follows.

> There may be privilege problems in creating triggers. You usually can't set triggers on tables you didn't create. You can deal with this problem in one of the following ways:
>
> (i) The database administrator (DBA) may be able to grant you permission to set triggers on others' tables. You must also check that you have the privilege to create a trigger in your account (to determine whether you have this privilege, check the data dictionary view "session_privs").
> (ii) You can create an identical table to the table provided. For example, you can create a table called Student1 that is identical to Student by typing: CREATE TABLE Student1 AS SELECT * FROM Student;

1. To create the script file that will contain the CREATE OR REPLACE TRIGGER command, type:

```
EDIT Trigger1
```

2. This will open up your editor. Type in the following CREATE OR REPLACE TRIGGER script:

```
CREATE OR REPLACE TRIGGER upd_student_trig
BEFORE UPDATE
OF major
ON Student
FOR EACH ROW
BEGIN
    IF :new.major = 'MACS' THEN :new.class := 6;
    END IF;
END upd_student_trig;
```

3. Save the script file.

4. To compile the trigger, type:

```
@Trigger1
```

This will give:

```
Trigger created
```

You have now created a trigger called `upd_student_trig`.

If you get errors upon compiling the CREATE OR REPLACE TRIGGER script, you will need to use the SHOW ERRORS command as shown below:

```
SHOW ERRORS trigger trigger_name;
```

In our case, this would be:

```
SHOW ERRORS trigger upd_student_trig;
```

5. Now suppose we want to issue an UPDATE command on the `Student` table that will change the `major` to MACS for the student with `stno` (student number) = 2. We could type in the following UPDATE command:

```
UPDATE Student
SET major = 'MACS'
WHERE stno = 2;
```

> We didn't include any comments in our CREATE OR REPLACE TRIGGER script, but it's generally a good idea to include some comments in your trigger script. Comments can include the trigger's function, who you are, and the date you created the trigger.

273

Introduction to Triggers

We will get:

```
1 row updated.
```

6. If we now want to see all the students whose `major` is MACS, we would type:

```
SELECT *
FROM Student
WHERE major = 'MACS';
```

And we would get:

```
STNO SNAME        MAJO CLASS  BDATE
───── ──────────  ──   ─────  ─────
    2 Lineas       MACS 6      15-APR-80
```

How the Trigger Worked

Our UPDATE command was updating the `major` to MACS where the student number (`stno`) was equal to 2. Our trigger, `upd_student_trig`, was a BEFORE UPDATE trigger, so if the new `major` was MACS, it changed the `class` of the student to 6 before the update (as shown by the output above).

This is a BEFORE UPDATE trigger on the `Student` table for updates involving the `major` attribute. BEFORE is necessary because you want to compute the value of `class` before the row is UPDATED. The "FOR EACH ROW" part of the trigger is necessary when each row in the table might change and should be checked. In this case, although we are updating only one row, the FOR EACH ROW is necessary to use "new" and "old" references (which are not allowed in statement-level triggers). `:new.major` refers to the new value for `major` per the UPDATE command that caused the trigger to fire. If you tried to run this example without FOR EACH ROW, you would get an error message that told you that this could not be a statement-level trigger (and hence you must add FOR EACH ROW).

Row-Level Triggers versus Statement-Level Triggers

Row-level triggers execute once for each row affected by a command. *Statement-level triggers* execute once for each table-modifying command. For example, if a DELETE command deleted 100 rows into a table, a statement-level trigger would execute only once. Statement-level triggers can be used to enforce undeclared security measures on transactions performed on a table.

Enabling and Disabling Triggers

Triggers are automatically enabled after they are created and compiled (unless they are specifically disabled). Triggers only affect commands of specific types (table modifying commands), and only while the triggers are enabled. Any transaction created prior to a trigger's creation will not be affected by the trigger; triggers do not retroactively check the database. To enable or disable a trigger after it has been created, the ALTER TRIGGER command is used as shown below:

```
ALTER TRIGGER trigger trigger_name ENABLE;
```

or

```
ALTER TRIGGER trigger_name DISABLE;
```

Enabling All Triggers for a Table

If a table in Oracle has multiple triggers, the command to enable all triggers for a particular table is:

```
ALTER TABLE table_name ENABLE ALL TRIGGERS;
```

Deleting Triggers

Triggers have to be dropped in order to be deleted. Triggers may be dropped by the DROP TRIGGER command:

```
DROP TRIGGER trigger_name;
```

Values in the Trigger

When referring to values in the table being modified in row level triggers, the general format is :new.attribute or :old.attribute (with the colons and periods).

In the PL/SQL body, you indicate the attributes in the tables with (colon)(new/old)(.)(attribute-name). For example:

```
:old.stno
```

or

```
:new.class
```

would stand for the old value of `stno` or the new value of `class`, respectively.

Our first trigger example (called `upd_student_trig`) illustrated a trigger which affected the values being placed into the table. The trigger would be fired with any UPDATE statement involving the `major` attribute in the Student table, and action would ensue when the new value of the `major` attribute is set to MACS. Nothing happens if the `major` is *not* UPDATEd to MACS. The action in the `upd_student_trig` example was that you would set the new value of `major` to MACS, but you would also set the new value of `class` to 6 (essentially automatically).

Using WHEN

Another way to handle the syntax of the PL/SQL body is to use the WHEN statement. The previous trigger creation (the `upd_student_trig` trigger) with a WHEN would look like this:

```
CREATE OR REPLACE TRIGGER upd_student_trig
BEFORE UPDATE
OF major
ON Student
FOR EACH ROW
WHEN (new.major = 'MACS')
BEGIN
    :new.class := 6;
END upd_student_trig;
```

Syntactically, the FOR EACH ROW is necessary if you use the WHEN clause. Also, there is a slight change in the syntax of the "new/old" modifier in the WHEN clause in that it doesn't use a colon before "new" or "old."

Performance Issues Using WHEN

There are some performance issues regarding triggers in general and the WHEN clause in particular. Triggers as a group were not compiled before version 7 of Oracle. If triggers are used, there may be multiple triggers on the same table—one for DELETE (BEFORE and AFTER), one for UPDATE (with a separate trigger for each different attribute), more BEFORE and AFTER triggers, statement- and row-level triggers, and so on. Generally, the more triggers you put into play, the poorer the performance (but, possibly, the better the integrity).

The WHEN clause of a trigger is executed first. If the trigger is meant to fire only under a restricted set of circumstances, and particularly if the trigger contains a lot of PL/SQL code, it is prudent to use a WHEN to bypass the PL/SQL if it isn't necessary to execute it. In this sense, the WHEN is not strictly an alternative to using IF logic inside of the PL/SQL block—it is generally better to use WHEN.

A Trigger Where One Table Affects Another Trigger

We will now consider several examples of triggers to illustrate their utility. What follows is an example that illustrates a trigger that checks one table and updates another table based on what happens in the first table. Suppose you create a table called Atrig with attributes stno, name, and class, and load data into the Atrig table such that if we type:

> The table Atrig has not been created. You have to create it.

```
SQL> SELECT *
FROM Atrig;
```

We get:

STNO	NAME	CLASS
100	Adam	1
200	Bob	2
300	Chuck	3
400	Dave	1
500	Ed	2
600	Frank	4
700	George	2
777	Extra	3

Also suppose further that you create another "mirror" table called `Btrig` with attributes `st`, `name`, and `cl` (these are the same attribute types as the `Atrig` table, but with different attribute names) as follows:

```
SQL> CREATE TABLE Btrig (st, name, cl)
AS SELECT *
FROM Atrig;
```

We will get:

```
8 rows created.
```

Now, if you type:

```
SELECT *
FROM Btrig;
```

We will get:

ST	NAME	CL
100	Adam	1
200	Bob	2
300	Chuck	3
400	Dave	1
500	Ed	2
600	Frank	4
700	George	2
777	Extra	3

Now, suppose you want a signal if `class` is changed to 5. If putting a value of 5 in `class` is wrong, you would, of course, create the `Atrig` table in the first place with a CHECK constraint option on `class` to prevent anyone from changing `class` to a value of 5. However, let's suppose that changing `class` to a value of 5 is allowable, but that you want to get an indication if that change were made.

For your signal, you can perform an after-the-fact check on `class` by using a trigger that fires when the UPDATE to the `class` attribute makes its value 5. A BEFORE trigger is used to fix a value for a table BEFORE an INSERT or UPDATE takes place. You can also compute a value for

INSERTing into (or UPDATing) the table with a BEFORE trigger. An AFTER trigger may be used to "audit" what happened when you INSERTed, UPDATEd, or DELETEd. In this case, the action of notifying you of a change in the value of the class attribute to 5 is more of an auditing action, so we choose to use an AFTER trigger.

To illustrate this trigger, create a script file called Trig1, which contains the CREATE TRIGGER command. This trigger is row-level, AFTER UPDATE trigger. It looks like this:

```
CREATE OR REPLACE TRIGGER Trig1
AFTER UPDATE
OF class
ON Atrig
FOR EACH ROW
WHEN (new.class=5)
BEGIN
    UPDATE Btrig SET Btrig.name = UPPER (Btrig.name)
    WHERE Btrig.st = :old.stno;
END;
```

When this script is run, it creates a trigger whose name is Trig1. Now, after an UPDATE on table Atrig is performed, the trigger fires if an UPDATE occurs on the class attribute. As the trigger body indicates, the trigger fires after the UPDATing takes place and each row in the table is checked. If the value of class in the Atrig table is set to 5, the Btrig table gets updated. For example, if we type:

```
SQL> UPDATE Atrig
SET class = 5
WHERE stno = 200;
```

We will get:

```
1 row updated.
```

Now if we type:

```
SQL> SELECT *
FROM Btrig;
```

We will get:

ST	NAME	CL
100	Adam	1
200	BOB	2
300	Chuck	3
400	Dave	1
500	Ed	2
600	Frank	4
700	George	2
777	Extra	3

Here the Btrig table mirrors the Atrig table with the old values for the student number, the old values for the class, and a slightly modified value for name (now shown in capital letters)—again, the result of the trigger being fired after the UPDATE was issued.

Mutating Tables

A mutating trigger is a trigger that attempts to modify the same table that initiated the trigger in the first place. You can't issue an INSERT, DELETE, or UDPATE command from a trigger on the table that is causing the trigger to fire. Note that in the first example (where we created the trigger called upd_student_trig), we simply used "old" and "new" to modify an attribute because the table in question was identified by the trigger. In the second case (where we created the trigger called Trig1), we modified the Btrig table when the problem that caused the trigger was in the Atrig table. When you are modifying the Atrig table, it is said to be "mutating."

In the script below, we create an example of a mutating trigger, Trig. This is an AFTER UPDATE trigger, so after an update has been made to the Atrig table, the trigger, Trig, is supposed to fire by inserting values into the Atrig table. So, type in the following script in a script file called mtrig:

```
CREATE OR REPLACE TRIGGER Trig
AFTER UPDATE
OF class
ON Atrig
FOR EACH ROW
WHEN (new.class=5)
BEGIN
    INSERT INTO Atrig VALUES (555,'XXX',1);
END;
```

Then, save mtrig. Now compile the trigger by:

```
@mtrig
```

This will give:

```
Trigger created.
```

The CREATE TRIGGER compiles without errors and everything looks okay. But look at what happens when we execute the following UPDATE command:

```
UPDATE Atrig
SET class = 5
WHERE stno = 700;
```

```
*
ERROR at line 1:
table ATRIG is mutating, trigger/function may not see it
at "TRIG", line 2
error during execution of trigger 'TRIG'
```

This error occurs because you can't issue an INSERT command on the Atrig table when you have already issued another table-modifying command on the same table. The workaround to this could be to use a temporary table, as shown in earlier chapters, or create a view that is identical to the target table, and then update the view.

CHAPTER 13 EXERCISES

For these exercises you must create two tables, called Atrig and Btrig, in your account. Populate the Atrig table with data as shown in the chapter. Do *not* populate the Btrig table. Then, write the following triggers. Be sure to save the CREATE OR REPLACE trigger code.

1. A row-level trigger that fires AFTER a row is DELETEd from the Atrig table—the trigger will INSERT the values that were in Atrig into Btrig. DELETE two tuples from the Atrig table. Show the values in the Atrig and Btrig tables. (This is like an automatic backup.)

2. A row-level trigger that fires BEFORE UPDATE or INSERT of a value for class = 6 that puts the old and the new values for the Atrig rows affected into the Btrig table. Show the values in the Atrig and Btrig tables. (This is like an "audit" table.)

3. In this exercise, you will create a statement-level trigger called st_trigger on the `Atrig` table using the same syntax as in Exercise 1. However, you will leave out the line that says FOR EACH ROW and the WHEN.

   a. First, create a table called `Resultx` that has one attribute called out of type VARCHAR2(50).

   b. Next create your trigger, st_trigger. Have the trigger INSERT a value into the `Resultx` table whenever an INSERT, DELETE, or UPDATE operation is performed on the `Atrig` table. Have the value of out be a message like "Atrig was modified" concatenated with the system date. (The system date is obtainable with the keyword SYSDATE and concatenation is accomplished with the concatenation operator.) Therefore, the INSERT command might look like this:

   ```
   INSERT INTO Resultx
   VALUES ('Atrig was modified'||SYSDATE);
   ```

   c. To trigger more than one action on a table, include the list of actions in the declaration part of the trigger. You would write it like this:

   ```
   CREATE OR REPLACE trigger_name
   AFTER UPDATE OR DELETE
   ON ...
   ```

4. You can embellish the trigger to perform different operations if you UPDATE, DELETE, and/or INSERT in the same trigger. You can test the action that caused the trigger with an IF statement like this:

   ```
   IF DELETING THEN
           operation
   END IF;
   ```

   Revise Exercise 3 to include all three operations (INSERT, DELETE, or UPDATE) in the message sent to the `Resultx` table so that the `Resultx` table will say that "Atrig was updated," "Atrig had a delete," or "something was inserted in Atrig," each concatenated with the system date.

5. Display a copy of USER_TRIGGERS from the data dictionary.

6. Create a partial copy of the `Student` table in your account like this:

   ```
   CREATE TABLE Student1
   AS
   SELECT *
   FROM Student
   WHERE rownum < 5;
   ```

   You can change the attribute names if you wish.

a. Write a BEFORE trigger for your `Student1` table that changes the value of the `class` attribute to 7 if you change the `major` attribute to MAAC (master's in accounting). Do this in two ways: once using an IF statement and once using the WHEN.

b. Write an INSERT trigger for the `Student1` table such that if you enter any new student, the `major` is recorded as "UNKN" (unknown). Test the trigger by using an INSERT like this:

```
INSERT INTO Student1
VALUES ('Juan',777666555,null,null);
```

Also test it using an INSERT like this:

```
INSERT INTO Student1
VALUES ('Juan',777666555,1,'COSC');
```

Does putting an actual `major` into the INSERT cause the `major` to be COSC or does the trigger prevail and make the major UNKN?

c. Re-create your trigger (or copy to a new trigger name) and use an AFTER trigger. (You only need to do it one way, with the IF or with the WHEN—it is your choice which you use.) What happens? Try this with a statement-level trigger and note the result. As you will see, it may not work. Why?

REFERENCE

Earp, R. and Bagui, S. (2001). Oracle's Triggers, *Oracle Internals*. Vol. 2(10), 14–20.

Getting Started with Oracle in the UNIX System

This chapter is written for those readers who will be using Oracle on the UNIX system. However, basic familiarity with the UNIX system is assumed.

Getting Started on Oracle in UNIX

Before you can sign onto Oracle in UNIX, you need to first log into the UNIX system. For logging into UNIX, access the host UNIX machine (directly or via teleprocessing) and sign onto your UNIX account. Once you are at the UNIX prompt, you are now ready to sign onto Oracle.

Signing onto Oracle in UNIX

To sign onto Oracle and use SQL, type "sqlplus" from the UNIX prompt. The UNIX prompt is shown as the following in Figure A1.1:

```
whelk%
```

Once you type in sqlplus at the unix prompt, as shown in Figure A1.1, the system will begin loading Oracle, and you will be asked to supply your SQL username and password. After you have typed in your SQL username and password, you will get the following SQL prompt:

```
SQL>
```

> sqlplus must be in lowercase letters because UNIX is case sensitive. While Oracle refers to SQL*Plus with the mixed uppercase and lowercase letters and the "*", you do not type the invocation of the language with the * and the mixture of uppercase and lowercase letters; you just type "sqlplus."

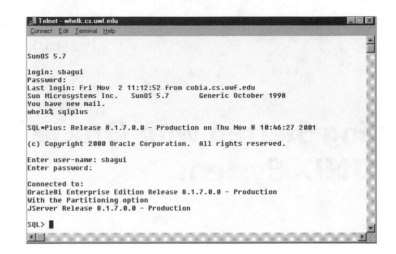

FIGURE A1.1 The SQL Prompt

The HELP Command with Oracle Under UNIX

If Oracle's HELP sub-system has been loaded into the UNIX system, you can type:

    SQL>HELP<Enter>

This will give you:

```
HELP
--
    Accesses the SQL*Plus help system.  Enter HELP INDEX for a
    list of topics.

HELP [topic]
```

To find what topics you can get HELP on, type:

    SQL> HELP INDEX

This will give the list of topics that HELP is available on, as shown below:

```
@               COPY            PAUSE           SHUTDOWN
@@              DEFINE          PRINT           SPOOL
/               DEL             PROMPT          SQLPLUS
ACCEPT          DESCRIBE        QUIT            START
```

```
APPEND          DISCONNECT      RECOVER                  STARTUP
ARCHIVE LOG     EDIT            REMARK                   STORE
ATTRIBUTE       EXECUTE         REPFOOTER                TIMING
BREAK           EXIT            REPHEADER                TTITLE
BTITLE          GET             RESERVED WORDS (SQL)     UNDEFINE
CHANGE          HELP            RESERVED WORDS (PL/SQL)  VARIABLE
CLEAR           HOST            RUN                      WHENEVER
                                                           OSERROR
COLUMN          INPUT           SAVE                     WHENEVER
                                                           SQLERROR
COMPUTE         LIST            SET
CONNECT         PASSWORD        SHOW
```

We recommend that you explore a few of these HELP topics. For example, to explore the help on "clear," you can type:

```
SQL> HELP CLEAR
```

This will give you:

```
CLEAR
———
 Resets or erases the current value or setting for the
 option, CL[EAR] option ...

 where option is one of the following clauses:
      BRE[AKS]
      BUFF[ER]
      COL[UMNS]
      COMP[UTES]
      SCR[EEN]
      SQL
      TIMI[NG]
```

Editing SQL Commands in UNIX

There are two ways to edit SQL commands in UNIX. You can edit them in an editor (the preferred method), or you can edit them using SQLPLUS commands (such as CHANGE, HOST, EDIT APPEND, INPUT, and DELETE [or some combination of these]). You should use whichever is the most comfortable for you when you need to change a command; you should, however, become familiar with both basic methods. We'll illustrate how to use each of these methods in the following sections.

Option 1: Editing SQL Commands Using an Editor

If a command is entered at the SQL prompt and if a change is desired, most programmers prefer to use an editor. An editor allows you to save your query as you are developing it.

Defining an Editor

If you are using a Sun terminal, you do not need to define an editor. If you are dialing up, you will have to first define an editor before you can effectively use EDIT.

If You are Using a Sun Terminal: To use EDIT on the Sun workstations to edit the current buffer, simply type EDIT. You will see what is basically a full screen editor, where you can add, delete, or change a command.

If You Are Dialing Up: To effectively use EDIT with a remote terminal, you must first define the editor that you will use. Common choices for use with terminals are "vi," "pico," and "joe." Pick whichever editor you want by typing (as shown in Figure A1.2):

```
SQL> define _editor = vi
```

(or pico, joe, or whatever editor) before you use EDIT. If you do not define the editor, UNIX and SQLPLUS will choose something for you (most likely "ex.").

FIGURE A1.2 Defining the Editor in UNIX

Editing the Buffer

After defining the editor you want to use, type in the following query at the SQL prompt:

```
SQL> SELECT cou
FROM rearp.Prereq;
```

You will get an error message because cou is not a valid attribute name in the Prereq table. To correct this query (while it is in the buffer) using an editor, you can type:

```
SQL> EDIT
```

The vi Editor Screen will appear (as shown in Figure A1.3). You can now edit your query using normal vi commands (vi commands are covered in detail at the end of this chapter). Once you have finished editing your query, press <Esc> :wq to save and quit vi. The buffer will be saved in a file named "afiedt.buf" (this is the default buffer name).

You can now execute the buffer with "/".

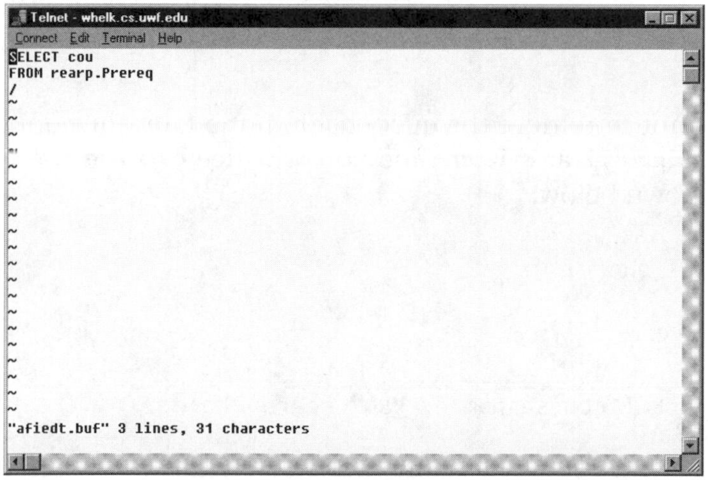

> See the section "Using vi as Your Editor " later in the chapter for HELP on vi if you need it. You can also use the "man vi" command in UNIX for help on the vi editor.

FIGURE A1.3 The vi Editor Screen

> You may want to read "HELP EDIT." This HELP screen will discuss editing options that may be useful. We recommend that you name the editor first. To name the editor the command is define_editor = vi (or you may use any other UNIX editor like pico).

If you invoke EDIT several times, you will be re-writing over your default buffer, afiedt.buf. However, if you just want to fix a command and go on to a different command, you may not need to save the contents of afiedt.buf.

Saving the Buffer

If you wish to save the contents of the buffer, afiedt.buf, into a file that you can later use, you can use the SAVE command as follows:

```
SQL> SAVE query1
```

You will get:

```
Created file query1
```

You have now saved the contents of your buffer, afiedt.buf, into a file called query1. Query1 will be saved until you delete it.

To re-save and write over the previous version of query1, type:

```
SQL>SAVE query1 REPLACE
```

The REPLACE saves over the previously saved version of query1.

Using GET

You may want to retrieve the query query1 at a later time and re-run it. To retrieve query1 at a later time you will need to use the GET command as shown below:

```
SQL> GET query1
```

This will give:

```
1* SELECT course_number FROM rearp.Prereq
```

This brings query1 back into the buffer. You can now edit query1 by typing:

```
SQL> EDIT query1
```

Using a Script File to Save Your Query

When you are writing longer queries, you won't want to use the default buffer, but you will want to write and save your query in a script file using the editor. To create a script file using the editor, type:

```
SQL> EDIT filename
```

This will open a blank vi screen (similar to that shown in Figure A1.3) where you can use vi commands and type in a query. When you save your query, it will be saved in a script file called `filename` instead of in the default buffer afiedt.buf.

To run this script file, type:

```
SQL> @filename
```

Option 2: Editing SQL Commands Using SQLPLUS

SQLPLUS supplies several commands to make minor changes to commands.

Using the CHANGE Command

If your change is simple (such as a misspelled word), you can use the CHANGE command. The format for CHANGE is:

```
CHANGE /old string/new string/
```

> The last "/" after "new string" is not required.

The CHANGE command works on one line at a time. For example, if you type:

```
SQL> SELECT * FROM rearp.Studens;
```

You get an error message because of the misspelled word "Student" spelled as "Studens." You can change the query by typing:

```
SQL> CHANGE /ens/ent/
```

or

```
SQL> c/ens/ent
```

> c is an abbreviation for the CHANGE command.

This will repair the current (last) line of the command in the buffer. You should then display the buffer from which you "/" the command to re-execute it.

Using the LIST Command

If the command is multi-line, you should use LIST first to see the whole command. Then, put in the line number that you want to CHANGE, CHANGE the line, type LIST again, and then "/" to re-execute the command. For example if you type:

```
SQL> SELECT cou          [press <Enter>]
FROM rearp.Prereq;       [press <Enter>]
```

you get an error on "SELECT cou" because "cou" is not a valid attribute name. To correct the error with the line editor, complete the following steps:

1. To see the whole buffer, type:

```
SQL> LIST
```

> l is an abbreviation for the LIST command.

This will give you:

```
     1 SELECT cou
     2* FROM rearp.Prereq
SQL>
```

2. To correct line 1 of the buffer, type:

```
SQL> 1 <Enter>
```

This will give you:

```
1 SELECT cou
```

3. To change cou to course_number, type:

```
SQL> CHANGE /cou/course_number/
```

This will give you:

```
1* SELECT course_number
```

4. To see the whole buffer again, use LIST. In this case, you will see lines 1 and 2. If you type:

```
SQL> LIST
```

This will give you:

```
    1 SELECT course_number
    2* FROM rearp.Prereq
SQL>
```

5. Finally, to re-execute the corrected command, type:

```
SQL> /
```

This produces the following output:

```
COURSE_N
____
ACCT3333
COSC3320
COSC3380
COSC3380
COSC5234
ENGL1011
ENGL3401
ENGL3520
MATH5501
POLY2103
POLY5501

COURSE_N
____
CHEM3001

12 rows selected.
```

Using Other Commands

As we stated earlier, most SQL programmers use an editor to make changes other than simple modifications. In addition to the CHANGE [c] and LIST [l] commands, you can use other line editor commands (although their use is rare nowadays). For example, if you want to add one line to the last line of a SQL command, you can use APPEND. In addition, you can use INPUT to add a line to a command anywhere, and DELETE will allow you to use the line editor to delete a line from a SQL command.

Some UNIX Commands

You will find UNIX much like DOS because one was derived from the other. The following are some useful commands you might try:

From a UNIX prompt, such as goblin%

To display your userid:

```
goblin% whoami
```

To list the files in your directory:

```
goblin% ls
```

To list the files in your directory with size and date:

```
goblin% ls -l
```

To list the files in your directory with size and date that start with the letter m:

```
goblin% ls -l m*
```

To list the files in your directory that start with the letters ma (no size, date):

```
goblin% ls ma*
```

To see how to use the "ls" command, invoke the UNIX built-in manual for ls:

```
goblin% man ls
```

To see what directory you are in:

```
goblin% pwd
```

To display the contents of a file:

```
cat filename
```

Example: `goblin% cat showc.sql`

For a longer file, to stop at the end of each page (and hit the space bar to continue) use the pipe operator and pipe the "cat" result to "more."

```
cat filename | more
```

Examples of piping to more:

```
goblin% cat showc.sql | more
```

or

```
goblin% more showc.sql
```

> You may find it easier to *view* a file from an editor like vi or joe than to LIST it with cat. Sometimes cat listings go by too quickly.

To *copy* three files, ex11, ex12, and ex13, into one file, ex1all:

```
goblin% cat ex11 ex12 ex13 > ex1all
```

To copy a file:

```
cp fromfile tofile
```

For example, at a UNIX prompt, goblin, type:

```
goblin% cp ex1.lst ex1.bak
```

To rename a file:

```
mv oldname newname
golbin% mv ex1.lst oldex1.lst
```

To move up one directory (change directory):

```
goblin% cd ..
```

To create a subdirectory, mysub, in your directory:

```
goblin% mkdir mysub
```

To move up to your newly created subdirectory:

```
goblin% cd mysub
```

To get back to your home directory:

```
goblin% cd
```

To see who else is signed on to this machine:

```
goblin% who
```

or, even better:

```
goblin% finger
```

To delete (remove) the file named frog:

```
goblin% rm frog
```

To print file ex1all on the printer:

```
goblin% lp ex1all
```

Summary Table

Several of the commands used in UNIX can be abbreviated. Below is a list of some important commands and their abbreviations:

Change directory: cd

Copy: cp

Delete: rm

Display: cat or more

Help: man

List: ls

Move: mv

Show directory: pwd

Other Miscellaneous Commands

The following are some additional UNIX commands:

To display a 2002 calendar, you can type:

```
cal 2002
```

To show the first 10 lines of a file, you can type:

```
head filename
```

To show the last 20 lines of a file, type:

```
tail -20 filename
```

To show the time and date, type:

```
date
```

To see what processes you are running, type:

```
ps
```

To kill a process by number, type:

```
kill
```

> ps and kill are useful if you lock up and have to sign back on to kill a previous session.

Editors

There are several editors you can use for editing text files in UNIX. Most UNIX gurus use the vi editor. Many people find vi cumbersome and prefer one of the "easier-to-use" editors, such as joe or pico. Some notes on each of these follow.

Using vi as Your Editor

To use the vi editor from a UNIX machine like triton%, type:

```
triton% vi filename     [initiates the file and gives it a
                        name]
```

To get into the insert mode in vi, press <Esc> and then press *i* to insert, and then start typing in your script.

> In the vi editor, you need to get into the habit of hitting <Esc> a lot. <Esc> is used to change from one mode to another in the vi editor.

From within vi,

Press <Esc> and *x* to delete a character

Press <Esc> and *:wq* to write and quit

Press <Esc> *:q!* to quit *without* saving (generally to start over)

Other vi Commands

> Remember that <Esc> is used to change from any mode to another mode in vi.

Below are some additional vi commands. You will need to hit the <Esc> key before you can use any of the following commands.

a: appends to the end of a line if you are at the end of a line (*<Esc>* to quit)

<Shift>a: moves to the end of a line and then appends (and *<Esc>* to quit)

o (lowercase): opens a new line below the present line

O (uppercase): opens the line above

dd: deletes a line

5dd: deletes 5 lines

To move a line, dd it, then place the cursor on the line *before* the point where you want the deleted line to be placed and press p.

Using Joe as Your Editor

If you use joe as your editor, invoke it as follows:

```
joe filename
```

To use joe, after you start it, press <ctrl>KH (hold down the control key and press KH). This gives you a HELP screen that stays at the top of the screen and guides you as to what to do when editing.

APPENDIX 1 EXERCISES

Since this appendix was meant to help UNIX users as they started working with Chapter 1 of this book, this appendix has no exercises. Instead we suggest that you complete the exercises at the end of Chapter 1, at this point.

The Data Dictionary

The data dictionary contains the meta-data (the data about data) for an Oracle database. Koch and Loney (1997) refer to the data dictionary as "Oracle's Yellow Pages." The contents of the data dictionary are available through a series of built-in views. Many of the views are restricted to the database administrator (DBA), but there are other views that are an excellent source of information for each user. What views are there in the dictionary that are available from your account? To see the available views, use the following command:

```
SELECT *     /* SET PAUSE ON or let it scroll */
FROM DICT    /* "DICT" is a public synonym for "dictionary" */
;
```

Note that the above query will give you too much information for you to digest without a SET PAUSE ON, so make sure to SET PAUSE ON first. Also, in all queries where the number of rows of output is unknown, you may want to get a count of how many rows you will be looking at first, so type:

```
SELECT COUNT(*)
FROM DICT;
```

This will give you a large number like:

```
COUNT(*)
--------
     817
```

As you peruse the dictionary table with SELECT * FROM DICT, you will note that several types of views can be ascertained by the prefix of the view:

Prefix	Example
ALL_	ALL_CATALOG
DBA_	DBA_CONSTRAINTS
USER_	USER_TABLES
Other views	V$VERSION or ROLE_ROLE_PRIVS

These views represent information about tables, constraints, database links, and other objects (like triggers, procedures, synonyms, and so on) that are accessible at the level of the USER, ALL, and DBA. These levels are explained below:

USER_　　　　These are objects owned by (created by) the account doing the query

ALL_　　　　This will display all of the USER_ information plus information on other objects to which access privileges have been given to the user or to the Public

DBA_　　　　These are database objects (some of which you may not have access to)

And other tables that are like ALL_ type tables.

Beginning to Explore the Data Dictionary

To begin exploring the data dictionary, enter the following command:

```
SELECT *
FROM DICT
WHERE rownum < 10;
```

Again, WHERE rownum < 10 will prevent excessive output when a particular command might otherwise give too many rows to handle effectively. The command as it stands ends after nine rows; you can, of course, use larger rownum values or delete the WHERE clause and see the whole table; but when exploring, we suggest you keep the view short or use pause (SET PAUSE ON).

To sample specific portions of the dictionary, type:

```
SELECT *
FROM DICT
WHERE table_name LIKE 'ALL%'  /* USER is case sensitive
                                 because it is stored that way
                                 in the dictionary */

;
```

This query will display only the table_names in DICT that begin with "ALL."

or

```
SELECT *
FROM DICT
WHERE table_name LIKE 'USER%' /* USER is case sensitive
                                 because it is stored that way
                                 in the dictionary */

;
```

This query will display only the table_names in DICT that begin with "USER," as shown below:

```
TABLE_NAME
----------------
COMMENTS
----------------------------------------
USER_ALL_TABLES
Description of all object and relational tables owned by the
user

USER_ARGUMENTS
Arguments in object accessible to the user

USER_AUDIT_OBJECT
Audit trail records for statements concerning objects,
specifically: table, cluster, view, index, sequence, [public]
database link, [public] synonym, procedure, trigger, rollback
segment, tablespace, role, user

USER_AUDIT_SESSION
All audit trail records concerning CONNECT and DISCONNECT
```

```
USER_AUDIT_STATEMENT
Audit trail records concerning  grant, revoke, audit, noaudit
and alter system

USER_AUDIT_TRAIL
Audit trail entries relevant to the user
.

.

.
USER_VARRAYS
Description of varrays contained in the user's own tables

USER_VIEWS
Description of the user's own views

USER_HISTOGRAMS
Synonym for USER_TAB_HISTOGRAMS

143 rows selected.
```

As you can see, the output for the dictionary queries may be large, so you may want to get into the practice of getting a count of the number of rows you will be getting in the output first, for example:

```
SELECT COUNT(*)
FROM DICT
WHERE table_name LIKE 'USER%';
```

This would show you that you would get 143 rows, as shown below:

```
COUNT(*)
-----
     143
```

A Paradigm for Choosing a View from the Dictionary

How do you begin exploring a particular view and find out which views are most useful? The paradigm for data dictionary view exploration is to

choose a likely view,

describe it,

select all or part of it.

To illustrate the paradigm, we will choose a view and follow the steps. We will illustrate two choices: CATALOG and TABLES.

Describing the Dictionary Itself

Before you begin looking in the dictionary, you should begin by looking at the names of the attributes in the dictionary itself and then look at a couple of rows. To look at the attributes of the dictionary we use DESC, as shown below:

```
SQL>DESC DICT;
```

This will give:

Name	Null?	Type
TABLE_NAME		VARCHAR2(30)
COMMENTS		VARCHAR2(2000)

Now, to display the first couple lines of the DICT table, type:

```
SQL>SELECT *
FROM DICT
WHERE rownum < 3;
```

This will give:

```
TABLE_NAME
----------------
COMMENTS
-----------------------------------------
ALL_ALL_TABLES
Description of all object and relational tables accessible to
the user

ALL_ARGUMENTS
Arguments in object accessible to the user
```

> Table names in the dictionary (DICT) are in all capital letters and the comments about the tables are in mixed case.

Choosing the View You Want to See

Use the dictionary table and look for a view that you want to find some information about. The dictionary is actually a series of views, but the dictionary description calls the view name, table_name. For example, if you want to know something about the system catalog, you can execute a command like this:

```
SQL>SELECT *
FROM DICT
WHERE UPPER(comments) LIKE '%CATAL%';
```

This produces the following output:

```
TABLE_NAME
————————————
COMMENTS
————————————————————————————————————————
CAT
Synonym for USER_CATALOG
```

This output gives the exact name of the table in the dictionary that you want to see: USER_CATALOG. The result also tells you that USER_CATA-LOG has a public synonym called CAT.

If you browsed a bit, you might also try:

```
SQL> SELECT *
FROM DICT
WHERE table_name LIKE '%CATA%'          /* Now querying
                                        table_name instead of
                                        comments */

;
```

This would tell you that there are other tables that deal with the catalog as well: ALL_CATALOG as well as USER_CATALOG.

ALL_CATALOG contains "All tables, views, synonyms, sequences accessible to the user."

Describing the View You Want to See (DESC ALL_CATALOG)

This step shows the columns that you might expect to see when you select from the view. For example, if you type:

```
SQL>DESC ALL_CATALOG;
```

It shows that you have three attributes:

Name	Null?	Type
OWNER	NOT NULL	VARCHAR2(30)
TABLE_NAME	NOT NULL	VARCHAR2(30)
TABLE_TYPE		VARCHAR2(11)

The reason that you want to describe the view is that some dictionary tables are very wide—perhaps 25 or so attributes. If you do not restrict what you want to look at, you will get long, hard-to-read listings.

Finding the Right Attributes

Because ALL_CATALOG is narrow (only three attributes), you will likely want to use

```
SELECT * ...
```

If there were a lot of columns (attributes), you might want to use less than the full complement of columns, like:

```
SELECT table_type, table_name ...
```

Finding out How Many Rows There Are in the View

You should always check to see how many rows you would get before you actually try to look at all of them. For example, to see how many rows there are in ALL_CATALOG, type:

```
SELECT COUNT (*)
FROM ALL_CATALOG;
```

This may give a large number such as shown below:

COUNT(*)
6681

If this number is very large (giving you a very long, perhaps useless, display), you can sample the table with a rownum as follows:

```
SELECT *
FROM ALL_CATALOG
WHERE rownum < 10;
```

Now look at the dictionary with some WHERE criterion to filter out some of the rows. For example, the following query displays the `table_name` and `table_type` from ALL_CATALOG where the owner is not 'SYS':

```
SELECT table_name, table_type
FROM ALL_CATALOG
WHERE owner <> 'SYS';
```

Views of TABLES

The information in ..TABLES (.. = USER_TABLES, ALL_TABLES, DBA_TABLES) tells you about the storage characteristics of the physical tables. Much of this information can be specified when tables are created and much of it can be changed with ALTER TABLE.

TABS is a synonym for USER_TABLES. Also, there is a useful, "old-fashioned" synonym, which has been carried forward in later versions of Oracle, called TAB. Although TAB is more limited than TABS, many people like the brevity because it gives an abbreviated list of tables, views, clusters, and so on that you own (that is, a restricted view of USER_OBJECTS).

Other Objects: Tablespaces and Constraints

Both ..CATALOG and ..TABLE views tell you about tables and tablespaces. If you have created or use other objects (such as synonyms), you can access a view called ..OBJECTS, which will tell you what "other" objects you may have. "Other" objects include clusters, functions, procedures, packages, sequences, synonyms, tables, triggers, and views.

Another useful table is USER_TAB_COLUMNS (synonym COLS), which tells you which columns you have in which tables. However, be aware that it contains a lot of data and lots of information about columns in tables. This table could be useful after an ANALYZE TABLES COMPUTE STATISTICS command because it would tell you the number of nulls, the high and low values, and so on for each column in a table.

Views of Tablespaces

Every table belongs to a tablespace, which is a division of a database. Some authors make the analogy that a database is like a city, the tablespace is like a block in the city, and a table is like a house on some block.

Usually, you use the default database as set up by the database Administrator (DBA). Also, you usually don't need to know the database name unless you're doing teleprocessing. In addition to the database, your account is set up to default to some tablespace. Tablespaces were also set by the DBA prior to your account being created. Every tablespace has some size to it that was defined when the tablespace was created.

A CREATE TABLESPACE command might look like this:

```
CREATE TABLESPACE TEMP
DATAFILE 'dog1.dbf' SIZE 100K
```

Such a CREATE TABLESPACE command would reserve 100K of diskspace under the filename `dog1.dbf` for your tablespace in your default database. In this command, there are options for MAXSIZE, which sets the maximum size of the tablespace, as well as AUTOEXTEND options, which allow your tablespace to automatically expand, if necessary.

> The MAXSIZE is set at the individual datafile level and not at the tablespace level. MAXSIZE is used only in conjunction with AUTOEXTEND ON.

As far as you and the dictionary are concerned, you may first want to know which tablespaces you have available. This is done by looking at the USER_TABLESPACES view as follows:

```
SELECT *
FROM USER_TABLESPACES;
```

This command might give you a display that looks like this:

TABLESPACE_NAME	INITIAL_EXTENT	NEXT_EXTENT	MIN_EXTENTS
MAX_EXTENTS	PCT_INCREASE	STATUS	CONTENTS
MYSPACE	10240	10240	1
121	50	ONLINE	PERMANENT

This output says that tablespace, MYSPACE, is available to you and that when you create tables, your initial extent for a table will be 10,240 bytes. If you put a lot of data in your table, the tablespace will allow you another 10,240 bytes (NEXT_EXTENT), up to 121 times (MAX_EXTENTS). The PCT_INCREASE means that when the next extent is allocated, it will increase by 50 percent each time. STATUS = ONLINE means that your tablespace is available. The tablespace owner might make it OFFLINE if they choose to—usually for maintenance purposes.

> Tablespaces are not owned by users. All tablespaces reside at the database level and can be taken offline by any user that has the appropriate privileges to do so.

Suppose you want to look at the space available in your tablespace. How do you do this? There are two views of interest: USER_FREE_SPACE and USER_TS_QUOTAS.

If you type:

```
SELECT *
FROM USER_FREE_SPACE ;
```

You will get an output that looks like this:

TABLESPACE_NAME	FILE_ID	BLOCK_ID	BYTES	BLOCKS
MYSPACE	12	4	45056	22
OTHERSPACE	11	2	305152	149

Here, the tablespaces listed are those that you have access to as a user. Suppose that MYSPACE is the tablespace of interest. If you type:

```
SELECT *
FROM USER_TS_QUOTAS;
```

You will get the following output (and perhaps some other tablespaces):

TABLESPACE_NAME	BYTES	MAX_BYTES	BLOCKS	MAX_BLOCKS
MYSPACE	104448	-1	51	-1

USER_FREE_SPACE tells you that you have 45,056 bytes available and USER_TS_QUOTAS tells you that you have used 104,448 bytes. The original allocation of space to this tablespace was 150,000 bytes. The "-1" means "unlimited."

Views of Constraints

When you have created tables in a tablespace in a database, you usually have constraints that are placed on the values. These constraints include:

• primary keys (P),

• unique constraints (U),

• foreign keys (R),

- checks (C), and

- a special option you can put on views called WITH CHECK OPTION (V).

The letters in the parentheses above indicate how the various options are referred to in the USER_CONSTRAINTS table. The attributes of USER_CONSTRAINTS can be viewed by:

```
SQL> DESCRIBE USER_CONSTRAINTS;
```

This gives you the columns (attributes) available in USER_CONSTRAINTS, shown below:

Name	Null?	Type
OWNER	NOT NULL	VARCHAR2(30)
CONSTRAINT_NAME	NOT NULL	VARCHAR2(30)
CONSTRAINT_TYPE		VARCHAR2(1)
TABLE_NAME	NOT NULL	VARCHAR2(30)
SEARCH_CONDITION		LONG
R_OWNER		VARCHAR2(30)
R_CONSTRAINT_NAME		VARCHAR2(30)
DELETE_RULE		VARCHAR2(9)
STATUS		VARCHAR2(8)

> These are the columns for the USER_CONSTRAINTS view in version 8.1.5. There are additional columns for later versions of Oracle.

APPENDIX 2 EXERCISES

1. How many objects are there in DICT?

2. How many objects start with USER? With ALL? With DBA? With something other than USER, ALL, or DBA?

3. Which tables in the catalog pertain to synonyms? To tables? To views?

4. How many rows are there in ALL_CATALOG?

5. Display the USER_CATALOG. Contrast the contents of USER_CATALOG with ALL_CATALOG. How many rows are there in USER_CATALOG? A synonym for USER_CATALOG is CAT. Try the command SELECT * FROM CAT and verify that it is the same as SELECT * FROM USER_CATALOG. How do the rows in USER_CATALOG differ from ALL_CATALOG?

6. Investigate and report on the following x_TABLES, where x = USER, ALL and DBA.

How many columns are there in USER_TABLES? In ALL_TABLES? In DBA_TABLES? How many rows are there in USER_TABLES? In ALL_TABLES?

7. Display a list of the tables you have created. Show the owner, table_name, and tablespace_name. Use USER_TABLES, TAB, COLS, and TABS.

8. Carefully look at ALL_OBJECTS (use ROWNUM, COUNTs, and DESC to explore first). If more information is sought on these other objects, there are tables at various levels (USER, ALL, DBA) for VIEWS, CLUSTERS, SYNONYMS, and SEQUENCES. USER_SYN-ONYMS and USER_VIEWS that are particularly useful.

9. Investigate and report on the constraints associated with the Student table.

REFERENCE

Koch, G., & Loney, K. *Oracle: The Complete Reference*. Berkeley, CA: Osborne-Oracle Press, 1997.

The Student Database and Other Tables Used in this Book

The Student-course Database

```
Student
    stno        NOT NULL        NUMBER(3)       PRIMARY KEY NOT NULL
    sname                       VARCHAR2(20)
    major                       CHAR(4)
    class                       NUMBER(1)
    bdate                       DATE

Grade_report
    student_number    NOT NULL      NUMBER(3)
    section_id        NOT NULL      NUMBER(6)
    grade                          CHAR(1)
            PRIMARY KEY(student_number, section_id)

Section
    section_id    NOT NULL      NUMBER(6)
                                PRIMARY KEY NOT NULL
    course_num                  CHAR(8)
    semester                    VARCHAR2(6)
    year                        CHAR(2)
    instructor                  CHAR(10)
    bldg                        NUMBER(3)
    room                        NUMBER(3)
```

```
Department_to_major
    dcode  NOT NULL       CHAR(4)        PRIMARY KEY NOT NULL
    dname                 CHAR(20)

Course
    course_name                   CHAR(20)
    course_number  NOT NULL       CHAR(8)
                                  PRIMARY KEY NOT NULL
    credit_hours                  NUMBER(2)
    offering_dept                 CHAR(4)

Room
    bldg       NOT NULL       NUMBER(3)
    room       NOT NULL       NUMBER(3)
    capacity                  NUMBER(4)
    ohead                     CHAR(1)
                              PRIMARY KEY(bldg, room)

Prereq
    course_number             CHAR(8)
    prereq                    CHAR(8)
        PRIMARY KEY (course_number, prereq)
```

Entity Relationship Diagram of the Student-course Database

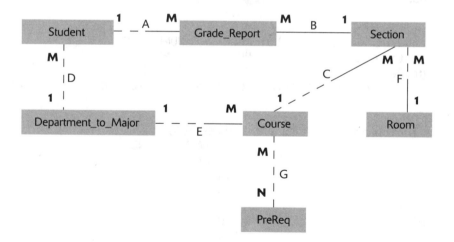

A. A Student MAY be registered in one or more (M) Grade_Reports. (Grade_report is for a specific course.)

A Grade_Report MUST relate to one and only one (1) Student.

(Students may be in the database and not registered for any courses, but if a course is recorded in the Grade_report table, it must be related to one and only one student.)

B.   A Section MUST have one or more (M) Grade_Reports. (Sections only exist if they have students in them.)

A Grade_Report MUST relate to one and only one (1) Section.

C.   A Section MUST relate to one and only one (1) Course.

A Course MAY be offered as one or more (M) Sections.

(Courses may exist where they are not offered in a section, but a section, if offered, must relate to one and only one course.)

D.   A Student MAY be related to one and only one (1) Department_to_major. (A student may or may not have declared a major.)

A Department_to_major may have one or more (M) Students. (A department may or may not have student who major in that department.)

E.   A Course MUST be related to one and only one (1) Department_to_major.

A Department_to_major MAY offer one or more (M) Courses

F.   A Section MUST be offered in one and only one (1) Room.

A Room MAY host one or more (M) Sections.

G.   A Course MAY have one or more (M) Prereq. (A course may have one or more prerequisites.)

A Prereq MAY be a prerequisite for one or more (M) Courses.

Other Tables Used in this Book

```
Plants
   company       VARCHAR2(20)
   plantlo       VARCHAR2(15)
         PRIMARY KEY(company, plantlo)
```

```
Cap
    name            VARCHAR2(9)
    langu           VARCHAR2(7)
            PRIMARY KEY(name, langu)

AA
    X               NUMBER(2)

Worker
    name            VARCHAR2(20)
    state           CHAR(2)
    salary          NUMBER(6)
    dept            NUMBER(3)
```

Improvements in Oracle 8*i* and 9*i*

Several features have been added to Oracle 8i and 9i. Following is a list of some of the major improvements in Oracle 8i and 9i. This is certainly not a comprehensive list. For a comprehensive list, visit Oracle's home website at www.oracle.com.

Improvements in Oracle 8*i*

This section lists some general features that have been added to Oracle 8i.

A DROP COLUMN Feature

An Index-Organized Tables Feature

Locally Managed Tablespace

Reverse Key Index

Multiple Block Size Support

Bulk Binds

Native Dynamic SQL

Trigger Bodies

Correlation Identifiers in Row-Level Triggers

NOCOPY

TO_LOB(long_column)

Improvements in Data Dictionary Features in Oracle 8*i*

This section lists some features that have been added to the data dictionary views in Oracle 8i.

To view partially dropped tables

ALL_PARTIAL_DROP_TABS

DBA_PARTIAL_DROP_TABS

USER_PARTIAL DROP_TABS

To view unused columns

DBA_UNUSED_COL_TABS

USER_UNUSED_COL_TABS

To view information on varrays

ALL_VARRAYS

DBA_VARRAYS

To view statistics on subpartitions

DBA_SUBPART_COL_STATISTICS

USER_SUBPART_COL_STATISTICS

DBA_LOB_SUBPARTITIONS

ALL_LOB_SUBPARTITIONS

USER_LOB_SUBPARTITIONS

To view information on index types

ALL_INDEXTYPES

DBA_INDEXTYPES

USER_INDEXTYPES

To view information on materialized views

ALL_MVIEW_ANALYSIS

DBA_MVIEW_ANALYSIS

USER_MVIEW_ANALYSIS

To view summaries

ALL_SUMMARIES

DBA_SUMMARIES

USER_SUMMARIES

To view information on internal triggers

ALL_INTERNAL_TRIGGERS

DBA_INTERNAL_TRIGGERS

USER_INTERNAL_TRIGGERS

Packages Added in Oracle 8*i*

This section lists and briefly explains some packages that have been added to Oracle 8i.

DBMS_BACKUP_RESTORE

DBMS_LOGMNR

DBMS_LOGMNR_D

DBMS_OFFLINE_SNAPSHOT

DBMS_REPAIR

DBMS_STATS

DBMS_TRACE

UTL_SMTP

UTL_TCP

Improvements in Oracle 9*i*

This section lists some general features that have been added to Oracle 9i.

GUI utility for Log Miner

Automated Managed Stand-By Database

Online Data Evolution (Active, Online Change Management)

Real Application Clusters

Dynamic Memory Allocation for SGA

LDAP Support

Oracle Label Security (Formerly Known as Trusted Oracle)

Undo Tablespaces (Instead of Rollback Segments)

Automatic Data History Retention for Flashback Queries (Using Undo Tablespaces)

XML Support

Shared Workspaces for Project Collaboration

Pipelined Table Functions

SAVE EXCEPTIONS

OVER

GROUP_ID()

GROUPING

GROUPING_ID

PERCENT_RANK

RANK

NULLIF(a,b)

NVL2(expr1,expr2,expr3)

VSIZE(x)

ASCIISTR(string)

BIN_TO_NUM

COMPOSE(string)

DECOMPOSE(string)

TO_NCHAR

TO_NCLOB(string)

Improvements in Data Dictionary Features in Oracle 9*i*

This section lists and briefly explains some features that have been added to the data dictionary views in Oracle 9i.

To view information on external tables

ALL_EXTERNAL_TABLES

DBA_EXTERNAL_TABLES

USER_EXTERNAL_TABLES

Packages added in Oracle 9*i*

This section lists and briefly explains some packages that have been added to Oracle 9i.

DBMS_FGA

DBMS_FLASHBACK

DBMS_METADATA

DBMS_MVIEW

DBMS_REDEFINITION

DBMS_RESUMABLE

DBMS_TYPES

UTL_ENCODE

UTL_URL

REFERENCE

Urman, S. *Oracle 9i PL/SQL Programming*. Oracle Press, Berkeley, CA, 2002.

Glossary of Terms

Abstract Data Type A user defined data type that allows you to define operations explicitly (in methods).

Administrator In this book, the administrator refers to the database administrator (DBA) who has the DBA role. See DBA.

Aggregate Functions A function that returns a result based on multiple rows.

Alias A temporary substitute for a name. There can be table aliases and column aliases.

Alphanumeric A data type that will accept a combination of characters as well as numbers.

Anomaly An undesirable consequence of a data modification.

Anonymous Block A set of PL/SQL statements which may be used to perform a series of tasks using the PL/SQL language.

Attribute Columns in a table or relation are called attributes.

Binary Large Objects (BLOB) A new data type, available in Oracle 8 and beyond, used for binary large objects.

Binary Intersection A set operation on two sets that generates unique values in common between two sets.

Binary Set Difference A set operation on two sets that gives us values in one set less those contained in another.

Binary Union A set operation on two sets where the result contains all unique elements of both sets.

Boolean A data type that can only take on True or False values (PL/SQL only). Boolean data type can also be NULL.

Buffer In general terms this is an area in the computer's memory where data is stored temporarily. The buffer, in Oracle's context is the SQL*Plus buffer, which is actually a file called afiedt.buf, stored at the operating system level.

Candidate Key An attribute (or group of attributes) that identifies a unique row in a relation. One of the candidate keys is chosen to be the primary key.

Cardinality In a binary relationship, this specifies the minimum and maximum number of relationship instances that an entity can participate in.

Cartesian Product A relational operation on two relations, R and S, producing a third relation T, with T containing the combination of every row in R with every row in S.

CHAR(size) Data type that gives fixed-length character data, size characters long.

Character Large Objects (CLOB) A new data type available in Oracle 8 and beyond. CLOB declares variables that hold a LOB locator pointing to a large block of single-byte, fixed-width character data.

Columns Attributes of a table. Columns hold the same kind of values.

Comments Syntax provided for inserting explanatory statements within a query or program. Comments enhance the readability of a program. They are not read, compiled, or executed by a compiler.

Conceptual Schema In Oracle, a schema is the collection of objects owned by a single user. Each user has their own schema.

Column Alias A temporary column name.

Copy Command to copy a file in Windows.

Correlated Subquery A subquery in which the information in the subquery is referenced by the outer, main query. A correlated subquery cannot stand alone; it depends on the outer query.

cp Command to copy a file in UNIX.

Cursor The simple definition of cursor is a marker such as a blinking square or line that marks your current position on the screen. In Oracle, the cursor is also used as a synonym for the context area. (The context area is the work area in memory where Oracle stores the current SQL statement.)

Data Facts concerning entities such as people, objects, or events.

Database A shared collection of logically associated or related data.

Data Dictionary Stores catalog information about schemas and constraints, design decisions, usage standards, application program descriptions, and user information. This information can be directly accessed by users or the DBA when needed.

Database Administrator (DBA) See DBA.

DATE Data type that is used to date and time data.

DBA (Database Administrator) The DBA (database administrator) has all system privileges and the ability to grant all privileges to other users. The DBA creates and drops users and space.

DDL (Data Definition Language) Used by the DBA and database designers to define the internal schema and conceptual schema.

DML (Data Manipulation Language) Users have the ability to manipulate (INSERT, UPDATE, and DELETE) data with the data manipulation language.

Domain The set of all possible values that an attribute can have.

Driving Table The table that is accessed first in a join.

Entity "Something" in the real world that is of importance to a user and that needs to be represented in a database. An entity may have physical existence (such as a student or building) or it may have conceptual existence (such as a course).

Entity Set The collection of all entities of a particular entity type in a database.

Entity Integrity Constraint A constraint that states that no key value can be null.

Entity Type A collection of entities that have the same attributes.

Equi-join A join condition with equality comparisons only.

File A collection of logically related records.

First Normal Form (1NF) Where the domain of an attribute must include only atomic (simple, indivisible) values and the value of any attribute in a tuple (or row) must be a single value from the domain of that attribute.

Foreign Account Account that you do not own.

Foreign Key An attribute that is a primary key of another relation (table). A foreign key is how relationships are implemented in relational databases.

Float A data type that accepts numbers with decimals (this data type is rarely used).

Function Named PL/SQL blocks that return a value and can be called with arguments.

Functionally Dependent A relationship between two attributes in a relation. Attribute Y is functionally dependent on attribute X if attribute X identifies attribute Y.

Group Function A function that returns a result based on multiple rows is a group function. Also known as an aggregate function.

Hierarchical Database A data model that represents all relationships using hierarchical trees, where a record represents a node of a tree and all relationships in the tree are represented by a parent-child relationship type. Each record in a hierarchical model may have several offspring but only one parent record.

Hierarchical Model In a hierarchical model, all the data is logically arranged in a hierarchical fashion (also known as a parent-child relationship).

Inline View A view that exists only during the execution of a query.

Integer A data type that accepts only whole numbers and no decimals.

Internal Schema Describes the physical storage structure of the database.

Join The join operation is used to combine related tuples (rows) from two relations into single tuples (rows) based on a logical comparison of column values.

Key An attribute or data item that uniquely identifies a record instance or tuple in a relation.

Logical Model Conceptualizing how data will be organized. It can be considered as the mapping of the conceptual model into a processible data model.

Login The process of signing onto a system. Logging in usually requires you to provide your userid and your password.

Large Object Data Type (LOB) Available in Oracle 8 and beyond, LOBs can store large amounts (up to four gigabytes) of raw data, binary data (such as images), or character text data.

lp UNIX command to send your file to a "line printer."

Many-to-Many (M:N) Relationship Where many tuples (rows) of one relation can be related to many tuples (rows) in another relation.

Meta-data Data concerning the structure of data in a database is stored in the data dictionary. Meta-data is used to describe tables, columns, constraints, indexes, and so on.

National Character Large Object (NCLOB) A new data type available in Oracle 8 and beyond. NCLOB declares variables that hold a LOB locator pointing to a large block of single-byte, fixed-width character data.

Nested Table Available in PL/SQL 8.0 and higher, is a table structure with a single dimensioned, unbounded collection of homogeneous elements.

Network Database Represents data as record types, where each record type may have relationships of any cardinality with any other record type in that network.

Network Model A data model where you are not restricted to having one parent per child. Many-to-one (M:1) and many-to-many (M:N) relationships are acceptable.

Noncorrelated Subquery A subquery that is independent of the outer query.

Normal Forms The process of decomposing complex data structures into simple relations according to a set of dependency rules.

Object Any named element in an Oracle database such as a table, index, synonym, procedure, or trigger.

Object Privileges Specifies how another user can manipulate the object to which a privilege has been granted (usually by the database administrator).

One-to-One (1:1) Relationship Where one tuple (or row) of one relation can be related to only one tuple (row) in another relation.

One-to-Many (1:M) Relationship Where one tuple (or row) of one relation can be related to more than one tuple (or row) in another relation.

Optionality A constraint that specifies whether the existence of an entity depends on its being related to another entity via a relationship type (also known as participation).

Optimizer Part of an Oracle kernel that determines the best way to use the tables and indexes to complete the request made by a SQL statement.

Outer Join A join condition where all the rows from one table (for example, the first table) are kept in the result set although those rows did not have matching rows in the other table (the second table).

Package Groups of procedures, functions, variables, and SQL statements grouped together into a single unit.

Parse Parsing is the mapping of a SQL statement to a cursor. At parse time, several validation checks are made, such as determining whether grants are proper, whether the syntax of the statement is correct, and so on. Decisions regarding execution and optimization are also made during parse time.

Participation A constraint that specifies whether the existence of an entity depends on its being related to another entity via a relationship type (also known as optionality).

Physical Model A representation of the form and details of how data is stored in the computer.

PL/SQL A programming language that provides procedural extensions to SQL.

Primary Key A candidate key selected to be the key of a relation. The primary key will uniquely identify a row or tuple in a relation or table.

Privileges Privileges specify what the user can do when he or she is logged on.

Procedure A PL/SQL block that can be used to perform a set of SQL commands and operations.

Qualifier A prefix used to identify the owner of a table or a particular attribute of a table. For example, in rearp.Student, rearp is the qualifier for the table Student.

Queries A SQL instruction to retrieve data from one or more tables or views. Queries begin with the SQL keyword SELECT.

Record A named collection of data items. In a relational model, a record is a physical realization of a row and tuple.

Recursive Relationship Relationships among entities in the same class.

Redundancy Storing the same data multiple times.

Referential Integrity The property that guarantees that values from one column that depend on values from another column are present in the "other column."

Relation A two-dimensional array containing single-value entries and no duplicate rows. The meaning of the columns is the same in every row, and the order of the rows and columns is immaterial. Often a relation is defined as a populated table. See also Table.

Relational Algebra A data manipulation language that provides a set of operators for manipulating relations.

Relational Database A database consisting of relations. A relational database is structured according to the principles of normalization.

Relational Model A logical data model in which all data are represented as a collection of normalized relations.

Relational Select A conditional relational algebra operation performed on a relation, R, producing a relation, S, with S containing only the rows in R that meet the restrictions specified in the condition.

Relationship An association between two entities.

Result Set Output of a SQL statement.

Rows A group of columns in a table. All the columns in a row pertain to the same entity. A row is the same as a tuple.

Row Filters A command that is used to select rows based on certain criteria.

Row Functions A function that is performed on every single row of a table.

Script A set of PL/SQL statements that may be used to perform a series of tasks.

Second Normal Form (2NF) A relation that is in first normal form and in which each nonkey attribute is fully functionally dependent on the primary key.

Session When you log on to your account, you begin a session.

Set A data structure that represents a collection of values with no order and no duplicate values.

Set Compatibility For two sets (or tables) to be set compatible, both sets must match in number of items and must have compatible data types. Set compatibility is also referred to as union compatibility.

Snapshot A means of creating a local copy of remote data.

Software Engineering A discipline that aims at production of fault-free software that satisfies the user's needs.

Spool Copying information from one place to another.

Spurious Tuples Tuples (rows) generated as a result of a join of tables which were decomposed incorrectly.

SQL (Structured Query Language) A language for defining the structure and processing of a relational database.

SQL Statements Are used to issue commands to a database.

Start Files Files or scripts that contain SQLPLUS commands.

Statements There are two kinds of statements: procedural and SQL. Examples of procedural statements are assignments, procedure calls, or loops. Examples of SQL statements can be divided into DML, DDL, transaction control, or session control.

Statement Buffer A file called afiedt.buf that contains the last executed SQL command.

String A mixture of letters, numbers, spaces, and other symbols.

String Function A function used to manipulate string data.

Structural Constraint Structural constraints indicate how many of one type of a record is related to another and whether the record must have such a relationship. The cardinality ratio and participation constraints taken together form the structural constraints.

Subquery The inner query within the outer (main) query; usually one SELECT query within another SELECT query.

Subset Some group of objects taken from a set.

Synonym A name assigned to a table or view that may thereafter be used to refer to the table or view.

System Privileges Privileges that allow the user to execute specific sets of commands.

Table A table is made of one or more rows of information, each of which contains the same kind of values (columns). It is also referred to as a Relation in the Relational Model.

Table Alias A temporary name given to a table.

Temporary Table A derived structure or table where the result of a SELECT can be intermediarily saved and then used in another SELECT.

Theta Join A join with one of the following comparison operators =, <, <=, >, >=, and not =.

Third Normal Form (3NF) A relation that is in second normal form and in which no nonkey attribute is functionally dependent on another nonkey attribute (that is, there are no transitive dependencies in the relation).

Transaction A series of operations between COMMITs.

Trigger A PL/SQL block that gets fired when a table-modifying event occurs.

Tuples Rows in a table or relation.

Union Compatibility When working with sets (tables), for two sets to have union compatibility, both sets must match in number of items and must have compatible data types.

User An Oracle user who has a name (userid) and password and can use tables, views, and other resources that he or she has privileges to use.

VARCHAR An older version of VARCHAR2.

VARCHAR2 A data type that allows you to define a Oracle variable-length string.

View A view is a query that is stored in the data dictionary and is resolved when accessed by a user or some other process.

Waterfall Model A series of steps that software undergoes, from concept exploration through final retirement.

Glossary of Important Commands and Functions

ACCEPT SQLPLUS command that takes input from a keyboard and puts it in a named variable.

ALTER TABLE SQL command that allows a user to add to, or modify a table.

ALTER TRIGGER SQL command that allows a user to modify a trigger.

APPEND SQLPLUS command that allows a user to add text to the end of the current line.

AVG SQL function that averages a group of attributes.

BEGIN PL/SQL statement used as an opening statement of a PL/SQL block's executable section.

BREAK SQLPLUS command that performs the action that is specified in the BREAK command.

BTITILE SQLPLUS command that puts text (a title) at the bottom of each page.

CASCADE SQL command that is usually used in conjunction with DELETE. CASCADE drops (deletes) all referential integrity constraints referring to keys in a dropped table.

CHANGE SQLPLUS command that changes old text to new text.

CHECK With a CHECK constraint the user can specify a range of values or a set of conditions that a column must have.

CLEAR COLUMNS SQLPLUS command that clears options set by the COLUMN command.

COMMIT SQLPLUS command that, when issued, makes changes un-ROLLBACKable. Therefore, when issued, changes to a table, INSERTs, UPDATEs, and DELETEs will become permanent.

COMPUTE SQLPLUS command that performs computations on columns or expressions selected from a table.

CONSTRAINTS Restrictions that can be placed when creating database objects such as tables and views.

COUNT(*) SQL function that counts the total number of rows in a table.

COUNT(attribute) SQL group function that counts the number of rows where attribute is not NULL.

CREATE FUNCTION SQL command that creates a function.

CREATE PACKAGE SQL command that sets up the specification for a PL/SQL package.

CREATE PACKAGE BODY SQL command that builds the body of a previously specified package.

CREATE OR REPLACE PROCEDURE SQL command that creates the specification and body of a procedure.

CREATE OR REPLACE TRIGGER SQL command that creates and automatically enables a database trigger.

CREATE OR REPLACE VIEW SQL command that creates a view.

CREATE SCHEMA SQL command that creates a collection of tables, views, and privilege grants as a single transaction.

CREATE SNAPSHOT SQL command that creates a snapshot (a table that holds the results of a query).

CREATE SYNONYM SQL command that creates a synonym for a table or view.

CREATE TABLE SQL command that creates a table.

CREATE TABLESPACE SQL command used to reserve diskspace under a filename for your tablespace in your default database.

CREATE TYPE SQL command used to create abstract data types in Oracle.

CURSOR SQL command used as a pointer to a context area. Used in the PL/SQL packages; it is declared in the package body.

DECODE SQL command that allows if-then-else logic.

DEL SQLPLUS command that deletes the current line in the buffer.

DELETE SQL command that deletes all rows in a table that satisfy a particular condition.

DESCRIBE (DESC) SQLPLUS command that displays a table's definition (its attributes and types).

DIFFERENCE SQL function which returns only those rows from the result of the first query that are not in the result of the second query.

DIR DOS command that gives a listing of the current directory.

DISABLE SQL command that disables an integrity constraint or trigger.

DISTINCT SQL function that shows unique values that are selected with the DISTINCT(attribute_name). DISTINCT also makes group functions summarize unique values.

DROP FUNCTION SQL command that deletes a specified function.

DROP PACKAGE SQL command that deletes a specified package.

DROP PROCEDURE SQL command that deletes a specified procedure.

DROP SYNONYM SQL command that deletes a synonym.

DROP TABLE SQL command that deletes a table.

DROP TRIGGER SQL command that deletes a trigger.

EDIT SQLPLUS command that calls an external text editor.

ENABLE SQL command clause that enables an integrity constraint or trigger.

EXECUTE SQL command that executes a procedure, package, or function.

EXISTS SQL operator that returns true in a WHERE clause if the subquery following it returns at least one row.

EXIT PL/SQL function that takes you out of the current loop.

FORCE Option that allows the SQL user to create a view if the underlying tables do not exist or if the user does not have privileges on the underlying table.

FOR EACH ROW SQL command that executes a row at a time in a trigger.

FOR . . LOOP SQL command that performs a series of statements a certain number of times in PL/SQL.

GET SQLPLUS command that loads a file from the host system into the statement buffer.

GRANT SQL command that allows someone to pass on a privilege to another user.

GREATEST SQL function that returns the highest of a list of values.

GROUP BY SQL clause that produces one summary row for all selected rows that have identical values for the attributes specified in the GROUP BY.

HAVING SQL clause used to determine which groups the GROUP BY will include in the result set.

HELP SQLPLUS command that provides help on various topics.

HOST SQLPLUS command that temporarily takes the user back to the operating system on which Oracle is running.

INDEX BY SQL feature that creates an index on a table. The index will be created by the attribute specified in the INDEX BY.

IF .. THEN .. ELSE The IF statement will execute one or more statements when a condition evaluates to TRUE. If the condition evaluates to FALSE, the statements in the ELSE section are executed. This is usually used with PL/SQL.

IN A logical operator for a WHERE clause, which tests for inclusion in a named set.

INPUT SQLPLUS line editor command that allows for the addition of a new line of text after the current line in the buffer.

INTERSECT SQL command that combines two queries and returns only those rows from the result of the first query that are identical to the result of the second query.

INSTR SQL function that returns the location of a pattern in a given string.

INSERT SQL command that allows for the addition of new rows to a table or view.

LEAST SQL function that returns the lowest value of a list of values.

LENGTH SQL function that returns the length of a expression, string, number, or date.

LIKE SQL command that matches a particular pattern.

LIST SQLPLUS line editor command that lists lines of the current buffer.

LOOP PL/SQL statement that performs the statements after the LOOP until a constraint has been met.

LOWER SQL function that converts every letter in a string to lowercase.

LPAD SQL function that stands for "left pad." LPAD makes a string a certain length by adding characters to the left of the string.

LTRIM SQL function that stands for "left trim." LTRIM trims (removes) a certain set of characters from the left side of a string.

MAX SQL function that gives the highest of all values from an attribute in a set of rows.

MIN SQL function that gives the lowest of all values from an attribute in a set of rows.

MINUS SQL function which returns only those rows from the result of the first query that are not in the result of the second query.

NOT SQL operator that comes before and reverses the effect of any logical operator like IN, LIKE, and EXISTS.

NOT EXISTS SQL operator that returns false in a WHERE clause if the subquery following it returns at least one row.

NOT NULL SQL operator that is True if an attribute has a non-null value.

NULL SQL command value that is unknown.

NVL SQL function that allows something to be substituted in place of a NULL value.

OR Logical SQL operator that returns a True value if either one of the expressions are true.

ORDER BY SQL clause that sorts the results of a query before they are displayed.

PRIMARY KEY SQL command; a CONSTRAINT used to create a primary key in a table.

PRIVILEGE SQL command used in granting permission to a user. There are SYSTEM PRIVILEGEs and OBJECT PRIVILEGEs.

PROMPT SQLPLUS command that displays text to a user's screen.

REFERENCE A CONSTRAINT that defines the table name and key used to reference another table.

REM (short for REMARK) This is like a comment line. It is not read, compiled, or executed by a compiler. It is good for documentation purposes.

RETURN Causes control to pass from a function or procedure back to the calling environment.

RESTRICT CONSTRAINT that prevents you from deleting a key attribute or value referenced by another table.

REVOKE SQL command that takes specific privileges away from a user.

ROLLBACK SQL command that reverses changes made to tables in a database since the last COMMIT.

ROWNUM A pseudo-column created by Oracle. Rownum returns the sequence number in which a row was returned when first selected from a table. The first row has a ROWNUM of 1, the second has a ROWNUM of 2, and so on.

RPAD SQL function that stands for "right pad." RPAD makes a string a certain length by adding characters to the right of the string.

RTRIM SQL function that stands for "right trim." RTRIM trims (removes) a certain set of characters from the right side of a string.

SAVE SQLPLUS command that saves contents of the statement buffer into a file on the host.

SAVEPOINT SQL command that allows you to save a transaction at different points.

SELECT SQL command that allows you to retrieve rows from tables (or view or snapshots) in a database.

SET SQLPLUS command that values a SQLPLUS feature.

SET ECHO ON/OFF SQLPLUS command that allows you to control the listing of each command in a file when the file is run with a start command.

SET FEEDBACK ON/OFF/n SQLPLUS command that allows you to control SQLPLUS's feedback. For example, SET FEEDBACK OFF will stop the row count from being displayed in a SELECT * statement.

SET HEADSEP SQLPLUS command that identifies the character that tells SQLPLUS to split a title.

SET LINESIZE SQLPLUS command that allows you to specify the maximum number of characters that can appear on each line.

SET NEWPAGE SQLPLUS command that allows you to specify how many lines there will be before the top line on each page.

SET PAGESIZE SQLPLUS command that allows you to set the total number of lines SQLPLUS will place on each page.

SET PAUSE ON/OFF/character expression SQLPLUS command that will cause output to be displayed a page at a time.

SET SQLPROMPT SQLPLUS command that allows you to change the default prompt.

SET TIMING ON/OFF SQLPLUS command that allows you to show (or not show) timing statistics.

SHOW ALL SQLPLUS command that gives a list of all your system parameters.

SHOW ERRORS SQLPLUS command that will display line and column number for each error, as well as the text of the error message.

SPOOL SQLPLUS command that shows the name of the current (or most recent) spool file.

SPOOL filename SQLPLUS command that writes the output of a query to the file specified in the SPOOL command.

SPOOL ON SQLPLUS command that, once it is turned on, everything that happens from that point is recorded in a host system file until you SPOOL OFF or SPOOL OUT.

SPOOL OFF SQLPLUS command that stops spooling.

SPOOL OUT SQLPLUS command that stops spooling and sends the spooled file to the printer.

SQLLOADER Utility for loading data from external files into Oracle.

SQLPLUS (SQL*PLUS) Oracle product that takes your instructions for Oracle, checks them for correctness, submits them to Oracle, and then modifies and reformats the response Oracle gives.

START filename SQLPLUS command that tells SQLPLUS to execute the instructions contained in the filename.

SUBSTR SQL function that allows SQL to retrieve only a portion of a whole string. The starting position is specified; the ending position may be specified.

SUM SQL group function that adds up all the values for an attribute in a set of rows.

TO_CHAR SQL function that reformats a number or date into a specified character format.

TO_DATE SQL function that converts a string into a given date format.

TTITLE SQLPLUS command that places a title at the top of each page.

TYPE DOS command that gives the contents of a file.

%TYPE A %TYPE attribute can be applied to a variable or table column. It returns the type of the object and is used to make your program more flexible.

UNION SQL function that combines two queries such that it returns all distinct rows for the result of both queries.

UNION ALL SQL function that combines two queries and returns all rows from both the SELECT statements (queries). A UNION ALL also includes duplicate rows.

UNIQUE Another attribute integrity constraint. UNIQUE disallows duplicate entries for an attribute even though the attribute is not a primary key. UNIQUE does not necessitate NOT NULL like the primary key.

UPDATE SQL command that changes values in specified columns in specified tables.

UPPER SQL function that converts every letter in a string into uppercase.

WHERE SQL clause that allows you to specify qualifiers on columns for rows that are being selected from a table. It is a row filter.

Index of Terms

I

Inline View
Integer
Internal Schema

J

Join

K

Key

L

Logical Model
Login
Large Object data type (LOB)
lp

M

Many-to-Many (M:N) Relationship
Meta-data

N

National Character Large Object (NCLOB)
Nested Table
Network Database
Network Model
Noncorrelated Subquery
Normal Forms

O

Object
Object Privileges
One-to-One (1:1) Relationship
One-to-Many (1:M) Relationship

Optionality
Optimizer
Outer Join

P

Package
Parse
Participation
Physical Model
PL/SQL
Primary Key
Privileges
Procedure

Q

Qualifier
Queries

R

Record
Recursive Relationship
Redundancy
Referential Integrity
Relation
Relational Algebra
Relational Database
Relational Model
Relational Select
Relationship
Result Set
Row
Row Filter
Row Functions
Row-level triggers

S

Script
Second Normal Form (2NF)
Session
Set

Set Compatibility
Snapshot
Software Engineering
Spool
Spurious Tuples
SQL (Structured Query Language)
SQL Statements
Start Files
Statement-level triggers
Statements
Statement Buffer
String
String Function
Structural Constraint
Subquery
Subset
Synonym
System Privileges

T

Table
Table Alias
Temporary Table
Theta Join
Third Normal Form
Transaction
Trigger
Tuple

U

Union Compatibility
User

V

VARCHAR
VARCHAR2
View

W

Waterfall Model

Index of Terms

Index of Important Commands and Functions

LTRIM
MAX
MIN
MINUS
NOT
NOT EXISTS
NOT NULL
NULL
NVL
OR
ORDER BY
PRIMARY KEY
PRIVILEGE
PROMPT
REFERENCE
REM
RETURN
RESTRICT
REVOKE
ROLLBACK
ROWNUM
RPAD
RTRIM
SAVE
SAVEPOINT
SELECT
SET
SET ECHO ON/OFF
SET FEEDBACK
   ON/OFF/n
SET HEADSEP
SET LINESIZE
SET NEWPAGE
SET PAGESIZE
SET PAUSE
   ON/OFF/character
   expression
SET SQLPROMPT
SET TIMING ON/OFF
SHOW ALL
SHOW ERRORS
SPOOL

SPOOL filename
SPOOL ON
SPOOL OFF
SPOOL OUT
SQLLOADER
SQLPLUS (SQL*PLUS)
START filename
SUBSTR
SUM
TO_CHAR
TO_DATE
TTITLE
TYPE
%TYPE
UNION
UNION ALL
UNIQUE
UPDATE
UPPER

Index

A

abstract data type (ADT), 63

ACCEPT command, 247–248

access to tables, 28–29, 121–122

actions in procedures, 258–259

adding
  comments to statements, 29–30
  concatenated primary keys, 220
  foreign keys, 224
  parameter lists to procedures, 258
  reporting commands, 242–246

aggregates
  column functions, 167
  functions, 89, 92–94
  GROUP BY clause, 174
    HAVING clause, 174–176
    nulls, 179–182

aliases. *See also* naming
  columns, 79–81
  tables, 74

ALTER TABLE command, 60, 217

analysts, software engineering, 17

anomalies, 12

anonymous blocks, 254–255

APPEND command, 35

Application
  Development command (Start menu), 20

applying
  CHANGE command, 34
  GET command, 33
  HOST, 24–26
  LIST command, 34–35
  PL/SQL tables, 269–270
  Rownum variables, 82–84

attributes, 2, 7
  NOT NULL constraint, 216–218
  Rownum, 82–84
  searching, 305
  selecting, 46–47

auditing subqueries, 176–179

B

binary intersections, 135

binary operations, Cartesian products, 71–72

binary set differences, 135

binary unions, 135

blocks, anonymous, 254–255

BOOLEAN data type, 62–63

buffers
  editing, 289–290
  saving, 290